The State of the World

Edited by António Pinto Ribeiro

CARCANET

and
FUNDAÇÃO CALOUSTE GULBENKIAN

First published in Great Britain in 2006 by
Carcanet Press Limited
Alliance House
Cross Street
Manchester M2 7AQ

Co-published with
Fundação Calouste Gulbenkian

CALOUSTE
GULBENKIAN
FOUNDATION

Copyright © João Barrento, John Frow, Paul Gilroy, Wang Hui,
Santiago Kovadloff, Surendra Munshi,Carlos Pacheco, Rosângela Rennó,
António Pinto Ribeiro, Colin Richards, Moira Simpson, Peter Sloterdijk,
Emílio Rui Vilar, Ghassan Zaqtan 2006

A CIP catalogue record for this book is available from the British Library

ISBN 1 85754 917 1
978 1 85754 917 1

Set in Monotype Dante by XL Publishing Services, Tiverton
Printed and bound in England by SRP Ltd, Exeter

Contents

Foreword

As part of the planned activities to celebrate the fiftieth anniversary of the Calouste Gulbenkian Foundation, it struck me as both important and opportune to organise a forum that would reflect on and analyse current cultural work, and simultaneously select emerging themes so as to establish paths for future work and action.

We live in an age that is rich in experiences but also heavily burdened by uncertainties and risks. This age is also one of perplexity – if not relativism – when we are faced with so many contradictions, not to mention striking absurdities: the availability of knowledge and practices that seem to ignore it; abundance and waste existing alongside scarcity and hunger; apparently standardised information alongside radical claims for the right to difference.

When planning this Cultural Forum, which includes publishing a book of ten essays, a set of poems and a portfolio of art – all of which have been specially produced for this project – our goal was to demonstrate how important contemporary reflection and creation are for the Calouste Gulbenkian Foundation.

The Calouste Gulbenkian Foundation is much more than a space where cultural activities are held: it is also a place where knowledge is produced, a place for open debate, a place where ideas, theories, proposals and art emerge. This book contains contributions by philosophers, a poet, writers, essayists, a plastic artist, sociologists and historians, all of whom took the present as their fundamental material for reflection and creation. As we read these texts and see the images, we are delighted by and grateful for the intellectual input that all the authors have provided.

As citizens of the world, they are not concerned just about the place where they live, their country, house, religion or personal pleasure. They are concerned and consequently alert us – if such an alert is necessary – to the consequences of the wars that are taking place and loom on the horizon, the deepening of asymmetries as the most negative aspect of globalisation, and the varied forms of violence that characterise today's world. They all point out that what is going on in the world is unfair and agree that something has to change. Nothing could be further from the utopia than this state of ruin, yet through their reflections, these authors make us believe that hope can emerge from among chaos.

I would like to thank the authors and António Pinto Ribeiro, the project co-ordinator. I trust that the following articles will form the basis for this newly-created path to develop positively, making a broad contribution to the debate as well as encouraging discovery and creative participation.

EMÍLIO RUI VILAR
April 2006

Introduction

The world's cultural situation has altered dramatically over the past twenty years. The independence movements which emerged in the 1950s created new countries that started to revise their histories of both the nation and the arts, and have already produced new forms of cultural expression, some of which now circulate worldwide. The end of the millennium, with the fall of the Berlin Wall and the appearance of new countries in Eastern Europe (to some extent part of the postcolonial movement) posed new questions as to the notion of Europe and the legacy of Western philosophy. Likewise, the emergence in the West of industrialised cultural practices from Oriental countries such as India, China and Japan meant a complete revision of the rules governing the reception of art and aesthetics. The violence dictated by cultural dogmas and expressed by 11 September 2001 caused a 'cooling down' in the intercultural strategy and triggered a slump in the significance of ongoing cultural negotiations. The globalisation of the markets for art and culture, coupled with the communication technology that accelerates the processes of cultural information and distribution, together require new epistemological frameworks and demand profound and ongoing reflection that goes beyond the analytical tools of the anthropology, aesthetics, sociology and economics of culture which were still valid and maintained some efficacy until ten years ago.

The current *State of the Cultural World* appears as a confused nebula whose evolution cannot be predicted and whose newly generated figures cannot be understood.

As practising citizens and as participants in various cultural practices, we not only have an instrumental or utilitarian vision of culture, but also ethical concerns, not forgetting the political and ideological options that condition the production of and citizens' access to artistic, technological and scientific culture. Yet nor can we distance ourselves from the initial dynamics involved in producing these new cultural values, the innovative artistic languages, and the production of a critical mass that this must necessarily entail. Thanks to its Atlantic/Mediterranean location, the Calouste Gulbenkian Foundation has become a forum for discussion, particularly for the Portuguese. As such, it has decided to help create a period of reflection. This period, which is simultaneously a cultural space, requires that the Foundation act as more than just a place for the consumption of artistic exhibitions or performances, no matter how interesting they may be.

This *State of the World* is designed to be a place where the future is challenged, a place for questioning cultural production and of what seems obvious but is not, where passive acceptance of a 'one-way' cultural market is criticised, a place *par excellence* for debating current themes and emerging problems that perhaps cannot yet be overcome, a place where the new culture can emerge from discussion (organised into various platforms) of cultural problems and the presentation of a complementary programme of performances, exhibitions and film as examples of the current *State of the World*.

The *State of the World* programme is organised into three platforms, the first of which is the publication of this book (in Portuguese and English) and an opening conference. The second is a programme of major conferences, lectures, performances, workshops by artists, touring exhibitions, a market of ideas and theories and cinema, performances of opera, dance and theatre. Finally, the third is the publication of a book of 'Conclusions' and an exhibition of the visual arts.

In order to create this book, we invited a select group of intellectuals, an artist and a poet, and asked them – based on a series of 'entries' – to write texts and create a portfolio that alone would be an evaluation of the State of the World. The 'entries' proposed as themes for reflection were: memory and artistic innovation; transatlantic relations: the white Atlantic and the black Atlantic; new forms of political action; today's myths and heroes; autobiography and artistic fiction; artistic internationalism; what comes after the market economy and democracy?; revising the concept of peace in the light of new world conflicts and new cultural semantics.

The invitation went out to the following authors: Carlos Pacheco, Colin Richards, Ghassan Zaqtan, João Barrento, John Frow, Moira Simpson, Paul Gilroy, Peter Sloterdijk, Santiago Kovadloff, Surendra Munshi, Rosângela Rennó and Wang Hui – all of whom I would like to thank them all for their great generosity and intellectual and artistic input. We hope and expect that the resulting book, published here and with international distribution in English, will help to find solutions within the new framework of cultural referents, thereby reviving some hope in our unique world.

ANTÓNIO PINTO RIBEIRO

Notes on Contributors

António Pinto Ribeiro
António Pinto Ribeiro was born in Lisbon. His academic background is in philosophy, communication science and cultural studies, where he has carried out research and produced theoretical work published in specialist journals. He is a lecturer and visiting speaker at several international universities. Alongside his research work and lecturing, he has also been responsible for artistic programming and cultural management, organising several programmes and exhibitions in Portugal and abroad. He was the Artistic Director at Culturgest (cultural centre) from its set-up in 1992 until April 2004. His most significant publications include: *A Dança da Idade do Cinema* (Dance from the Age of Cinema, 1991), *Dança temporariamente Contemporânea* (Temporarily Contemporary Dance, 1994), *Por Exemplo a Cadeira – Ensaio Sobre as Artes do Corpo* (For Example the Chair – Essay on the Arts of the Body, 1997), *Corpo a Corpo – Sobre as Possibilidades e os Limites da Crítica* (Body to Body – On the Possibilities and the Limits of Criticism, 1997), *Ser Feliz é Imoral? – Ensaios Sobre Cultura, Cidades e Distribuição* (Is Being Happy Immoral? – Essays on Culture, Cities and Distribution, 2000), *Melancolia* (Melancholy, 2003), *Abrigos – Condições das Cidades e Energia da Cultura* (Shelters – The Condition of Cities and the Energy of Culture, 2004).

Carlos Pacheco
Carlos Pacheco was born in Luanda, Angola, in 1945. He has studied History and Philosophy at the University of Lourenço Marques in Mozambique and at the University of São Paulo in Brazil. He writes regularly in the Portuguese daily newspaper *Público* and he has contributed extensively to Portuguese,

Brazilian and Angolan newspapers. Carlos Pacheco has published several books and articles about Angolan and African issues, colonialism and on Angolan poetry, among other subjects. In recent years he has addressed conferences in different Portuguese and Brazilian universities. Currently, he is the Vice-President of the Humberto Delgado Foundation.

Colin Richards

Colin Richards currently lectures in art criticism, studio practice and art theory in the Division of Visual Arts in the Wits School of Arts, Wits University where he is Professor. He studied at the University of South Africa, the University of London (Goldsmiths' College) and Wits University, where he was awarded his PhD in 1995. He has published widely on South African art and curated a number of major exhibitions. He has also presented conference papers on contemporary South African art locally and in Nigeria, Japan, India, Australia, the United States, England, Scotland, and Sweden. His most recent text is a book-length monograph on the artist Sandile Zulu. Richards is also a practising artist, having exhibited in South Africa, Europe and North America. His work is represented in the major public collections in the country.

Emílio Rui Vilar

Emílio Rui Vilar was born in Oporto in 1939. He graduated in Law from Coimbra University (1961) and, since May 2002, has been President of the Board of Trustees of the Calouste Gulbenkian Foundation and Chairman of the Board of Directors of Partex Oil and Gas (Holdings) Corporation. He has also, since 1998, been Guest Professor at the School of Economics and Management (Portuguese Catholic University) and since 1996 Chairman of the Audit Commission of the Banco de Portugal. He is Vice-Chairman of the European Foundation Centre, President of the Portuguese Foundation Centre, Trustee of the initiative 'A Soul for Europe', President of the Steering Committee of the European Foundation Centre project 'Europe in the World', Senator of the European Cultural Parliament and Founding Member of the Portuguese Institute of Corporate Governance. Co-opted Trustee of the Calouste Gulbenkian Foundation in 1996; Chairman of Galp Energia SGPS (2001–2); from 1989 to 1996, Chairman and CEO of Caixa Geral de Depósitos (National Savings Bank); General Commissioner Europalia Portugal (1989–92); Director General at the European Community Commission, (1986–9); Deputy-Governor, Banco de Portugal (1975–84); Minister of Transport and Communications (1976–8); Minister of the Economy (1974–5); Secretary of State for External Trade and Tourism (1974); Founder and first president of SEDES; Manager, Banco Português do Atlântico, from 1969 to 1973.

Ghassan Zaqtan

Ghassan Zaqtan was born in 1954 near Bethlehem. He obtained a teachers' training degree from Jordan and became a physical education teacher. Zaqtan worked with the Palestinian resistance movement and was editor of *Bayader*, literary magazine of the PLO. He is the editor of the literary page of the Al-

Ayyam daily newspaper in Ramallah, and the editor of the new poetry quarterly Al-Shou'ara. He has published a number of poetry collections, and his first novel appeared in 1995. His poetry abounds with luminous imagery, ranging in topics from life and death to the particular themes running through contemporary life. He has participated in countless international poetry festivals, and his works have also been translated into French. He lives in Ramallah.

João Barrento
João Barrento is an essayist and a translator. He has published widely on literary criticism, essays books and he has translated German literature from the last few centuries as well as contemporary German literature. He is a regular contributor to most Portuguese literary magazines and also the daily newspaper *Público*. João Barrento is also the President of Portuguese PEN Club. He has received several awards including the Calouste Gulbenkian Sciences Academy Award (Poetry Translation, 1979); the Translation Great Prize (1993 and 1999); the Essay Award of the Literary Critics Portuguese Association (1996); Literary Essay Great Prize of the Portuguese Writers Association (1996); PEN Club Essay Award (2001); and the Latin League Scientific and Technical Translation Award (2005). In 1991 he received the German Merit Cross and in 1998 the Goethe Medal.

John Frow
John Frow is Professor of English at the University of Melbourne, and has previously taught at the University of Edinburgh, Queensland University, the University of Minnesota, and Murdoch University. He was educated at the Australian National University and Cornell University, where he completed a PhD in Comparative Literature in 1978. He is the author of *Marxism and Literary History* (Harvard, 1986); *Cultural Studies and Cultural Value* (Clarendon Press, 1995); *Time and Commodity Culture* (Clarendon Press, 1997); *Accounting for Tastes: Australian Everyday Cultures* (with Tony Bennett and Michael Emmison, Cambridge, 1999); and *Genre* (Routledge, 2005).

Moira Simpson
Moira Simpson is an academic, author and museum consultant with interests in museums, visual arts, ethnography and education. She has written extensively about museums, cultural property and Indigenous peoples. Her publications include *Making Representations: Museums in the Post-Colonial Era* (Routledge, 1996/2001) and *Museums and Repatriation* (Museums Association, 1997). In the 1990s, she was a member of the national Museums Standing Advisory Group on Repatriation and Related Cultural Property Issues and carried out research on behalf of the Museums Association of Great Britain, which led to the introduction of national repatriation guidelines for UK museums. Now living in Adelaide, Australia, she is researching the influence of Indigenous cultural beliefs on contemporary museology; repatriation as a stimulus for cultural revitalisation; and new museum models based on Indigenous approaches to heritage preservation.

Paul Gilroy
Paul Gilroy was born in London in 1956. He is the first holder of the Anthony Giddens Professorship in Social Theory at the London School of Economics. His intellectual background is multi-disciplinary and he has extensive interests in literature, art, music and cultural history as well as in social science. He is best known for his work on racism, nationalism and ethnicity and his original approach to the history of the African diaspora into the western hemisphere. Gilroy received his PhD from the Centre for Contemporary Cultural Studies at Birmingham University where he was part of the group which collectively produced *The Empire Strikes Back* (Routledge, 1982). After that, he worked at the GLC for a number of years before taking up academic positions at South Bank and at Essex, where one of his principal responsibilities was teaching on the joint degree in Sociology and Literature. Gilroy moved to Goldsmiths College in 1991 and was appointed Professor of Sociology and Cultural Studies there in 1995. Before joining the LSE in the summer of 2005, he taught at Yale University where he was Charlotte Marian Saden Professor of Sociology and African American studies as well as chair of the African American Studies department. Gilroy has worked, among other things, as a guest curator at the Tate Gallery and the House of World Cultures in Berlin. He has lectured in universities all over the world. His work has been translated into French, Italian, Portuguese, Danish, Swedish, Japanese, Arabic, Spanish and German.

Peter Sloterdijk
Peter Sloterdijk was born in 1947 in Karlsruhe and he has studied philosophy, germanism and history in Munich and Hamburg. He is acclaimed as one of the most important philosphical thinkers of today, at least since the publication of *Kritik der zynischen Vernunft* [Critique of Cynical Reason], which was an instant success. This book quickly became the philosophy best seller in Germany of the last fifteen years. In the last few years he has been working on his monumental trilogy *Sphären* [Spheres], first published in Germany in 1998, in which he deals with the umbilical connection between the man and his environment. He has taught at the Vienna University and at the Karlsruhe Arts School, of which he is the Dean, since 1999. He directs a TV show in the state network ZDF, *The Philosophical Quartet*.

Rosangela Rennó
Rosângela Rennó (Belo Horizonte, 1962) graduated in Architecture at the Minas Gerais Federal University in 1986 and in Fine Arts at the Guignard School in 1987. She has also a PhD in Fine Arts from the School of Communication and Arts of the University of São Paulo (1997). She now lives and works in Rio de Janeiro. Rosangella has received scholarships from the Civitella Ranieri Foundation (1996), Fundação Vitae (1998) and from the John Simon Guggenheim Memorial Foundation (1999). She has exhibited in several arts institutions including The Appel Foundation (Amsterdam, 1995), The Museum of Contemporary Art (Los Angeles, 1996), Australian Centre for Photography (Sydney, 1999), Museu do Chiado (Lisboa, 2000), Museu de Arte da Pampulha (Belo Horizonte, 2002), Centro Cultural Banco do Brasil

(Rio de Janeiro, 2003) or at the Passage du Désir (Festival d'Automne à Paris, 2005). Her work has been present at international exhibitions like *Aperto93*, 45th Venice Bienale (1993), *Cocido y Crudo*, Centro Cultural Reina Sofia (Madrid, 1994), 22nd São Paulo International Biennale (1994), *Insite97* (San Diego e Tijuana, 1997), 2nd Berlim Biennale (2001), *La Mirada*, Daros LatinAmerica (Zurique, 2002), Pavilhão Brasileiro, 50th Bienal Internacional de Veneza (2003), and others. In 2003 she published the book *The Universal Archive and other Archives*.

Santiago Kovadloff

Santiago Kovadloff (Buenos Aires, 1942) graduated in Philosophy at the Buenos Aires University. He is an essayist, poet and writer of children books. He is also a regular contributor to the daily newspaper *La Nación* in Buenos Aires. In 1992, as an essayist, he was awarded the Repubic of Argentina Literary First Prize and in 2000 the City of Buenos Aires Poetry First Prize. He is a member of the Argentinian Academy and a correspondent of the Royal Spanish Academy. Santiago is translator of Portuguese and in 2000 he translated into Spanish Fernando Pessoa's *The Book of Disquiet*. He has received several scholarships from the Calouste Gulbenkian Foundation and from Portugal's Ministry of Culture In 2005 he was awarded the Infante D. Enrique Order by the Portuguese government in recognition for his contribution for the promotion of Portuguese literature.

Surendra Munshi

Surendra Munshi is Professor of Sociology at the Indian Institute of Management, Calcutta. He has researched and taught in India and abroad in the fields of classical sociological theory, sociology of culture and industrial sociology. His current research interests include good governance. Until recently, he has been leading an international project on good governance with the support of the European Commission in which several European institutions of higher education took part. The outcome of this project has appeared as a book published by SAGE under the title *Good Governance, Democratic Societies and Globalisation*. He spoke on invitation at the Second European Cultural Forum held at Luxembourg, 15 to 17 April 2005. His paper at the Third World Congress of ISBEE held at Melbourne is due to appear soon under the title 'Ethics in the Era of Globalisation'.

Wang Hui

Wang Hui is an intellectual historian, Professor at the School of Humanities and Social Sciences, Tsinghua University as well as the chief editor of *Dushu* magazine, the most influential intellectual journal in China. Before moving to Tsinghua University, Wang Hui was a senior fellow at the Institute of Literature of Chinese Academy of Social Sciences. His early book entitled *Resisting Despair: Lu Xun and His Literary World* (1990) is considered one of the best achievements in the Lu Xun and modern Chinese literature studies. The most important works among his numerous writings are the four-volume *The Rise of Modern Chinese Thought* (2004) and *China's New Order: Society, Economy and Politics in Transition* (2003).

Reflecting the Abysm

CARLOS PACHECO

... the world has probably been living in the worst possible way since the beginning of the twentieth century. The number of countries that are not underdeveloped but undernourished; plagues such as Aids; the hole in the ozone layer and its relationship with the way current society produces; the chance that the world may run out of food within fifty years ... this is all the result of the total failure of a thought system that began at the end of the Renaissance.

Abdelardo Castillo, Argentine writer, interviewed for
La Nacion newspaper (Buenos Aires), 25 February 2006

Introduction

During recent decades, thanks to the adoption of new technological and political strategies, the structure of the world has undergone such swift transformations and on such a scale that simply stating these facts might lull us into the utopian assumption that humanity is heading towards something better.

In fact, transnational communication networks and circuits have destroyed distance and made the separations between men, countries and continents fluid. As the resources of cyberspace are inexhaustible, information on an event taking place in one part of the planet can be instantaneously transmitted to every last corner of the globe. The individual's behaviour and his or her vision of the world have changed, largely because of migratory movements and mass tourism. The nation state and its ethnic borders have been denationalised; the old notions of territory are making way for a new conception of space. Productive, commercial, financial and cultural processes are now all becoming transnational, toppling the old models of individual and collective identity.

Twenty-five years after the fall of the Berlin Wall, some thinkers point to such changes as the dawn of a new historical and social movement in the global world, which they call post-modernity.

Despite these mutations and the significant advances made in the sciences and medicine, in industrial and food production, and even in the struggle for civil and social rights, is it reasonable to talk about a fairer and more balanced world society?

It seems to me that the following real situation provides a convincing answer: out of a world population of 6,000 million, 4,700 million are poor and over 1,000 million survive on less than a dollar a day, while some 2,700 million people have to make do with two dollars a day. In addition to the drama of such extreme poverty, there are an estimated 840 million who are sick due to hunger and malnutrition, including 300 million who are children. All these people live in Southern Asia and Sub-Saharan Africa.[1]

The Middle East offers another drastic situation. Unending bloodbaths take place in Iraq due to the presence of occupying troops and death squads, where the latter are responsible for summary executions and torture in illegal prisons. Entire cities have all but disappeared. Fallujah [360,000 inhabitants] is just one example of a place where vast numbers of people who have died.[2] Prior to the economic sanctions imposed in 1991, the country had the highest standards of living in the region, with excellent factories, health care facilities equivalent to those found in the First World, and a very modern education system. The nation now lies in ruins, with serious water and sanitation problems, unable even to maintain its buildings. As British journalist Robert Fisk said, it is a 'monumental tragedy' that has turned into a 'routine, amorphous and incipient civil war'.[3] Meanwhile, there are political tensions in Lebanon, Egypt and Saudi Arabia produced by intolerant régimes that the United States trumpets as models of 'flourishing democracy'.

The third situation concerns Europe, which is far from being a haven of security. First came the Islamic fundamentalist attacks on Madrid and London, then the social revolt in France with the so-called 'battles for recognition' by the 'human dregs', as Polish sociologist Zygmunt Bauman defined the migrants or children of migrants.[4] The French authorities had always settled for seeing these pariahs of the universe as people who were incapable of reacting against the difficulties that afflicted them. The thinking was that 'they have no choice': 'Given the alternative of living in France or returning to where they came from, they'd prefer to stay here and put up with it.' This is the frightening and 'negative utopia' described by Loïc J.D. Wacquant, supported by the neo-liberal, technocratic short-sightedness that triggers the decomposition of urban suburbs with the full force of 'discrimination, violence, poverty and social isolation'.[5] Therefore, in Bauman's words, all you need is a single 'speck of dust'[6] to make all these anachronistic solutions explode. The end result is that the excluded are now demanding their rightful place within the Republic; they demand at least fair rights, if not the same prerogatives as French citizens. Unless the French élites integrate them, the situation will tend to worsen in the near future, leading to more violent conflicts which the other member states of the European Union that take in immigrant communities – such as Portugal – will be unable to escape.

The World Adrift

It is undeniably true that over the last fifty years, the contemporary world has achieved high levels of material and technological progress. However, at the same time, the world has become less safe and less caring. I would even go so far as to say it is more dangerous and, on occasion, incomprehensible. Nothing is fixed or stable any longer. The very limits of reality have been blurred; everything is contradictory and nebulous. The common ground and the bonds that tie individuals to communities – a legacy from the Renaissance and traditional societies, expressing the concept of security and the possibility of belonging to something – are now on the verge of extinction. Man feels that he is 'scared and alone', a mariner without a compass, sailing an unknown sea. The present-future is heavily laden with uncertainties: lack of work; fear of losing one's job or of immigration; the possibility of social and family collapse; shortages in food; lack of transport; poverty; the rise in delinquency and crime; declining safety for people and their possessions; the risk of terrorism, of armed conflicts and of epidemic disease. This maelstrom catches us up and spits us out, 'shipwrecked' on the beaches of suffering and frustration.

Such is the scale of the neglect shown by their respective states and governments that entire African peoples can no longer survive. In the rich world, the shallowness of governments and politicians reduces them to *insignificance*, as noted by French philosopher and sociologist Cornelius Castoriadis (1922–97). Lacking any programme, politicians are interested only in 'hanging onto power', and are prepared to do anything to try and get back into power.[7] Meanwhile, in Africa, the reality is a thousand times more serious. Ever since national independence, the power structures have been in the hands of élites that override national interests and maintain authoritarian hegemonic systems characterised by coercion, by ideological confrontations and – all too frequently – by ethnic violence. Not even so-called democratic elections have proven able to break this dominance; they have instead ultimately strengthened it. Cronyism, corruption and tyranny have prevailed over the universal values of human rights and democratic pluralism, and the consequence is the crystallisation of trends and forces that increasingly impede Africa's development.

Robert Kaplan, the North American essayist, believes that the current global conjuncture is bad and that the planet's social fabric is being profoundly affected by scarce resources, excess population, environmental decline, multiplying diseases, tribalism, the crimes of transnational terrorism and the emergence of private armies. He claims that a series of states almost all over the world – in Asia, in the Hispano-American hemisphere, even in Europe's Balkans and the Caucuses, but above all in Africa – are showing signs of territorial fragmentation, as the central power of the state is being broken up. In other words, 'they are turning feudal'. The new lords of these domains, leaders of militia hordes, enforce obedience through the most varied forms of strict loyalty.[8] Their agendas, and those of their accompanying *condottieri*, are further enhanced by crime. In conversation with Kaplan, a state employee from Sierra Leone provided a stark profile of the country's new leaders, men who had seized power: their first concern was to appropriate the official vehicles – Mercedes, Volvos and BMWs – and then to kill the people who had helped them, even in their own education.[9]

This state of affairs is far from new: it merely reflects the weakness or collapse of historically incomplete states, which are marked by cycles of poverty and instability and by internal struggles that place élites in direct confrontation. Their objective is to gain control of the country's natural resources, which will simultaneously help them to 'get rich quick' and to acquire weapons and enter the circuits of world trade. In this type of state, where the vague presence of the authorities is purely symbolic and governments are unable to carry out the modern state's tasks, institutions are shorn of even a bare minimum of credibility. Bureaucracy exists solely as a means to oppress the citizens.[10]

Any prognosis about the future of our civilisation is truly disturbing. It seems that the majority of underdeveloped peoples are condemned to being left behind as history advances, trammelled by poverty and ecological disaster. The United Nations has forecast that by 2015 51% of the world's poor will be concentrated in Africa, while the contrasting minority will enjoy exceptionally high standards of living.

Although Kaplan and other scholars recognise this cruel reality, they say nothing about the role played by global capitalism in creating the most severe of civilisational imbalances. They merely feel that anarchy is coming and that it may harm the United States. This then becomes the reason behind their claim that the strategic imperative of the 'imperial administration' is to defend itself and battle on all fronts, and in particular the military. In a recent article, I showed precisely how the global capitalist system, with its tendency towards concentration and exclusion, is responsible for the ever greater injustices that are to be found in the international sphere:

The rules of the World Trade Organisation speak for themselves, creating dramatic imbalances between the North and the South, threatening the agriculture and industry of peripheral countries, particularly the poorest. So do the shock therapies of the IMF [the Washington Consensus] based on the inappropriate economic concepts of austerity and structural adjustment [as identified already by the former president of the World Bank and Nobel prize winner, Joseph Stiglitz], which create the illusion that the countries helped are staging an economic and financial recovery, when what really happens is that poverty and social inequality get worse. So does the lack of transparency shown by transnational corporation business dealings, whose negative impact [the result of brutal pillaging] threatens the very survival of states that are already suffering from structural deficiencies or breaking up. Not to mention other phenomena whose effects are a thousand times worse: armed interventions, civil wars, massacres, bombardments and coups against legitimately elected governments that undermined [and continue to do so] the stability of Latin America, Africa, Asia and the Middle East throughout the twentieth century. All this was to protect and safeguard the geopolitical interests of industrialised nations.[11]

Chossudovsky goes further still, warning that the great threat hanging over mankind is the growing militarisation of the major powers and their open warfare to impose the neo-liberal economic model on every country.[12] Naturally, the biggest victims in the midst of all this militarisation are the weakest states, which become battlefields for the world powers, which not only foster local conflicts, but also supply weapons to warring groups. The United Kingdom is among the G8 countries that have quadrupled their revenues since 1999 and is currently in second place on the list of the world's major arms exporters.[13]

Given the complexity of the problems, the issue is clearly not whether there is a choice between accepting or rejecting capitalism. Rather, the aim is to warn of the destructive effects of the games played out by multinationals that are forcing the agricultural and industrial systems of the poorest countries into a cul-de-sac, forcing the people's spiralling hunger ever higher.[14]

Disarming Chaos

The situation in Iraq is intolerable. The creators of chaos are only thinking about business. The Bush administration and North American businessmen are more concerned with Iraqi oil and the reconstruction of infrastructures than with the incipient civil war and the humanitarian disaster caused by the invasion. Comparable events can be seen in the Democratic Republic of the Congo, where foreign gold mining corporations deliberately violate the norms of cooperation with the host country by contracting brigands to help them locate veins of the ore and simultaneously encourage conflict between the local populations so that they can exploit the wealth found in the region.[15] These gross violations are being repeated everywhere, ultimately acting as ways to stimulate violence and plunge societies into disorder.

It is evident that the future will be dangerous, and continuing down the current path means accepting that the 'desert of the Real', Slavoj Žižek's well-coined term for the Third World,[16] will become a terrible memory for forthcoming generations. What then can be done to avoid the spread of poverty and the destruction of humanity? We must disarm chaos, which means disarming the invisible fist that lies behind that chaos: the world system that rules us based on the close ties linking militarist beliefs and the capitalist global market system.

Translated by Richard Trewinnard

Notes

1 According to estimates and comparisons made up to 2001, the percentage of the world's population earning under a dollar a day is divided as follows: Sub-Saharan Africa 46.4%, Southern Asia 29.9%, East Asia 16.6%, Southern Asia and Oceania 19.2%, Latin America and the Caribbean 9.5%, Community of Independent States 5.3%, Northern and Western Asia 2.7%, Southern and Eastern European economies in transition 2.0%. However, although the battle against extreme poverty has gained some ground in much of Asia, this is less true in Latin America, while the situation has worsened in Southern Africa and Western Asia. Yet the most worrying statistics concern Sub-Saharan Africa, where poverty levels are at record levels. It is hard to see how to turn this tide in the short and medium term. Indeed, in general terms, the setbacks in the battle against hunger have outstripped any progress made

(United Nations. 'Millennium Development Objectives, The 2005 Report', New York).

2   Accounts of the acts of barbarism carried out by the USA and its allies may be read in *Iraq Solidaridad*, 2004–5 editions.

3   Robert Fisk, 'La derrota es victoria y la muerte, vida', *La Jornada* [Mexico], Sunday 26 February 2006.

4   'Náufragos num mundo líquido', interview with Zygmunt Bauman by José Castello, *No Mínimo* [Rio de Janeiro] magazine, Saturday 18 February 2006.

5   Loïc J.D. Wacquant, 'Da América como utopia às avessas'. In Pierre Bourdieu, *A Miséria do Mundo* (Petrópolis, third edition, 1999), p. 175.

6   Zygmunt Bauman, *Em Busca da Política* [translation by Marcos Penchel] (Rio de Janeiro, 2000), p. 23.

7   Cornelius Castoriadis, *Diálogo Seguido de Post Scriptum sobre a Insignificância* [translation by Miguel Serras Pereira] (Lisbon, 2004), p. 112.

8   In Latin America, Colombia is the case that best illustrates the phenomenon of co-governability of regions by guerrilla forces and legally established institutions.

9   Robert Kaplan, 'The Coming Anarchy', *The Atlantic Monthly*, Vol. 273, No. 2, February 1994.

10   In failed states – as Rotberg rightly noted – economic opportunities continue to be a privilege of the dominant élites. Corruption prospers, birth rates are negative, inflation is high and the lack of food results in widespread hunger (Robert I. Rotberg, *Nation-State failure: a recurring phenomenon?*, 6 November 2003, p. 3 [paper for North Islan College]). Document available on the internet: http://www.cia.gov/nic/PDF_GIF_2020_Support/2003_11_06_papers/panel2_nov6.pdf.

11   'O primeiro mundo recusa-se a entender' (The first world refuses to understand), *Público*, No. 5620, Monday 15 August 2005, p. 6.

12   Michel Chossudovsky, *Guerra y Globalização. Antes y Después del XI-IX-MMI* [translation by Bertha Ruiz de la Concha] (México/Argentina, 2002), p. 132.

13   Richard F. Grimmet, *Conventional Arms Transfers to Developing Nations, 1996-2003*, Congressional Research Service Report for Congress, 24 August 2004.

14   Carlos Pacheco, 'Ambiguidades na ajuda à África' [duas partes] (Ambiguities to aid to Africa [two parts]), *Público*, issues No. 5558, Monday 13 June 2005, p. 6; and No. 5579, Monday 4 July 2005, p. 6.

15   Human Rights Watch. *Rapport Mondial* 2003 – Congo.

16   Slavoj Žižek. *Bem Vindo ao Deserto Real. Estado de Sítio* (São Paulo, 2002), p. 49.

The Wounds of Discovery

COLIN RICHARDS

… man is a *yes*. I will never stop reiterating that. *Yes* to life. *Yes* to love. *Yes* to generosity. But man is also a *no*. *No* to scorn of man. *No* to degradation of man. *No* to exploitation of man. *No* to the butchery of what is most human in man: Freedom.

Frantz Fanon, Black Skin, White Masks

Shame at having to hear, having to say, fainter than the faintest murmur, so many lies, so many times the same lie lyingly denied, whose the screaming silence of no's knife in yes's wound

Samuel Beckett, 'Texts for Nothing 13'

I: The Other Side of the World

I begin this text as I end it; with an emblem. But, being elaborate and without the economy of an emblem, this text is more like an allegory. Its place is what António Pinto Ribeiro calls a 'cultural site', its time is the last two decades, its energy what the curator calls a 'perplexing nebula', and image that of inapprehensibility. I start with a meditation on a street name.

Vascoda Gama is a street name in the small east coast South African resort town of Kenton-on-Sea. The name is incorrectly transcribed. There is an error in spacing. It should read 'Vasco da Gama' (1469–1524), the Portuguese explorer who passed these parts in the 1490s in search of a safe all-water trade route between the Occident and the Orient. Africa was then simply a way-station with food and sweet water, a mere interval supporting the grander narrative of East and West. If you stand at one point in Vascoda Gama Street and look south-west, you may glimpse a promontory in the distance. On some days, heat and mist make this outcrop look like an island. And, on a clear day, you see the silhouette of what looks like a column or post atop the high-point.

The column is in fact a padrão, a stone landmark capped by a cross. This particular padrão marks the southernmost landing point of Bartolomeu Dias (*c.* 1450?–1500), da Gama's precursor, whose pilot sailed with da Gama. It was Dias who named the southernmost region of Africa as *Cabo Tormentoso* (Cape of Storms). The place of this padrão is called *Kwaaihoek*; literally, an 'angry', 'wild' or 'dangerous' corner. The outcrop is also called *False Islet*, as, according to one scholar, from the seaward side 'the illusion of an island is complete'. Illusion and emotion are both deeply part of this site. When Dias turned back from *Kwaaihoek,* one historian (Barros) noted that the explorer 'watched the cross disappear in the distance with a heavy heart, as if he were leaving behind a son in lonely exile'.

There was also destruction. The Dias documentation in the archives of Lisbon was consumed by fire following an earthquake in Portugal in 1755. The entire archive was destroyed, leaving unfillable gaps in the historical record. The padrão too suffered the fate of destruction. This 'oldest recorded monument in South Africa' – a scarcely tenable conceit, but a familiar one – was in pieces by the late eighteenth century. The record shows that in 1786, one Colonel R.J. Gordon 'carried away three stones covered with inscriptions' from the site, all of which have disappeared. The site in *False Islet* was itself 'lost to memory'. It was rediscovered in 1938 by Eric Axelson by a process of research and deduction. Initially, Axelson was unaware of similar deductions by two Portuguese sources which placed the lost padrão on False Island; Admiral Ernesto de Vasconcelos published later in 1938, and one Captain Fontoura da Costa, published in 1935.

Such padrões or beacons carried by the explorers of the late 1400s were of a crystalline white limestone of a non-local origin, and were ceremonially consecrated before a fleet set sail. A South African historian offered the rather outlandish opinion that by current standards these voyages of discovery 'must rank equal to modern space travelling'. The material and symbolic presence of padrões announced that a place had been 'discovered' by the authority of God and King. The God was Christian; the king,

Portuguese. The padrão was proof of priority of title and possession – actual occupation was not required by incipient international law at the time. It was also a symbol of sovereignty, and the sign of Christianity.

It also signalled colonialism. The efforts, energy and ingenuity of these Portuguese luminaries and the labour of the nameless who toiled under them brought European colonialism to this part of the world. Colonialism and competition. The Martellus map (*c.* 1489) of that time showed the Cape at a latitude of over 40 degrees South, when in fact Dias knew the latitude was 35 degrees (the precise co-ordinates are Lat 33° 44' S and Long 26° 38' E). This deception was apparently necessary to scupper Spanish competition. These voyages proved more lucrative than those of Columbus, and, according to American historian Daniel Boorstin, they 'changed the course of both Western and Eastern History'.

They also changed Africa. In his diary, de Gama writes of seeing 'about 10 or 12 negroes overthrow both the cross and the padrão' at São Bras, anglicised first as St Blaize, and later renamed as Mossel Bay by the Dutch. This was some 400 miles to the south west of *Kwaaihoek*. The destruction of the Diaz padrão itself was a matter of speculation. The first idea – rejected – was that it was struck by lightning. The 'defacement' (as some accounts have it) was more likely deliberate, 'done by a craftsman who could use a mallet and chisel as a trained man would'. In this theory, vandal ships and vagrant 'foreigners' would likely have been the culprits. Their motive may have been 'anti-catholic, or, more probably, simply prejudice against "foreigners" on the part of some visiting vessel of another nationality'. This cultural site was the playground of the powerful. Here indigenous peoples seem not to be have been even foreign, but only nominally visible aliens.

One writer does suggest greater agency to indigenous inhabitants, only to dismiss this. Natives may, he suggests, have been involved in such destruction; but even so 'one cannot picture natives taking the trouble to chip painstakingly at the decoration, so that it came away in thin flakes and left the block still a fairly uniform, true-faced surface. Nor had they the tools.' Elsewhere we are reminded fragments of limestone 'from the "padrão"' – much 'more attractive... than the local rock' – were 'shattered by... unknown means. Probably lightning was the villain of the peace. Interloping Frenchman may just conceivably have been responsible. Once shattered, the work was probably carried further by aborigines.'

De Gama's observations about the overthrowing of the padrões, the worrying at who defaced the these structures – defacement being 'the wound of sacrilege wrought by desecration' (Michael Taussig) – all open another perspective on the scene before us; that of indigenous peoples and the claims they might make. From a simple mistake in the spelling or spacing of the street name to the whole symbolic and material enterprise of raising the cross and all that followed, we can begin to imagine different dimensions of a visual history being disclosed.

The spacing (spelling?) error in the street name speaks of mistranslation, of literacy of another kind, of literal mimicry. If error is a strategy, mimicry and mockery converge. Homi Bhabha articulated this in an early text, suggesting that the 'effect of mimicry on the authority of colonial discourse is profound and disturbing'. Mimicry is a form of appropriation, and appropriation cuts both ways (or every way) in a colonial and post-colonial world. It prepares a stage for cultural acts of self and other possession, sometimes as if by magic. An error can be an opportunity stolen from correctness, and reinserted into a discourse imagination and creativity; in short, into the discourses of art. Through error as affirmation, the habits which lay siege to our imagination, our creative begin to disintegrate. If I make too much of what might be a simple error in transcription, forcing it into some culturally significant choreography of spacing, I do so because of the context from which I write: post-Apartheid South Africa and the shadow it casts over Africa and beyond.

If we add to this 'error' the fact that the Dias padrão at *Kwaaihoek* is a replica, we can begin to enflesh other, sometimes subversive more spectral stories; stories of deception, betrayal, self-aggrandisement, venality and violence we know but deny. Tales of resistance and resentment, of rage and revenge, animated by the anxiety at the centre of so many claims of origin. This last is often the claim of a 'first' discovery of the already discovered. But these are not always tales of racial supremacy and bad faith, of naming and blaming. Our thoughts can also shade into more subtle, more nuanced, less consolingly antagonistic lines. There are always those fertile moments of compromise, complicity and the commonality even, the last anyway being the ground and condition of any conflict. Such moments allow us to learn from each other.

The question of error, transcription and naming (*Kwaaihoek, False Islet, Cabo Tormentoso*), the deception in mapping the co-ordinates (five degrees off) of a claim made in the name of one god and one king (Christian, Portuguese), mimicry, the fact that the padrão *in situ* is a replica: all these amount to tales of almost magical completeness, that kind of completeness we sense when we read coincidence and contingency as teleological. More familiar in religious rather than secular terms, such completeness – or the acceptance of its impossibility – lies at the heart of our imagination of which art is a concrete part.

The aesthetic, the visionary and the political lie in close proximity in the world of our imagination and what we make of that imagination. These are the things which give an emotional, even sentimental edge to our otherwise hard-edged cynicism which knows the price of everything and value of nothing. Coincidences and contingencies concatenate events, subjects and objects in a way which allows us to imagine afresh the state of our world now. The ambitions, acts and anxieties, the historical convergences and conflicts, the hubris and the hesitations of being alive in this wired, post-millennial moment connects us now in unprecedented ways. And this is what contemporary art shows like nothing else.

The scene sketched in this long opening, with its calibrations of the imagination, of desire, of failure and frustration, of risk and reward, could *mutatis mutandis* be mapped onto virtually any part of the globe. While it is specific, it is not parochial. Embedded here too, sometimes clearly, sometime obliquely, are many of themes curator António Pinto Ribeiro took up in his notes; memory, artistic fiction and innovation, myths and heroes of today, autobiography, transatlantic relations, 'multi-cultural' Europe, artistic internationalism, art and trade in the age of the 'free market', art, democracy and civil society, contested histories, new histories... the list is long.

II: States

The 'State of the World' cultural forum is ambitious. Curator António Pinto Ribeiro developed short background notes which proved pointed and provocative to me. Some I have already mentioned. Many overlap or are intimately interrelated and some struck me at a quite personal level. So, where better to start than at this personal register, with memory and the fictions of autobiography, both of which are so much part of the contemporary artworld.

Two artistic projects were important here. The first was 'Faultlines: Inquiries around Truth and Reconciliation', which opened on 16 June 1996 at The Castle of Good Hope, Cape Town. This exhibition was curated by Jane Taylor and included artistic responses to the work of the South African Truth and Reconciliation Commission. The second was 'memórias íntimas marcas', curated by Fernando Alvim with Sussuta Boé which opened on 25 April 1998 in Johannesburg.

My most intense encounter with the Lusophone Africans occurred when I was conscripted for 'border' duty in 1975–6 in an infantry battalion of the then South African Defence Force (SADF). After an interminable diesel- and dust-ventilated night ride, we found ourselves looking at Portuguese road signs. We were in Angola, without warning, unable to understand the signs. We had been deceived about where we were and what we were there for.

The colonial chains linking Angola to Portugal had only recently been struck, and Angola was enduring the painful throes of massive change. This pain became Angola's signature for most of the world until quite recently. Portugal, unlike other European countries, relinquished its colonies in Africa very rapidly. On 25 April 1974, the Carnation revolution in that country ousted the government of Marcello Caetano, ending some five decades of dictatorship. Within a short time, the colonial wars in Angola and elsewhere were ending in independence for the colonies. The speed of this process was a mixed blessing, exhilarating and violent. After the coup in Portugal, one South African – an officer in the SADF and authored a book on this early Angolan 'campaign' – noted the beginning of the disintegration of stability ['*verkrummeling van stabilitiet*'] in that country in 1975. This view, with the increasingly overt framing of developments in terms of the Cold War, gave the military in Apartheid South Africa reasons (if reasons it needed) to get involved in that country. The *cordon sanitaire* along the northern border of then South-West Africa was at risk, and the threat of 'terrorism', of what the Apartheid State touted as 'total onslaught', sealed matters. Intervention (initially covert and with the support of the United States) was arrogated both as right and responsibility.

Like many white South African males conscripted in the 1970s and 1980s, I recall many things from that time. Some of these surfaced in works on exhibitions in the decade of our first democratic elections (1994). One scene is difficult to forget. We had been ordered to guard a group of refugees, mostly younger women and children. Some of the children were black, some mixed, and a few fair-haired and blue-eyed. The absent fathers were reportedly Portuguese citizens, mostly white, and who had repatriated to Portugal without their 'local' families. Abandoned, these hapless women and children were at the mercy of the madness of a disintegrating world and especially vulnerable to marauding private or partisan armies, including the South African Defence Force. The young women and older children were forced into providing sex for shelter, safety and subsistence. In short, survival. I recall looking into often listless, bewildered eyes, at bodies weighed by the recognition that any future was hostage to a terrifying present. This forced a paralysis which I found difficult to cope with. In exchange terms, a living human body became equivalent to the overripe corpse of a sinewy chicken, a handful of mielie meal, a half-full tin of *All Gold* condensed milk. And dog-biscuits, staple dry rations for infantry just about anywhere.

This image is overlaid by others, the relationship between these being obscure to me. One was our platoon section standing at frozen attention, sweating on some concrete part of an otherwise deserted landing-strip. It was dawn, but hot. Not dark, not light. All our webbing and our rifles were disassembled and laid out systematically on groundsheets in front of us. Military police and military intelligence were picking through these things, looking for live ammunition rounds and anything that could link us to where we had been and what we might have done. They even confiscated grenade rings troops routinely used as hat decorations. They did this with the same sense of ceremony as the *Pro Patria* medal awarded all soldiers who saw active service in Namibia and Angola.

The search produced mixed results. We lost all the undeveloped film we had taken clandestinely of people, patrols and camps in southern Angola. We had only verbal and mental images of the destroyed rooms of a vet, blood, broken bottles, syringes in a town empty but for dogs and chickens and wind. Of domesticated cattle gone wild (*bossies*) which we eventually hunted for food. Of green skin on the stagnant waters in reservoirs and the agony of unmilked cows. One of our troops was an apprentice butcher. We had buried the film in tins of condensed milk painstakingly opened and resealed with the tip of a bayonet. The tins had been boiled to caramelise the milk, which we then hollowed out to hide the film. We felt the loss of these images sorely, but we did managed to smuggle other things out – heavy bore shotgun cartridges and ammunition clips made in Luanda or Cuba, bits and pieces of uniform, pamphlets, and, in my case, some drawings I had made in letters home I never sent. These are the things – the cartridge, the clip of ammunition, the medal – which all found their way into assemblages and installations I made two decades later for the two exhibitions I mentioned earlier.

One, '*memórias íntimas marcas*' was structured around the work of memory and trauma, and what Angolan curator artist Fernando Alvim called 'the urgency of ethno psychiatry'. The memory work here appeared to have twofold purpose. The first was that of bringing lost or suppressed histories to the surface. The second was to allow a certain working through and coming to terms with what had happened. Art was ventilating unspeakable things and was, controversially, redemptive. In a recent interview Alvim restated part of what he felt drove the project:

> I think culture can be a very interesting tool for this passage from war to peace… it's quite clear everybody knows it's not history we need to revisit, but the old images and symptoms we had during wartime… In reality, the first war was against the Portuguese, then South Africa and Zaire, and then between us… eventually we can come to see all these historical moments, or all these wars… as an integral part of our history, aesthetics and culture.

During the first Johannesburg Biennial in 1995 (that is, one year after our first democratic elections) Alvim introduced me to a Cuban curator who had also served in Angola, obviously against South Africa. Reality overtook imagination in this impossible meeting, and it was an extraordinary moment in an extraordinary time.

The second exhibition – *'Faultlines: Inquiries around Truth and Reconciliation'* curated by Jane Taylor – was earlier than Alvim's Johannesburg project. This exhibition allowed artists an opportunity to access hitherto closed archives and create work which responded in some way to the upcoming TRC event. It is telling that while the TRC offered a stage for truth-telling and reconciliation – at least in stated intention – the activities of the old South African Defence Force were by and large absent from the process. There were, according to one commentator, 'two very important gaps' in the TRC report. Referring to the wars in Angola and Moçambique, this author pointed to 'an extraordinary conspiracy of silence' which 'enveloped those who served in these wars and campaigns… In all, only a handful of former soldiers – fewer than ten – made statements to the Commission, and all of them were conscripts.'

These two exhibitions offered a singular opportunity for me and other artists to look at what happened in the army within the framework of a future few of us could ever have imagined. Apartheid, like the Berlin Wall, felt impenetrable and immutable.

Both fell! The dissolution of the Soviet imperium and the triumph of an almost unfettered capitalism – and the corollary aggression – of an ascendent but increasingly fundamentalist United States re-organised the world in which these events happened. The reprise in two large-scale media-saturated wars against 'terror' in the East, the travails of Eastern Europe, 9/11, Rwanda and the central African disaster, Davos and beyond: all these things have rendered the world strange to many. Visual art – which at its best is perhaps a willed form of strangeness and estrangement – began to lose some of its comfortable familiarity on both a popular and a specialist level. It ceased to obey in any obvious way any easy historical logic of progress in art or in society. We might be tempted to say that one of the few spaces left for imagining a less managed and administered life, less structured by the iron fist of the market, lies in art. It is a temptation as powerful as it is ideal-istic and romantic.

Part of this strangeness in art and elsewhere, at another register, is the almost magical development of communication technolo-gies and connectivity all across (albeit unevenly) the globe. These have altered our sense of space, time, proximity and materiality in decisive ways. New artistic formats and forms of mediation – installation, internet and other media – and iconographies have become available to us. We have also perhaps begun to understand more intensely that objects and events, processes and structures largely outside the conventions of the artworld are part of a revised notion of performativity. This differently understood perfoma-tivity has relocated art on the body (which has a long, but somewhat differently focused history) and with this, the individual temperament and ideas of artistic agency.

In his notes for this 'cultural site' of the state of the world, António Pinto Ribeiro mentions a 'return to art' which is relevant here. What remains distinctive and beguiling about art? In one sense, a consciousness of contemporary art's relation to wider social and political dynamics, as well as broader imagined commu-nities has remained vital and fertile in our part of the world. Indeed, in South Africa at least, there has been an ongoing debate about the 'autonomy' of art *vis à vis* the social and political worlds in which it is embedded, and further precisely how the relationship between art and these worlds is best understood, and, importantly, creatively articulated. The lines of this debate echo those in African, European, English, American (South, central and North) and Asian which address the 'autonomy' of art.

Any 'return to art' seems recognise these as foundational questions. It also presupposes a leave-taking, perhaps exile. Such a return might be grounded in some decisive separation of spheres or the opposite, a hopeless indistinctness. It might owe something to constraints, political and economic, found to be hostile to the very project of independent creativity. Or if not hostile, infatuated in a way which suffocates sensuous specificity and particularity and assimilates difference. But it may be more accurate if crude to speak less of a 'return' than *rapprochement* between art and everyday living on the one hand, and between art and large-scale history on the other. Certainly we can and do speak of a reconstruction of forms of intimacy and connectedness, and of the critical reconstitution of art as a form of relation and resistance to reduction, be it in the form of an object, and event, an act.

Perhaps this return, if return it is, also shows most clearly that we do not benefit from thinking in oppositions, but can draw strength from thinking solidarities are provisional and mutable in shifting nests of connectivity. Here the emancipatory potential of technology becomes a little clearer, and the techno-magic enmeshed in the contemporary moment has the potential to re-imagine selves, communities and relations: perhaps even an improbable starting anew, following Michael Taussig's idea of magic as an unruly momentum within modernity. This democratic magic can of course become quite delusional if overstated, as it is when the taken-for-granted cultural and technical infrastructure present in the so-called developed world is extended to all the world. This said, the possibility of an emancipatory energy here persists. And this persistence is part of the challenge of making this forum a 'cultural site... where the future will be challenged and not just another setting for artistic consumption'. Or to ask how indeed we might produce spaces 'for critical review that goes beyond surface and the passive acceptance of a one-way cultural market' is to ask important and difficult questions. But ask them we must.

The desire for human distinctiveness and commonality, not as essence but as a experience remains one such question. This is still most often expressed in relation to the body and its extensions, natural or artificial (prosthetic), its sensations and feelings, its possibilities for extension, its limits, its material endurance, its animality. This distinctiveness, taken with the personal, is at the centre of such difficult notions as 'authenticity and 'truth'. The range of ways to be 'subjective' has multiplied. Within urban experience this has often resulted in a nomadic, paradoxically anonymous personhood, drifting and detached from durable community and constituency, with its only solidarities often embedded in those random accumulations we call the crowd or the mass. Or accumulations of atomised communities. The intersection of the body and the performance of confession also remains a significant resource for many contemporary artists, and part of the state of our world. One could say the same for the collectives we associate with forced migrations and the 'black' markets which accompany human dispersal. These migrations are often below the radar of regulation and administrative control, and have come to take on a special resonance for many contemporary artists.

Considered performatively, objects have biographies, events have histories and artists are actors of autobiography. This performativity may have a strongly intellectual bent, but this usually tends to a scepticism about its social effects. But I must also say that ambitious art-making in those parts of the world with colonial histories often seems to consider incarnated intellectual work is part of a politics of art. It is this possibility that might allow resistance to what António Pinto Ribeiro refers to as 'passive consumption'. I do not, however, want to overstate the case here (there are many caveats), nor to suggest that intellectual and 'rational' are interchangeable; reason requires enchantment if it is to approach anything like the richness and fullness of human life within and beyond any collectivity. It is rather that the division of faculties may be more fluid and negotiable. Another dimension of such performativity is the manipulation of contemporary secular magic of celebrity in an increasingly sign-saturated world. Temporally, such performativity extends from fleeting moments of contingency and drift to intense, elaborately structured duration. Space has become a material, a medium; haphazard, boundless, on the edge of dissolution or an emanation of a specific site. Time and space are less the trap they once seemed, insofar as these elemental co-ordinates (or the model of location and identification they offer) have become unstable. Our locations are liquid in unprecedented ways, something which permeates our senses of identity and community through and through.

The supreme aesthetic syntax of much contemporary art seems to be that of the pile, the dump, the fragment in haphazard accumulation and combination. Intense singularity, selection and studied indifference to selection exist in increasingly edgy and senseless proximity. Art mediates and meditates on such senselessness from an elastic and restless distance. The ready-made banalities of an increasingly homogenised daily life – commodities, thoughts, feelings – have become grist for the passive artistic mill. These states address some of the primary questions posed by António Pinto Ribeiro in his notes. I would hazard that the obsession with the particularities of site and subjectivity itself might actually amount to a peculiarly post-modern failure of nerve.

My use of the personal register is both a failure of nerve and an effort to acknowledge that autobiography and the voicing of hitherto occluded histories remain a crucial part of what artists and art writers now do. And it is not just that the content of such histories should be revealed, but the structures of knowing and organising new knowledge appropriate to such contents in our lived experience and our critical cultural work. So I write in the personal register not to claim undue authority, but to suggest something larger and more common than the incidental eccentricities of personal experience. Autobiography, taken one way, could be confessional, which to a degree is what has happened earlier in this text. But autobiography can also be a form of writing or rewriting (in the broadest sense) history. These ways are sometimes complementary, but they may equally exist in uncomfortable tension.

The imagined artistic 'constituencies' art addresses, or attempts to produce in contingent solidarity, could often be seen to be social antagonists: the indulgence of the wasteful guilt of privilege countered by experience once silenced but now increasingly vocal and visible. The first tends to be confessional and can appear solipsistic, culturally narcissistic, insular. The second can appear didactic, programmatic, parochial. Both seem to belong in a contracting world. Expansion requires us to continuously draw a line between the two, or to erase the lines we find too heavily drawn. There is a veritable 'post-colonial' and postmodern industry of confession, autobiography, memory and trauma, often located on or in the body which feels increasingly fatigued. There is both overproduction and a numbing, excessive flatness in this traumatophiliac culture industry. We seem exhausted less through resolution than wearying repetition. The personal has begun to pall, and the aesthetic appeals to 'trauma' as a fundamental organising principle is now less easy to stomach.

But macro-identities such as 'nation' also carry their own diminishing returns. In parts of this essay I have stuck quite closely to an understanding of forms of community and history in terms of State and the Nation (South Africa, Portugal), something always already implied in any notion of internationalism. This is partly a pragmatic choice, but it does also involve a politics of art. As a citizen of a recently liberated country, I am acutely aware of both the benefits and perils of seeing art and culture in terms of nations. The discourses and energies of nation-building are well-known to most South Africans, and the Nation-State remains a viable if high risk mechanism for interaction between regional specificities and global pressures.

However, from a different perspective, ideas of civil society and citizenhood beyond conventional national identity seem more compelling than anything nationalism might offer. It suggests to me that the relation between place and people is more flexible than allowed by static notions of nation. It allows different kinds of collaboration, solidarity and difference in a way which is less fixed, more responsive, more of the moment, between sensuous particular and discursive generality. It recognises the fact of human dispersal and the condition of diaspora. Further, nation tends to cut across what is eccentric, idiosyncratic and particular in cultural life, exactly what much art is about. And are these not the qualities we find so valuable to us? Put more rigidly than how I actually feel about this, one could say (not for the first time) that art serves civil society best when it serves itself, however complex that self-understanding may be.

How modernity is grounded and experienced in once colonised nation-states is a matter of argument and analysis. But surely no part of the globe has been untouched by modernity, however mediated, however uneven. Metropolitan cultures, the cultures of the city, may have more in common with each other than locales within the borders of the nation-state. This common urbanity or cosmopolitanism provides something of an antidote to the excesses of nationalism, as well as creating a critical interface between communities and the pressures of globalisation. Yet, nation-building is a critical dimension of modernity, and this often remains the form of collectivity still best able to negotiate, resist and find common cause with the forces of multi-national globalisation. The more interesting questions are those which perhaps in the relations between individuals, groups and communities and what we understand by democracy.

III: Crimes

Some two years ago, the late Edward Said published a book entitled *Humanism and Democratic Criticism*. In it, he presents a robust argument for the importance of that collection of ideas and practices we might bring under the rubric 'humanism'. Said's is a complex, free-ranging text linked to terms we hear almost every day – from 'humanitarian' interventions to crimes against humanity. Apartheid was one such crime against humanity, as declared by UN Resolution 3068 passed on 30 November 1973. Justice Richard Goldstone (Chief Prosecutor of the United Nations Criminal Trials for the former Yugoslavia and Rwanda) notes that the new offence – the 'crime against humanity' was first manifest in the London Agreement of 8 August 1945 which established the Nuremberg Tribunal after the Second World War. This was 'the first time in legal history that certain crimes were identified as being of such magnitude that they injured not only the immediate victims and not only the people of the country or on the continent where they were committed but also of all humankind'.

Clearly some idea of the pan-human animates, shapes and gives direction and purpose to this discourse. But as important is the link between what we might understand as the human and the idea of an almost transcendental crime, some supreme act of inhuman violence and violation. It is in this juncture between violence and humanism that I would argue much critical contemporary art is coming to operate. These operations are of course not explicitly articulated in this way, but this does not weaken the sense that such an articulation is, or can have, profound heuristic value. Perhaps trauma – our reaction to trauma, our suffering of trauma, our perpetration of trauma – is part of what our common humanity comprises. Perhaps the energy in the art we make is most closely associated with violence. Both trauma and violence can be frustratingly nebulous terms, but even so, much contemporary art and certainly South African contemporary art has exercised and taken liberties of the choices liberated by the end of Apartheid, arguably one of the most violent systems of modern times. The forms are as varied as there are artists, but we could understand each in terms of what it has become to be fully human in a violent society. We find performances with prosthetics in old black townships in the work of Steven Cohen, a range of *faux* subjectivities in the menageries of Tracey Rose, the visual culture of poverty and fashion in the almost shackchic photographic work of Zwelethu Mthethwa. Play, humour, irony, spirited and spiteful, have begun to lighten our art with its dark history.

A recognition of the entanglements of humanism and violence in our cultural work draws us away from the sentimentality we might associate with humanist practices, but also the often gratuitous and hypocritical temper of our attitude to violence. Perhaps this is partly what the gnomic Jean Baudrillard had in mind when he suggested, in the late 1990s, that our (*sic*) 'society has expelled violence (at the same time as it has expelled evil, illness, negativity and death – I don't mean it has eliminated them, but it has expelled them from its system of values)'. Closer to home, violence is part of the fabric of the postcolony, as Achille Mbembe shows when he writes that while the champions of state power 'invent entire constellations of ideas… adopt a distinct set of cultural repertoires and powerfully evocative concepts' they still resort 'if necessary, to the systematic application of pain'. Perhaps this is the case with history *tout court* and what Frederic Jameson means when he says history is what hurts.

Francesco Bonami, director of the fiftieth Venice Biennale, very strongly advocated 'creative irrelevance to attack the absurdity of war, violence and discrimination. I am for producing dreams to contain the madness of conflicts.' The problem with the first part of this 'creative irrelevance' (whatever we take the phrase to mean) is that claims implicitly to stand outside violence. In a very simple, obvious, ostensibly trivial way, this is wrongheaded. Perhaps more so because there was a specific act of erasure – or a no less benign 'overlooking' – on this biennale. This occurred in curator Gilane Tawadros' mix-and match show titled *Faultines: Contemporary African Art and Shifting Landscapes*. Included in this show was work by Moshekwa Langa, who presented an extraordinary work at the earlier *Faultlines* exhibition at the Cape Town Castle some years before, which I mentioned earlier. No history linked these two events, no argument, just the syntax of parachute curating, and a free-floating dreamy sense of difference. What kind of dream is Bonami's? Is it not more a symptom – as dreams may be – than a 'container' of a hidden violence? The dream is a mask. There is a violence to this erasure that raises questions not only about the work on the show, but about the entire project in all its complex ripples outwards (from work to the global phenomena of Biennales, triennales and the like). Had this violence been revealed rather than overlooked, we would have had something much more constructive to challenge us and for us to grapple with. Joining the lines of history remains a critical and necessary cultural act, the alleged 'end of history' notwithstanding.

Following Bonami, I do not believe non-violence is served by conceiving violence as absurd. Violence as act, event and representation characterises much contemporary art I have seen. Drawing the line between mutually contaminating phenomena and representation – when the violence of representation and the representation of violence collapse into the other – remains a necessary and important challenge. The recent furore over the cartoons of the prophet Mohammed is playing this out in spectacular form as I write. I am also left wondering about the implications for, for example, Paul Virilio's rather feverish rant against 'pitiless' and art as violence in this regard. And then we might recall the extraordinary project Iconoclash project of Bruno Latour and Peter Weibel in 2002.

What seems to lie deep in the heart of any dynamic of violence is a wavering – now strong, now weak – line between specific historical woundings and the limits of expressive liberation. And to speak of expressive liberation is to speak almost treacherously of redemptive trace in the acts of artistic imagination and indeed art itself. Violence – symbolic and actual – seems to be a necessary precondition for strengthening this redemptive trace. This, even though we need to understand that violence is complex and has a paradoxical edge in that we tend to understand human civility as a process which incrementally exiles violence from it spaces and its relations. And yet in effecting such an exile in thought and deed do we not we become like good civil servants and expel what is alive in life itself in the process? Violence, like fire, can turn both good and bad.

The link between violence and human *being* is central to the writings of Frantz Fanon, performing what Jean-Paul Sartre termed 'the striptease of our humanism'. Fanon reserved a special rage for the incessant talk of 'man' in colonial Europe: 'When I search for Man in the technique and style of Europe, I see only a succession of negations of man, and an avalanche of murders.' Fanon envisions – but does not spell out – a humanism which 'shakes off the heavy darkness in which we were plunged', one which does not 'set her face against all solicitude and tenderness', one in which we 'find something different'.

The resources of reinvigorated, historicised humanisms are

present in our cultures at large as well as our artistic efforts. K. Geyeke, for example, argues that if we were to seek a thorough-going, foundational idea 'in African socioethical thought', one that 'animates other intellectual activities and forms of behaviour, including religious behaviour, and provides continuity, resilience, nourishment, and meaning', that idea would most likely be humanism. In Africa these concepts are embedded in the older discourses of the human which would not have been unfamiliar to Fanon. Speaking of Julius Nyerere's heretical attempt overturn Western conceptions of 'the natural nature of the human', Anthony Bogues, writing in 2003, argues that Nyerere's 'heresy made him a consistent theorist of the Swahili precept that a human being is a human being because of other human beings'.

This particular conception of a relational human identity seems to run through much of Africa, and this form is present in the South Africa from which I write. Moeketsi Letseka argues that the humanisms of Africa find expression in *ubuntu: umuntu ngumuntu ngabantu (*Nguni languages) or *motho ke motho ka batho* (Sotho languages). The TRC was itself founded on these indigenous notions (which are subject to change) of what it is to be human; the report highlights 'the fundamental importance of *ubuntu...* [which] generally translated as "humanness", expresses itself metaphor-ically in umuntu ngumuntu ngabantu – people are people through other people'. The loss of ubuntu is a crisis in an ethical relation to the other, what Mark Sanders calls 'an ethics of reciprocity'. This reci-procity relates to both members of a community, and, importantly, to strangers.

An ethic of reciprocity (or its disavowal), violence (trauma) and the shifting contours of what we understand as humanity seems to ground much contemporary art of the last two decades. The forms this grounding takes, the processes by which those forms are produced must of necessity be extraordinarily varied – notwithstanding or perhaps even resistant to the flattening effects of global art circuits. If I were to speculate on these forms I would describe theme in a rough and provisional way as follows.

Perhaps the most obvious form would be the depiction of excep-tional pain or violence – historical trauma, wounding and death.

Of course there is a strong and widely-held view of the intimate relation between pain and creativity. So depiction here should be seen in widest sense – as process, as act, object or event, and as iconography. Then, I would want to cite Achille Mbembe's description of two related discourses which constitute widespread negative interpretations of Africa:

> Africa is never seen as possessing things and attributes properly part of 'human nature'... It is this elementariness and primitiveness that makes Africa the world *par excellance* of all that is incomplete, mutilated, unfinished, its history reduced to a series of setbacks of nature in its quest for humankind. At another level, discourse on Africa is almost always deployed in the framework (or in the fringes) of a meta-text about the animal – to be exact, about the beast: its experience, its world, and its spectacle.

These twin 'negations' gives rise to a second more diffuse sense of violence that involves relations between the wild and the domestic, often expressed as a relation between animal and human, bestiality and civility, normativity and monstrosity, the social and the singular.

A third aspect has to do with ritualised assaults on the body. This is a very broad category, but here I have in mind local art practices which interest themselves in circumcision rituals and the metropolitan representations of these rituals. This phenomenon would in part at least refer also to the contemporary phenomenon of extreme body art. A fourth aspect involves embodied language, the languages of carnality and multi-lingualism. Language is often taken as a defining characteristic of the uniquely human. Written into this complex are the dynamics of linguistic imperialism and aesthetic purism, to name but two. The scriptovisual violence of irony, parody, mimicry and the sentimental frozen nostalgias (and counter-nostalgias) for lost origins and lost futures would be important here; as is narrative form. Also important is the violence of militant discursivity in the visual field and the destruction of singularity by generality, the sensuous particular by abstraction.

There is a certain kind of conceptualism where idea dominates materiality, where the mental disavows the manual, where representation dominates thing.

In all these forms we find expansions and contractions of what it means to be human, ranging from infinitely regressive prosthetic subjectivities to play with authenticity, identity, dissent, resistance. I am reminded here of an aphorism of Nietzsche's in his *Maxims and Arrows*: 'Are you genuine? or only an actor? A representative? Or that itself which is represented? – Finally you are no more than an imitation of an actor...'

Lastly, a possible sixth form would be the insistence of an insurgent, aggressive 'presentness' or 'nowness'. In many cases this amounts to a rather unembarrassed ahistoricity. In a sense this development is a function of the spatial turn in culture and art, the invocation of mobility as a state of being, and the associated development of temporal modes of momentariness, drift and dawdle – the world as mall and waiting room. Also part of this is an assertion of the priority of the surfaces of the here and the now. What we might call the ethics of proximity are deeply enmeshed in these spatio-temporal turns. Zygmunt Baumann captures the ethical dimension of proximity eloquently:

> Being inextricably tied to human proximity, morality seems to conform to the law of optical perspective. It looms large and thick close to the eye. With the growth of distance, responsibility for the other shrivels, moral dimensions of the object blur, till both reach the vanishing point and disappear from view.

IV: Vanishing Points

I began this text with a story which seems to allegorise the current state of the world. It is a narrative of human ingenuity and venality, of human imagination and violence. There is no conclusion to this. I want to stop if not exactly end by returning to this register of narrative and continue to describe the contemporary fate of the padrão.

The remains of the 'original' structure are now housed in the William Cullen Library of the University of the Witwatersrand, my *alma mater*. Wits is over a thousand kilometers away from Kenton-on-Sea, and it was here at the University that the remains of the Dias padrão were authenticated in a scene described in almost divine terms by the discoverer: 'Professor Fouché rose from his examination... and exclaimed, "I have been on my knees before the true cross."' The Historical Monuments' Commission and the then Union of South African Government entrusted the structure to Wits's care. Fragments from the original – about one quarter to a third had disappeared – were cemented into a contemporary concrete construction which fills in what is missing and fixes the place of what is not. Several casts were made of this cross, one being erected at *Kwaaihoek* (unveiled 20 June 1940), another gifted to the Portuguese government (who also later received an original fragment), and a third presented to the people of Lourenço Marques (now Maputo) where it was housed in a museum.

When there are more than one, when there are copies, the original seems to intensify its claim to singularity. When I was researching the holdings of the University Library on the subject of the 'true cross', the librarian offered me a number of papers from their archives. The librarian also spoke darkly of a recent claim for cultural restoration; that is, repatriation of this padrão to its historical place or thereabouts. About a similar, if much grander challenge (Greece and the British Museum), Christopher Hitchens wrote: 'There is still time to make the act of restitution: not extorted by pressure or complaint but freely offered as a homage to the indivisibility of art and – why not say it without embarrassment? – of Justice too.' There is too much to say about the state of the world. And even more to do.

For some of the historical information I acknowledge the work of Eric Axelson, especially his *Vasco da Gama: The Diary of His Travels through African Waters 1497–1499* (Somerset West, 1998). Of course all errors are my own. Another primary general reference was Leonard Thompson's *A History of South Africa* (New Haven, Yale, 1990).

The Habit of Exiles

GHASSAN ZAQTAN

The Habit of Exiles

My heart is suspicious, my friend inexperienced
My dream is blind
I was bereaved by the news of Baghdad
Brought out by amateur exiles
What are they to us?
They just happened to be crossing the bridge

The intentions are in the ports
Confused, just as their owners had left them
Deficient as the dead had left them
And where our friend, you know him, pointed,
We went on, without looking back, without a second thought.

Our country is far
And our intentions are good

As is usual with exiles
We abandoned homes more beautiful
Than the road
Women more loyal than these transient ones
But that did not deter us
Or weaken our resolve

We dreamt as settled people do
Of roads more beautiful than home
Of women to inhabit our bodies and speak a new tongue
But that did not carry us to the hills
Or to the sea

Infantry appeared from a battlefield
Whose uproar we heard
But did not see
With haggard eyes and cracked feet
They wiped the mud off on the marble
Drying their boots on the posters of the
Founding father

And we watched
But it was as though we neither heard nor saw

One could have recalled their voluptuous dreams,
And chased their ghosts
Touching the thighs of women just to make sure

There is no mercy for the dead in these cold regions
No reward for those who know

One can only listen to the mountains where the caves multiply,
And darkness expands like a devouring plant

We were not carried away by the screech of the birds
With the advent of dawn
We were not held back by the judgement of our predecessors

And their fears
Yet what we saw
Deserves to be told

…then slaves began emerging from the chasm
Climbing the walls
While the doors were wide open
To descend upon the city,
Roam its markets,
Men and boys were there, shouting at the darkness
Chasing it away with drum and dance,
And women stripping naked at the edge of the abyss
To lure death away from their young
As an ordinary man explained to us
So we gave thanks to our exile and home.

We said to ourselves:
We are only exiles on the march
Whose shadows leave no traces on the ground
Like weavers we catch up threads
And weave them into memories that pant after us
As they follow our footsteps like distracted dogs

Who are we to hate what we do not know!
Who are we to love that which does not concern us!

When the amateur exiles who brought the news of Baghdad
Had gone
A jealous boy appeared
Whose jealousy
After he had left
Continued to gleam on the fence
And bar the way for cats,
Passersby and the scent of basil
Pressing on the breasts of a girl

Who, emerging from the shadows
Threw off her thick veil on the grass near the soldiers' boots.
Then I moved to another dream

All that could have been pondered and repeated
Had not a young philosopher in Ramallah died
At sixteen minutes past four that morning
Surrounded by his students, his admirers and three friends
– Two men and a woman!
We could remember sundry other details and add them
To reveal grief and expose the fullness of the treachery
Foremost of all:
The lilac statue of Buddha*

Or the picture of the landlord
In the hall of the furnished apartment
As he stares at us from
The classical pose of his death

The father's private reflections
His deep complicity with the 'girl'
As he lay dying in the oxygen tent

The woman's voice down the telephone line
Concealing under its ten thick layers
Her betrayal

His death could have been recorded,
Other things remembered
Like the weight of his body
The whites of his eyes
In a final act of perplexity
Before releasing the light in the carriage

---

* The reference here is to the Bamiyan Budhhas, two monumental statues of
  Buddha carved from the mountain in Bamiyan, Afghanistan and condemned
  by the Taliban as idolatrous, which were destroyed in March 2001.

Had his posture towards the world not been slightly askew
  As had happened with Constantine Cavafy,
For whom he did not care as much as for other poets

My heart is suspicious, brother
My stance is final
No one will guess
The storms in my head
I no longer have confidence in those
Who pass through at night.

Black Horses

The slain enemy
Think of me without mercy in their eternal sleep
Ghosts ascend the stairways of the house, rounding the corners
The ghosts I picked up from the roads
Collecting them from the sins around other people's necks.

The sin hangs at the throat like a burden
It is there I nurture my ghosts and feed them
The ghosts that float like black horses in my dreams.

With the vigor of the dead the latest Blues song rises
While I reflect on jealousy
The door is warped open, breath seeps through the cracks
The breath of the river
The breath of drunkards, the breath
Of the woman who awakes to her past in a public park.

When I sleep
        I see a horse grazing the grass
When I fall asleep,
        The horse watches over my dreams

On my table in Ramallah
There are unfinished letters
And pictures of old friends
The manuscript of a young poet from Gaza
An hourglass
And opening lines that flap in my head like wings?

I want to memorise you like that song in first grade
The one I hold onto
Complete and
With no mistakes
The lisp, the tilt of the head, off key
The small feet pounding the concrete so eagerly

The open palms pounding the benches.

They all died in the war
My friends and classmates
Their little feet
Their eager little hands... they still pound the floors of each room
They pound the tables;
And still pound the pavements, the backs of the passersby, their
                                                                shoulders.

Wherever I go
I see them
I hear them.

An Enemy Descends the Hill

As he descends,
As we watch him descend,
As he conveys to us that he is
About to descend

Warily, silently

His illicit presence
As he carefully listens at the shrubs.

His fear as he descends
The withheld silence
That he is not 'us'
Not 'here'
Death begins.

He seizes a flower
Just a flower
With no message to convey
No vase for it.

From the hill
He can see
The military checkpoint
The paratroopers
He can see the desperate people;
The slopes of the mountains;
The only path
Where their feet will leave imprints in the rocks
In mud and water.

He can also see
The losses from the hill
Left hurriedly behind

The equivocation of shadows
Where the moustached enemy
Resembles the dead Arabs here.
In the slopes of the mountains
The caves will all appear peaceful
The road always look the same.

As he descends
The caves in the mountains
Continue to stare
They blink in the cold.

The Trench

How strange are the days of salt
It is as if they belong to others
And like a well-plotted tragedy
Just brought to a close
They begin to breathe as we remember them

The hills forgotten in the boredom of the slopes
The mountains that aspire towards the west
The wandering caravans of death
The faith of the dead, complete.

The hands that emerge from the darkness
To tell you everything
The deep fraternity that does not lead to wisdom
The words no longer suitable for high places

Strange are the days of salt
Now alone in the abyss
Disparaged like rotten seed

And while we ascend,
Because that's all we can do
The days roll away into the distance behind us,
Abandoned, and can never return

Our dark complexions
Our attempts at sleep
…Names, endlessly long titles
Dialects also
Proclaiming a countryside
No longer necessary.

How strange are the days of salt
They are not even worthy to be remembered.

The Camp Prostitute

What those intend who visit her house
Is palpably felt
So pure, so proud.

Those who stayed late in the fields
Will find her hanging near the little trees
The five mossy steps
Then the bougainvillea plant by the door.

Her bracelets jingling in their sleep like a phantom horse
Her undergarments colouring their dreams
Her breasts well trodden like the path to the mill
Her ritual movements between the bed and the wash basin
Like a popular song all the rage.

The still life on the wall
The sheets and two pillows
The scent of cheap cologne
The nails behind the door
Where the smell of their clothes still lingers
The jasmine outside the window

The numbed convolutions of her body
The strain pervading her silence

The intentions of those passing through to her house
The passersby and the visitors,
The students, clerks and chickens
The vans, the guards and the dogs,
The porters, the cats and the vegetable sellers
The fathers and sons
All those who have left their smell in her broken sleep
They were all of them there
Behind the kids
The cart

The coffin
So pure, on their way to her destination.

The Sleeper's Song

I ascend the seven levels
Of sleep
In sleep you are
An elegy to the departed
An icon of censure

I ascend
The seven levels of sleep
All of them.

Nothing happens
Nothing ends.

I switch on the light
So that the dead
Can see the dream.

Additions to the Past

The letters in the widow's room
In the straw basket
On the bed purged of sleep
In the intention to fast which lurks
In the air of the corridor.

The vegetables, normally purchased in the morning
The tickets,
The dawn bus on a Thursday
The pillows
The candles
The forbearance… where holy phrases are
Gaudily etched
In the carvings

The edge of the cupboard from the crack of the door
The door itself… where the assembled hymns
Flutter like kerchiefs on the darkness of the plain.

The shadow of the air
The novel she has not returned to the shelf,
She cannot remember!
Its heroes fall dead to the ground
She sweeps them up
One after the other
With her broom, her reproaches and her prayers

The letters remain unopened
The dead
Return through the crack of the door
To steal the flower vase
The orange sheet
And the covers

Translated by May Khadra

The Devastated Garden and the Profile of Hope

JOÃO BARRENTO

> And be not conformed to this world
>
> St Paul, *Epistle to the Romans*, 12:2

> How can one distinguish the devastated garden in which we stand from the profile of hope? _____ All around me, I constantly hear people talking about the *world*, what's gone wrong, what should be changed, what could be better, but I don't know where I can place that different within it, because I can't see – can't even imagine – the form of the world.
>
> Maria Gabriela Llansol, *Lisboaleipzig 1.*
> *O Encontro Inesperado do Diverso*

The World Scene

Wittgenstein's first proposition in *Tractatus Logico-Philosophicus* reads: 'The world is everything that is the case.' The sub-proposition that follows it and is derived from it reads: 'The world is the totality of facts, not of things.' I have started with these fundamental definitions because they permit me immediately to distance myself from any metaphysical or ontological view of the 'world' and instead to emphasise a vision that foregrounds its performative, changing and poetic aspects. The world is what is done in it and comes from it, but it *is* not, at least for my purpose here, purely and simply an ontological entity (Heidegger's ontology also distinguishes between world and Being). As such, it seems impossible to describe the 'state of the world', let alone to understand the 'form of the world', since we are essentially dealing with an unstable group of events, relations and interactions. However, we can try to understand the *forms of that happening* within a defined and more or less broad historical and cultural group. For my purposes here, the patterns of our 'actuality' can easily be seen through references to the last decade, covering the last years of the twentieth century and the opening years of the twenty-first. Alternatively, if this time-span makes political and cultural sense (an issue I shall return to), we could be guided by 11 September 2001, a date which – while not marking a decisive rupture between a 'before' and an 'after' – fell exactly halfway through this period.

First Allegory: The Days of Judgement
Although we are clearly living in a time of *passage* and accelerated mutation (what we must try to understand is where to and how), let us imagine what a snapshot of our world, of the human and non-human world, might look like (but only after wondering if there is any truly non-human – or at least non-humanised – world in the current state of civilisation). In one essay from his latest work (*Profanazioni*, 2005), Giorgio Agamben defines photography as the place for the Final Judgement, the representation of the world as it will be on its last day, or rather, on that day after, the apocata-stasis. He was specifically referring to the earliest long exposure daguerreotypes, which showed no figures in the fragment of the world focused on. Although they were in fact there, they were moving and therefore did not appear in the final print. In such an apocatastic photograph, the gesture captured – which is not a static crystallisation but latency and anticipation, the fulcrum of a connection between past and present – becomes the focal point of a metonymic power that allows it to be a historical milestone for an age that is endlessly repeated and multiplied by millions, like the always identical gesture of the shadows of the dead in Hades. It simultaneously suggests another time, a more up-to-date and urgent time that has not yet come into being. We will try to imagine which figures can be seen and which signs can be read in such a snapshot of today's world, in a cross-section of the flow of temporality, suspending time in an apocatastic pause, or at the moment of death, as it is said that the hanged see their entire lives in a sort of intense, concentrated dream. In our case, the predom-

inant movements of the figures would be a drift without visible horizons, moving equally in the great cities and the deserts of Africa, and a chain of relocations, migrations and catastrophes of all kinds, natural and civilisational, alternating and contrasting with intense foci of great creations, of moments of euphoria, of 'triumphs of invention over the necessary, formatted death', to quote the key formula from one of Michel Serres' recent books (*Branches*). The background is an undefined grey mass with no apparent centre, no detectable form, an amorphous chaos, a homogeneous nebulosity under the uniform light of several invisible spotlights. Yet at the same moment, highly diverse dates, different times, contrasting profiles and forces in conflict emerge from this indistinct sea. Here and there, we see small images with poorly defined outlines: semi-formed, fleeting flashes of brilliance that point to that other, more urgent time, which can now be detected but has yet to arrive. It is a time when those many lost figures that stare out at me from the photograph will not force me (as they now do) to look away from this scene of the world, this time that was allocated to me – a time of shame, fear, shock, and of blindness, dazzled by the overwhelming civilisational brilliance created by human talents in the last century. Yet as I look, I realise that I am looking at myself. I am also part of the portrait of the world, and I cannot absent myself, nor ignore its sufferings and achievements, let alone withdraw from the responsibility of being part of it.

No power will look in this way at the state of the world, at its living portrait. As Montaigne knew and transmitted through the constant *exempla* in *Essays*, power is always on the 'obscene' side of the world, and knows nothing of 'shame'. Yet these terms must be clarified; this can be done by using Giorgio Agamben's *Idea of Prose*. First, we must recall that 'secret relations link power to potency', and that power is the negative form of potency, which does not permit the freeing of its intrinsic force and will be transformed into an act, as happens with pleasure. Moreover, potency that is not transformed into an act creates pain (Agamben writes that power 'is the isolation of potency in relation to its act, the organisation of potency', 'literally [leaving] man's pleasure incom-

plete'). Then, there are the feelings of obscenity and shame are
naturally part of the moral narrowness and human pettiness of the
modern world. The Ancients knew nothing of the feeling of misery
that torments (for example) Kafka's characters in a world without
God (which is still there today, but now in an unconscious and non-
tragic form, entertaining itself with simulations of the divine in
trompe l'oeil). What must urgently be recovered now for individual
consciousness from work such as Kafka's is that 'shame' of which
the powers know nothing and which Agamben defines as 'the pure
and empty form of the most intimate feeling of the I'. It is another
form of ethics, the freeing of that shame for human happiness, the
'only good' that we would still have in a universe without values.
Agamben concludes: 'To fulfil this mission, to at least maintain
shame for humanity, Kafka rediscovered something like an ancient
happiness.' The contemporary world's obscenity includes both the
return of a political discourse that uses God in the name of war and
the many forms of cacophony and anti-dialogue that know
nothing of and assault 'the most intimate feeling of the I' (and
which poets and philosophers from Kierkegaard to Heidegger and
from Paul Celan to Daniel Faria have resisted). This world ignores
the slow time that internalised discourse demands, far beyond the
strident shout of the ungrounded word, perhaps even the 'gabbling
that makes up language', to which Jean-Luc Nancy contrasts the
'resistance of poetry'.

No power will look in this way at the state of the world, at its
living portrait. Yet 'culture', which is also part of the picture (albeit
now on the periphery and informally dressed) will have to do this;
otherwise, it will be charged with promoting and enacting the act
of forgetting through strategies of illusion instead of stimulating
memory, cultivating criticism and upsetting the preconceptions of
the comfortable world. If it succeeds in doing this, as the dominant
culture of media-based populism does *not* nowadays, every day
will necessarily become a day of judgement, of permanent revision of the state of the world; because, in this totally secularised
world (but where politics seems to have re-appropriated religion
and all its manipulative paraphernalia – not only in the East), art
and culture may be the setting for the great courtroom, and the

Final Judgement will take place every day, here and now. Kafka knew this and wrote this at the time of modernism, when in the portrait of the world, the aesthetic and the ethical were far more strongly contrasted, so as to mask inner fragmentation. However, the remains of metaphysics, the nihilist dialectic, dualist visions of 'two cultures' were still active one hundred years ago. These things have since vanished from our pacified, indifferent and relativist cultural horizon. Not even the great allegory that opened the new century to yet another endless series of wars managed to shake this. The allegory in question was the explosive image of 11 September 2001, which razed the world temple of mercantile glory, the *skyline* of the power held by an abstract and blind deity that has no 'faithful' and is even now building ever greater shrines in China.

Second Allegory: Twin Towers
This is no abstract allegory, the product of an imaginative projection such as the allegory of a photograph of the world, but a historically grounded one, a symbol of the new century. Although it could be observed in 'real time', this made it doubly unreal. Initially, this sense of unreality was due to stupefaction at an event that went beyond all fiction, clearly seen through a virtual medium that has now donned the mantle of the sole reality: television. Secondly, because the event ('the sudden appearance of the formless'), which some tend to see as a decisive reference in gauging the current state of the world, was continued beyond the initial shock and beyond the next holy oil war that it triggered, essentially in the 'symbolic' sphere and at both the communicational and the ideological level: the deafening repetition of *discourses* on the event (the preferred form of repercussion and action of events in today's world, of its 'legibility'); and the *ritornello* of history, after its end had been proclaimed and following a relatively long 'strike of events' (Baudrillard), at least for America and Europe, which had not experienced internal war since 1945. The fall of the Berlin Wall did not in fact start any new cycle, but merely closed the Cold War phase. Its place would be taken in the new millennium by the 'infinite war' (Foucault) in which we now live. The 'strike of events',

merely enlivened by the end of Europe's last totalitarian and colonial régimes, and by the existence of abundance and security guaranteed by the armed peace of the second post-war, has been followed by a period of eagerness for events that characterises today's world. This includes a series of features that give it the profile of a time dominated by the culture of the *radical* and, to some extent, associated culture of the *sublime*, understood as an event that overcomes itself by being more real that reality itself: in the historical limits of our contemporaneity, and in a sort of inverted specular relationship, these two moments of a 'sublimity' that is the start and end of what is terrible, were Hiroshima and its *pendant*, the World Trade Centre. These were both symbols of imperial orders being shaken and of another phallic and patriarchal order that has, since the beginning of civilisation, been represented by towers, gates, ziggurats and metropolises, material forms of a 'culturalist verticality' that superimposes and imposes itself on the 'naturalised horizontality' (Fernando R. de La Flor).

The event in New York does not constitute any radical caesura in the flow of contemporary history: it does not establish a 'before' and an 'after'. It came like an unheard shock, a profane apocalypse that is far removed from the idea of the 'end of history' proclaimed by Francis Fukuyama, which corresponded more to the stagnation of a known and supposedly insuperable model. What it did do was to reposition something that we already knew on our immediate horizon, reopening the *discourse of separation* after the Cold War. This is now called (in Samuel Huntington's sorry expression that can only be explained by yet another return: of religious fundamentalism in this new age of crusades) 'the clash of civilizations', which Edward Said corrected to 'the clash of prejudices', rightly intuiting that civilisations and identities are not sealed entities but processes that result from interactions and contacts, historically grounded in practices of tolerance and living together. The state of the world is now again marked by the return of religion on the political front (albeit sometimes in a camouflage that fails to hide the osmosis between monotheism and absolutism in the world of empires), set against the grey but almighty backdrop of the globalised economy. This is what explains the new discourses of separation, of the Manichaean radicalisation of the movement towards theologising the political and towards the 'compulsive alternatives' in this field. In the 1950s, during the aftermath of Nazism, the philosopher Karl Jaspers wrote that this was a very Western tendency, yet it is equally present in the Orient, in the terrorist practices of the rulers of Saudi Arabia and so many Arab states in the Gulf who are 'friends' of Western democracies, and in the preaching and actions of that genuinely American figure: the 'electronic prophet' Bin Laden, 'a man for whom wealth and power are all that matters, regardless of the means' (as Alain Badiou noted at a conference in October 2001).

For the moment, that wealth and power comes from oil. We are witnessing – in this historical allegory that might be a restaging of Wagner's tetralogy – a new curse of gold (no longer in the Rhine, but in the Gulf) that is one of the great modern curses. Theologising the political, now seen in the 'political instrumentation of religion' by the Gulf monarchies, in turn instrumented by the USA itself (as again noted by Badiou), is nothing new. During the 1920s and 1930s, it was given one of its most important theoretical supports in the political philosophy of Carl Schmitt, with his theses of the political and anthropological need to create images of the enemy and the 'providential enemy' (rediscovered now both in American politics since the Gulf War and the fundamentalist excesses of a deformed Islam). His theory of salvation (the ideal tool of all totalitarian systems) demands that individual consciences be annulled in the name of collective interests to counter an absolute and absolutely 'necessary' enemy. Based on this, every war can be legitimised as an innate necessity, whereas they are in fact cultural artefacts. This is also the basis for all the Manichaean polarisations that have a vaguely religious background, which establish 'axes of evil' and the hypostasis of an 'us' (in which we immediately get trapped in the dualism of for and against) that is extended today – depending on convenience – into 'the West', 'our societies' or 'democracies'. Contemporary culture may be slipping down that perilous slope in several ways: in the anti-terrorist paranoia whipped up by 9/11, the proliferation of sects and widespread political apathy; as well as in some now-dominant forms of literature (mythical, myth-creating and alien-ating), and even in the positive opposite of the perversity of the political through the undeniable presence of diverse forms of voluntary work, philanthropy and 'mission spirit'. And naturally, this also appears in the conservative politicians who have an abso-lutist tendency, wrapped up in the dangerous liaisons – *à la* Carl Schmitt – that link power and salvation.

In order to face up to this new salvational constellation, we must revive the culture of productive conflict: a culture that creates rather than destroys, one that is based on communication and not violence, one in which Hesiod (in a poem from the seventh century BC) could contrast those who need enemies and not rivals with 'bad conflicts'. Europe's colonial history and all contemporary forms of warlike and mercantilist neo-colonialism are a part of a culture of non-communication and extermination. The Swedish historian Sven Lindquist has studied the roots of this culture in a series of books in which he tries to demonstrate how Europe's first export was violence, and how extermination was the consequence of a notion of culture based on the hostile and xenophobic relationship between peoples and cultures. It is a history of 'progress' that has a desperately high price. For some, it is an endless and triumphant straight line, for others a vicious or 'fixed' circle in which humanity 'treads water' (curiously, this is the position adopted by a revolu-tionary from the Paris Commune, Louis-Auguste Blanqui, in *Eternity Through the Stars*). Probably neither one nor the other is true to reality, which is more complex and vertiginous, being of the world in time. For a philosopher of human progress such as Hegel, there is a desire for history, for teleological meaning; yet in *Weltfremdheit* (World Strangeness) Peter Sloterdijk states that 'the heroes of history (...) are not men, but the rhythms and forces of the birth and positioning of the world, where men find their place'. Just as the aristocratic, conservative and Catholic Count of Leinsdorf in Robert Musil's *The Man without Qualities* says 'there are no voluntary regressions in the history of mankind', it is equally true that there have been spectacular plunges into the abyss of barbarity.

Turning Points and Centres

I will bring the allegories to a close and focus instead on some more blatantly obvious issues in the current state of the world, including the cultural world, fully aware that there is no single world, but multiple worlds in the world; that there is no single state, but a future of the world, that 'nothing was, everything is being' (Maria Gabriela Llansol). As Montaigne wrote, 'Man is undoubtedly a marvellously evanescent, diverse and ever-changing subject, and it is a hard task to try and form a constant and uniform judgement on him.' However, this does not prevent us from establishing that there is a historical memory that returns, cycles that are repeated with variations, problems which – since they are cultural rather than anthropological – seem to be recurrent obsessions.

In 1800, Friedrich Schlegel published a programme that rethought the parameters of cultural creation in *Athenäum*, the theoretical organ of the first centre of German Romanticism. Simply called *poesie* in the language of Romantic syncretism, this came after a century of rationalism, system and abstraction. The title of his text was 'Discourse on Mythology', and the underlying thesis was that culture at the turn of the century *lacked a centre* and new political and aesthetic paradigms, 'something like mythology for the Ancients'. In fact, the various preceding 'turns of the century' – where one set of values reaches its end and declines as a new set emerges – seem to have had a keen sense of this absence of a 'centre'. The Romantics from 1800 felt that a new mythology had to be subjective and sensitive in nature, centred on the present and with an aesthetic background. However, aesthetics was already understood as ethics, as can be seen from another significant text written four years earlier by an unconfirmed author (Hölderlin, or Hegel or Schelling, perhaps), 'The Oldest Programme of the System of German Idealism', which reads:

> I am convinced that the supreme act of reason – by which reason covers all ideas – is an aesthetic act, and that truth and goodness are only linked as sisters in the plane of beauty. ... Monotheism of reason and of the heart, polytheism of the imagination and

of art – that is what we need! ... We need a new mythology, yet it must serve ideas and must become a mythology of Reason.

Schlegel's proposal headed towards a new 'realism' (more of a philosophical than an aesthetic meaning, in response to the dominant idealism), founded in the emerging *physics* and Espinosa's materialist and organicist philosophy, fed on the 'beautiful chaos of the [living] imagination' and a moderating factor of individual particularities ('in Espinosa, you will find the beginning and end of all imagination, the general land on which your individual inventions rest').

In 1900, when the previous century turned to what would become 'our' century (one whose contradictions and unparalleled energy we are still experiencing), there was an awareness of the absence of a centre that was felt like a gaping wound and a dissolving force. This was particularly alive throughout the process of modernism, during which we witnessed the fragmentation of the nucleus that had acted as the sought-after 'centre' for the Romantics of Iena: the universes of the I and interiority. The Irish poet W.B. Yeats formulated, in the name of all the moderns (although it could have been, and also was, Pessoa who did this) that awareness of breaking away from a centre and nostalgia of the other in his poem 'The Second Coming': 'Things fall apart, the centre cannot hold.' All the movements of aesthetic modernity, from Baudelaire to the various modernisms, would focus on a negative centre, Nothing, acting as they did as the aesthetic expression of a philosophical nihilism which, in the second half of the nineteenth century and following Nietzsche, opened those two great craters of the *ethical void* (and the consequent aestheticisation of ethics itself, and later of totalitarian politics) and *scepticism* regarding the subject, whose 'dissociation' is accentuated, and regarding language, which becomes aware of its limitations.

Nowadays, in a social and cultural constellation that we must continue to see as 'post-modern' (as we have no other name for it, and not even 9/11 can act as a foundation stone), there does not seem to be any sense of lacking a centre. In cultural and social terms, the centre was disseminated in post-modernity through a series of multiple and mutating nuclei. It now acts and is experienced – and above all is 'lived' by the dominant mechanisms of the *media*, advertising and performance politics – in a land that belongs to all and to nobody, in an opacity that does not allow clear outlines to be seen or defined. The long and collective poem on 'The state of world / The brilliance of language' (part of the Coimbra Capital of Culture project on the internet in 2003), describes 'the world in a state of voracious erosion… / with its waters rotted by chemicals and the future, / bodies imploded by hunger, children who were never children, … / exoduses incinerated in fire with neither light nor salvation, migrations to nowhere / because the new world cannot break free from the other side of the mirror…'. Its efforts to describe the current situation of the surplus of events and the voiding of perspectives emerges in images such as the following: 'we now draw squares of nothing / a cortège of alphabets a fall / a Kafkanesque scream for atoms / a future in the shape of impulses / a territory voided to the maximum.' In *Accents*, Fernando Gil echoes the last sentence in Espinosa's *Ethics* – '*Omnia praeclara tam difficilia quam rara sunt*' ('All notable things are as difficult as they are rare') – and demands that we should 'see clearly', against the grey backdrop of the 'widespread falsification' that threatens us. Seeing clearly now means having one's conscience alert in the midst of a universe of appearances, criticising the bad faith and sophist perversity of political opportunism – namely the one that led to the great tragic/allegorical show of 9/11 and its consequences in Iraq and other areas of the world – while not forgetting that this clear vision includes the capacity for wonder and amazement at the beauty and admirable aspects of the world, our world, which is almost all upside down and with no centre in sight.

In cultural terms, the post-modern – with its aesthetics of the simulacrum, of imitation, of the kitsch and the virtual, with its genological hybridism, the interplay between reader/viewer, the idea of the I as an illusion of language and of reality as a mere possibility – focuses mainly on an evasive centre, that of *as if* (whatever it may be, this world is the best of worlds). In today's world, with its cult of appearance and contingency, one can only succeed through a soft dialectic of appearances where the world is (as

indeed it is) one of experiences without deep experience, dominated from one end to the other by a typically social-democrat
spirit that is the opposite of radical commitment, which mistrusts
the integrity of what is the whole being, and comes from inside,
which is lukewarm and based on good intentions that promise 'the
common good', using a mega-ideology that excludes pain and
death from its programme, which has a mentality of averageness
that (despite appearances) resists creativity. While this world may
never have been so alive and diverse, especially in terms of mass
culture, it tends to be uncritical, narcissistic, lightweight or
populist, shorn of originating power, made up of games and
effects. For a man like George Steiner, the embodiment of a
European culture that committed suicide when it killed its Jews
and is again killing itself by excluding the 'barbarians' that it has let
or enticed in, cultural Europe entered a period of the 'fascism of
vulgarity' (*The Idea of Europe*), while in *Language and Silence* (1967)
he spoke abut the 'treachery of the amanuenses' regarding the
great tradition of an idea of Europe that has now been reduced to
an economic and geographical concept. In Steiner's case, it may be
nostalgia for a *Mitteleuropa* that is long gone. Yet sooner or later,
in this post-colonial age, the cultural tedium and camouflaged
decline that have settled in Western civilisations will be definitively overcome. Indeed, this has already started through cultural
expressions from the ex-colonial world, which is politically and
economically weakened but which still holds a potential for
renewing culture.

The question is political, rather than merely cultural. Perhaps
more accurately, as Alain Badiou says, it is a 'metapolitical' question, if we consider its demand to abandon the swampland through
a political thought (now almost completely absent from politics,
but where culture would have to take a leading role) that essentially questions and again brings practices of resistance to the social
field. These are the 'movements of rage against the era' that
Deleuze also wanted for philosophy, because 'not resisting means
not thinking [...], and not thinking means risking risk' (Badiou,
Abrégé de métapolitique). This poses some questions that cannot be
easily answered at this moment in time, but that can be raised

before analysing some symptoms that will enable us to draw up a potential profile of the current state of the world. Will the art and culture of the future devote themselves to some form of commitment to life and experience that goes beyond the 'entertainment interests' which now dominate? Will we reach some sort of 'new mythology', which in this case would have to be trans-individual, reviving the 'living sources of imagination' (as Schlegel wished in 1800), of nature and of the symbolic, going beyond consumption? Will thinking overcome the current bulimia of cases and facts, again be accepted in the *polis*, and gain a new home in a language that can be heard and in a space of dialogue? Will ethics again have its place in aesthetics? Can future culture, after the market and soft democracy, concordats without productive conflict, become a culture of seriousness (without necessarily becoming solemn), breaking through the alienating lightness of advertising culture? Will art still have a place in a 'democratic' global society that is totally Americanised – a term which implies (although these defining lines are often forgotten) imperialism and bitter puritanism? In *The Idea of Europe*, Steiner also refers to societies such as America as 'provincial' due to the spread of sects, the widespread ignorance, the transformation of the local into the parochial and, last but not least, the absence of cafés! Steiner openly assumes his position as a Europeanist (albeit with a clear vein of outdated and now innocuous nostalgia) and adopts an openly anti-American stance. Accepting globalisation as a legitimate and desirable process (provided it will lead to tolerance and to the elimination of frontiers), he recalls that the genius of Europe lies in the 'sanctity of minute detail' (Blake) and in its diversity, which contrasts with the 'American greed for uniformity'. According to Steiner, the wave of Anglo-Americanism, that 'devouring Esperanto' whose greatest tool – besides economic and military power – is now a language that is never really a language, tends to nullify what is best in European individualism: its languages and its cultures, its languages *of* culture. Yet will the day ever come when Europe witnesses the 'counter-industrial revolution' whose need George Steiner advocates as an alternative, one that is now clearly utopian and clearly undesirable?

Format and Invention

The list of questions posed above has brought some responses from the most diverse sectors. Almost all are more philosophical than practical, all have a profile of hope; they are sometimes contradictory, but operate with similar concepts and seek the key to a different future through balance. These concepts are those of the singular and the common (or of the libido and the social, the desire and the technical), and the visions of the state of world and its future almost invariably involve different forms of functional articulation or disjunction between the two. In his latest work (*Branches*), Michel Serres focuses on what might be called a 'cosmo-genesis' that rewrites human history within the history of the universe, using an approach which, while not explicitly assumed, is undeniably of a Pascalian nature. He also focuses on what he likes to call 'the Great Narrative' of the human adventure, compared to which traditional history is just a minuscule layer of time. This is the starting point for his reflection on what he sees as the extreme level of 'formatting', i.e., of standardisation and abstraction reached by minds, behaviours, and rhythms of life in this age of globalisation. He also recognises that there are many counter-movements in the contemporary world, with a flourishing and 'evolving ramification' that emerges from the dominant trunks, from the figures of the Father that are condemned not to death, but to being overtaken by countless and inevitable Sons who bring changes, inventions and advances that – while never denying their legacy – will leave the withered stem behind. It is the point of view of a philosopher who has assimilated the forms of progress from science and aims to demonstrate that it has been like this since the beginning of the world, in the physical, civilisational and religious history of that world. The great paradigm for this plant metaphor and the escape from the 'format' is Saul-Paul on the road to Damascus, embodying an event (*événement*) that represents the advent (*avènement*) of the I over the we, the new spirit of a Christianity of the 'not-belonging of the soul' born from the common Judaeo-Roman trunk, from the spirit of the Father and of the Law, which then deterritorialises itself and opens up to all men. It is a metaphor that opposes – yet recovers, in a Hegelian dialectic – the format (rigidity, repetition, 'libido of belonging', the mother of all wars and all racisms, the law of the Father) to the event (the advent of the new, invention, the improbable, the possible, the place of the Son before the Father, seen as the great former/formatter).

It has always been like this. The specific difference between our contemporary world and his 'great narrative', based on the two great 'formats' of the laws of physics and the genetic code (nano- and bio-technologies), is where codification, format and informa- tion become a new metaphysics in which the support replaces the substance. This intuition alone offers us a far better understanding of what is happening in our time: the predominance of the virtual, performance politics, 'live' war, an entire era in which the sky and the weather do not lie outside, but on television.

On the other hand, our modern (enlightened) legacy created illusions that have gradually crumbled, even in science, or espe- cially in science, which has fed us with pseudo-certainties for centuries. Thus, the 'age of the Son' which were are now in appears as the age of doubt, of risk, of contingency, a state of tension between power's desire for format and the permanent eruption of invention, a moment marked by awareness that over-formatting means loss of freedom, yet at the same time features another fear of the contingent: that we do not control what we have created. Open society and democracy are the place of all the (un)certainties. It is this imbalance between the format and the informal that leads to these 'thousand blossoming branches' and – according to Serres – the need for a new synthesis (or perhaps a new mythology?).

A Multitude of Singularities?

The latest of Antonio Negri's works to deal with political philos- ophy (*Empire* and *Multitude*, written with Michael Hardt) offers proposals that are similar to other theses on the 'end of history'. In this case, he constructs an idea of global democracy that is open and inclusive, materialised and led by an immaterial entity that is decentred and chaotic, a 'multitude of singularities' that act as a function of a 'desire' for democracy and of new mechanisms to construct a unifying cement for what is 'common' and guaranteed by habit and based on the subjectivity of experience, on daily practices and behaviours. An unsustainable utopia, this projected new 'class' with no exterior (which is called 'multitude') comes from a theory of the 'common' that can never be transformed into a material to be produced and absorbed by the globalised masses of the future. If 'biopolitics' (a category proposed by Michel Foucault and adopted by other thinkers mentioned here – most notably Giorgio Agamben and Peter Sloterdijk) is now an established fact in the age that others call 'unpolitical', there is no indication of how a 'bio-resistance' to match it can develop in the resulting foreseen future. The paths along which the 'host', that mass of singularities with a collective conscience, can be the agent of such resistance are even less clear. The concept of the enlightened and saving 'host' can never be the basis for a 'global democracy' that is merely a projection, evidently one that comes from the order of desire. It is impossible to see how that host will discover the 'common' that will enable it to act and communicate effectively, or how the nature of work that we know can lead to forms of immaterial production, creating 'affections' appropriate for a resistance which, however, will have difficulty in effecting radical transformations.

The Absent World

While apparently less revolutionary, radicalism seems to be the diagnosis of the current state of the world, specifically in the field of cultural production and libidinal mechanisms, and in the future projections of a philosopher such as Bernard Stiegler. Like Stiegler, one could say that the defining characteristic of the current state of the world is the *absence of world*. The culture and civilisation of the absent world appear in a dual dimension that is both temporal and spatial. The current world has gone into exile from time in the sense that it tends to live solely in the present, which is not truly a dimension of time, but simply a permanent intersection of the extensions of time that we call past and future. However, our current experience of time is not one of being conscious of a rooted existential precariousness, as found in the verse by Rilke which reminds us that 'we live on the waves and have no refuge in time'. Rather, it is one of a culture that increasingly tends to ignore the past (has no historical consciousness) and lives an uncertain or non-existent future under constant threats that range from unemployment to social insecurity, and from 'infinite war' to ecological catastrophe. It has absented itself from natural and social space and moved to virtual space, living for much of its time in 'non-places' (Marc Augé), homogeneous spaces that have no memory, or in that alienation of the world to which Peter Sloterdijk gives the very German name *Weltfremdheit* (world strangeness), referring to the situation facing some ancient minorities (anchorites, mystics) and modern-day majorities (supporters of drugs or the virtual). His book aims to be 'a phenomenology of the spirit outside the world, or strange to the world', simultaneously pondering the possibility and meaning of 'denying the world' or absenting ourselves from it at the moment when that world – in an age of doubts, large-scale migrations, famine and wars – has ceased to be the great tent or global house, and the equation House=World has entered a period of crisis.

The absence of the world is thus expressed as the loss of nature's symbolic potential and presence, as nature has been absorbed by the overwhelming wave of consumption that brings everything to the same level, creating and spreading symbolic, existential and libidinal misery. At the same time, consumption is the main factor in neutralising the positive conflictive energy of current societies, through the 'strategy of forgetting' that it induces and which Aldous Huxley denounced in *Brave New World* (1932). Then, at the dawn of late-capitalist modernity and the centre of historical and civilisational recession caused by totalitarianisms (which implement mega-mechanisms of a more tribal than culturally symbolic 'belonging'), Huxley profiled the mechanisms of stabilising the *status quo* through an *emotional engineering* which the market engineering and advertising found in the globalised economy would perfect through the most sophisticated methods of managing the unstoppable balance between the creation and the satisfaction of desires. At the same time, this was also the political – political-theological – and conservative utopia of a writer who was very influential in Europe (the aforementioned Carl Schmitt: cf. *Political Theology*, 1922, and *The Concept of the Political*, 1932), which has been readopted by all men of power, advertisers and television of our time. It is the utopia of a 'good world' in which the most important and 'serious' is relegated to a secondary position in the name of a culture of entertainment and illusion, stripped of tensions: one which 'forgets' to pose the question of binding values and is therefore voided of any ethical dimension. Dominated by this forgetting, post-modernity brought a concept of struggle-free culture that was disseminated all over the 'world of life' and applicable to everything: from the body to laughter, from metropolises to wine, from gangs to fashion, from automobiles to free time. Culture shifted from the symbolic associated with the use-value of intellectual 'goods' to the cult of a contingent iconicity subject to any consumer product and with a mere 'exhibition value' (to use a known distinction created by Walter Benjamin). In the longest essay ('In Praise of Profanation') from his latest work, Giorgio Agamben suggests that this represents the death of the use-value in contemporary culture's 'capitalism as religion' (the term comes from a fragment of Benjamin's work). Everything is confused when 'televised game shows are part of a new liturgy; they secularize an unconsciously religious intention', merely changing the place of profanation in its etymological and ancient sense (to use, or make available for everybody's use), inexorably removing it from the sacred and integrating it in the game as *ludus* (libidinal investment), and not as a mere entertainment. The apparent profanation produced by capitalism is accompanied by its opposite, the absolute yet hollow consecration of the product, which leads Agamben to the conclusion that 'the capitalist religion in its extreme phase aims at creating something absolutely unprofanable'. There – in the devalued world turned into a museum for tourists, as in supermarkets, shopping centres or televisions – there is no use. Language itself is subjected to this neutralisation process in the media, and this impedes its liberation for other purposes.

'The profanation of the unprofanable is the political task of the coming generation': reclaiming culture (and the profane world) for use-values and for authentic playfulness.

Desire and Technics

In the 1930s, and specifically in *Being and Time*, Heidegger generically established the term 'technic' for the decisive factor that – in modernity – may have led to the evanescence of the substance of the world in individual existences and current forms of collective life. Today, it has gained more complex configurations and even more universal implications. Heidegger's question, which a philosopher like Bernard Stiegler again poses in order to reach proposals that can get past the non-productive withering of contemporary culture, deals with knowing how to articulate *being in the world* with *technic*. Heidegger believed that there was also a clash between technic (determination and calculation) and being (which implies a relationship with original time, death and incalculable non-determination). Stiegler believes that this opposition is now to be found in the state reached by Western metaphysics (the legacy of Plato, who fathered a fully rationalised capitalism that, under the mask of satisfying all desires, in fact kills the root of desire) and in the disjunction that we are now experiencing between *globalisation* (the ultimate expression of a broad notion of 'technic', in the most abstract form of the virtual domain) and *body* (apparently free, but actually controlled and manipulated by the mechanisms of today's bio-politics – as Stiegler claims already happened in Plato's *Republic*, whose fundamental idea was to channel the desire of bodies so that they could be subjected to the law). Stiegler's proposal develops in contrast to all the current positions of 'resistance' to the alienating action of capitalism and its technics. He states that 'technic must be placed at the very heart of desire', which is beyond immanence yet is not of the order of the transcendental. Rather, it informs another order that is essential to establish singularities in the current capitalist universe. Stiegler sees this as an order of 'consistency', a form of replete and

meaningful existence, beyond mere survival in the very heart of
the neo-liberal order of the hyper-industrial age in which we live
– and *with* which we can co-exist in a consistent manner. We must
seek – in capitalism itself and current technics – the forms for the
individual's fulfilment inside that system, the means to *create desire
with technique*. Today's capitalism stimulates what Stiegler terms
'grammatisation of the living': an ambivalent process with dual
potential, like Plato's *pharmakon*, simultaneously poison and medicine. On the one hand, this 'grammatisation' creates mechanisms
of control over and cloning of the individual; on the other, it
produces '*différance*' and the principles of singularity. It is – like
Joseph Beuys' artistic practice – a question of rethinking the relationship between the two directions of the dual myth of
Prometheus and Epimetheus: articulating the latter's gifts that
were granted to the non-human world, with the compensatory
prostheses brought to us by the technique that the former stole
from the gods, and thereby renouncing capital's strategy of simple
demonisation. Instead, we should move towards revaluing *life* in
its alliance with *technic*, and *re-intensify the libido*.

In other words: the state of the world can and should be thought
and rethought according to and in the name of the state of life –
the *states of life* that occur in it and essentially continue within it.
In the accessory and temporal plane, economics, politics, production, consumption and the 'environment' (now an inalienable part
of any well-behaved policy) clearly stand out. Yet, they are merely
attributes of the central category of life, in all planes of the being.
From this perspective and on an all-embracing scale that stretches
from micro-worlds to macro-universes, from the animal to the
human, from the universes of the I to the plane of the Pascalian
All, a new 'perspectivism' can be born for the world of the human
– because this is and always will be the issue. This new 'perspectivism' will be decentralised, without hierarchies, 'chaotic' and as
entropic as the very state of the world. The new 'mythology' for
the current and future world could then take as its reference one
of its most vital and fascinating images: the universe of fractals, a
structured chaos that self-generates new configurations, just as
nature itself does. The main question will shift from the state of

the world to the state of the *Being*, and will be of a more living and ethical question than a civilisational one: a question of a *contract with the Living*.

The State of the Being and the Place of the Human

This is the perspective found in a body of work that – in contemporary Portuguese literature, and particularly among books published in this new century – offers the most radical alternative to the epistemological and ethical/aesthetic 'cultural' parameters that dominate the current world: the work of Maria Gabriela Llansol. Books such as *Onde Vais, Drama-Poesia?* (2000), *Parasceve. Puzzles e ironias* (2001), *O Senhor de Herbais. Breves ensaios literários sobre a reprodução estética do world, e suas tentações* (2002) and *O Jogo da Liberdade da Alma* (2003) reorient an original project to revise history and the problem of the human in terms of a 'figural order of daily life'. Through these unparalleled literary works, Llansol intervenes in the great debate of post-humanism which, ever since Heidegger, has fuelled reflection on our post-modern condition, from Foucault to Lyotard, from Derrida to Bernard Stiegler, from Sloterdijk to Michel Serres. Yet there is a decisive difference: even though her work is often seen esoteric and mystical, Llansol's view neither declares the end of humanism nor a return to metaphysics in an age of pragmatism and contingency. In fact, its motivating force is of the order of pure physics, like Schlegel's 'mythology', carbon and the vibration of the Being. In contrast, the main issue that runs through her work, and which I would like to analyse here, is knowing *what today's* (real) *world lacks* to be (more) *human*. Following Espinosa and his pact of goodness and beauty, this question proposes a *hyper-human (or trans-human) vision of the human* that is free of the simplistic avatars of all autistic humanisms and of the theology, moral and all the webs of power.

Llansol would argue that what the world needs to be human is another integrating dimension of the human. What her work tells us is that nothing has yet changed the world and that it is possible and necessary 'to conceive of a human world that could live here', and that human history has yet to fulfil this. It also says that thought and creation, the culture of affections and the spirit of depossession – whose openness to multiple worlds, in seeking the diverse that they offer, in the true languages that they use and reinvent – weave 'what will come to man as fate'. On the basis of current horizons, what will come to man as fate can only be a return to the roots of Being and the 'living sources of imagination'. As Llansol stands at the opposite extreme to narrow anthropocentrism, this means the total de-hierarchisation of the Being and opening a notion of the world as a configuration or *Gestalt* that has multiple meanings, such as the 'unknown that accompanies us' in the form of a reality that always has one face and its opposite. 'Everything that is exists in an opposite', and the other side of that opposite holds extensions, new realities and echoes of other worlds. Naturally, one of the fundamental opposites (albeit no more important than others) is the one linking the human being to another human being, in the 'eternal return of the mutual'. An entire programme for a culture of the future opens up. If 'the world is purely aesthetic' – made up of the surprise and enigma of the unknown that is with us in our permanent passage through its diverse aesthetics (all one needs is to have one's eyes and senses open) in search of the impact of the new and the potential for amazement which that world still and always holds – then entering that landscape may bring access to new forms of creation at every level. This is achieved through a 'poetic gift', which does not aim to make everybody a poet, but to awaken faculties that enable all to see the unheard and most attractive beauty of the Being and open up to the multiplicity of worlds and express it in languages. It is also achieved through the 'freedom of conscience', which will transform that aesthetic capacity to be in the world and to pay it attention in an inevitably ethical stance, within a context of tolerance, similarity in difference and mutual non-annulment. A philosophical conjecture with this profile of 'pondered hope' (derived from Espinosa's revolutionary ethics and found in current nuclei of alternative thought) may form the basis for a culture of 'sensualethics' that is far removed from the forms of society known today and its ideologies and so-called 'liberal' practices. Yet it is not incompatible with relearning the desire beyond the name (the convention, the exteriority and the norm) and a new vision of the world as 'a story that does not deserve to be mourned'. It is one response (among many) to the exhaustion of all castrated humanisms, deprived of the 'remaining life', and a means to 'de-sculpt the human', to 'strip away the living from the form of the identical and of fear'. Although we live in an ethereal garden devastated by a world of uncertainties, it is our *duty* to be happy (Peter Sloterdijk, *Weltfremdheit*); we have to 'fight for after the catastrophe' (B. Stiegler).

In this landscape without territory (for territory – including territories of culture – is what the eye of the powerful covets and seizes as its own, while landscape is what the free eye sees and the body inhabits), the motive of the world shifts from the implacable laws of the market, which subject and submerge us all, to freer spaces where the history of that world and its aesthetic representation are different. Perhaps this history comes at the very reasonable and even desirable price of returning to forms that are 'poorer' than the spectacular and sophisticated ones of art and life. It certainly always has just one tenuous foundation in thinking and the beauty of things ('I am called / the just promise, but I can guarantee nothing', as Manuel Gusmão, a poet close to Llansol, says in *Teatros do Tempo*), but even so it is a safe horizon for that 'pondered hope', set against the catastrophe that is latent in the great bourgeois tradition of the novel and expressed in the tragic drive of the moderns. It is a potential path for precisely such a situation as the current one, where there are new signs of a cultural pessimism that is too unaware of itself to be nihilist, but clearly marked by the sense of disturbance and unease that have already established themselves in contemporary societies.

The Profile of Hope

St Paul, in his *Epistle to the Romans* (5:5) writes: 'And hope confoundeth not.' Ever since *Republic*, one of the most commonly present instruments of hope found in the history of culture has been the utopia. Yet every utopia since Plato has borne the sign of the inhuman, the mechanical and the hyper-regulated. Perhaps the only construction of a living and concrete utopia that still comes directly from the last century's 'hot line' of Marxism is the one by Ernst Bloch in *The Principle of Hope* (his masterpiece, written between 1938 and 1947, and published in 1959). This is the utopia of the daydream and the *docta spes*, the hope that knows there is a path of 'unrealities' that bear reality (as Llansol says: 'not real existing') and that puts its faith in the living latency of the Being to establish itself both against the 'cold currents' of the dark, nihilist existentialism of the century and against the *cool pathos* of the current generation, one which sadly does not know a philosopher such as Bloch. Yet he finds other contemporary projects of thought, such as those in Peter Sloterdijk's *Spheres* and in Giorgio Agamben's *The Coming Community* and more recently *The Open: Man and Animal*. The first is a very broad reflection along the lines of the 'end of humanism' that aims to rehabilitate the 'animised' space of the history of the human and the category (now marginalised by the break-up of solidarity caused by a narcissistic and success-based culture) of the 'relation' with the demand for a common constitution for men, machines, plants and animals, countering the humanist ideology of the 'naked man' with a posthumanism of the 'dressed and accompanied man', a new 'ontological constitution'. Meanwhile, in *The Coming Community* (1990), Agamben proposes that 'the coming being is the what-ever being' (*quod libet*), not an indifferent one, but the one who has the will (*libet*), the being-in-action that establishes an original relationship with *desire*. In this case, an ontology of the singular and of the 'excess of power' runs through his work, a proposal of thinking the political (and happiness) beyond the State. In *The Open: Man and Animal* (2002) the key idea is the inevitability – after so many nationalisms and imperialisms in the nineteenth century and the totalitarianisms of the twentieth – of societies assuming the post-historic and post-political condition of the 'naked life' when faced with their depolitisation by the power of the economy. The ultimate (un)political task would now be to assume the biological life, 'the complete humanisation of the animal and the complete animalisation of the man'.

Maria Gabriela Llansol offers an unmistakably parallel project that is aesthetic, or rather 'ethisthetic' rather than philosophical. The world anticipated by the concrete eudemonist conjecture of her text proposes a culture full of the human in a place of free liberty and more beautiful beauty – an 'Eden-like space', as the author calls it. She is not referring to the mythical garden from which we may have been expelled, but to another one that is latent and real because it is intrinsic to the Being. We have not yet entered this space as a body of community, but the 'intense', as Espinosa would say, have always lived there. In that place, in a 'more-than landscape' that is not a utopia because it can be experienced at every corner of reality, the 'human' is also what lies outside man (and he has subjugated and destroyed: all of the Living) and the more-than-human, the expansion of the known and visible world to the possible and the probable. In the view of this eudemonist uchronia founded on the energy of the Being and the brilliance of the world, a culture of the human would be one that managed to develop forms of acting and creating at some point between 'the pleasures of the game' and 'the dangers (that are assumed and can be overcome) of the well'. In other words, it is a culture that is simultaneously *grave* and *jubilant*, that is not fuelled by dead and predictable conventions or fleetingness that come more from boundless imagination than from the root of the body (as happens with most of today's culture), but instead – still using the language of Espinosa, the great inspiration for this work – from a libidinal energy that joyfully creates a potential to act. Thus, culture would be a motive for life, the 'double of living'. The free game to be played – which some have always played and that Llansol has transformed into figures in her text – at the heart of these forms of experiencing culture and of 'culturalising' life is the real 'game of the freedom of the soul'. In other words, returning to Manuel Gusmão's *Teatros do Tempo*, it is the game of the 'other birth: the unrememberableness of joy'. We need to believe, as do those authors among us who have poetically pondered the state of world, that we still have, 'against all evidence to the contrary, happiness' (*Theatres of Time*).

Translated by Richard Trewinnard

References

Giorgio Agamben, *A Comunidade Que Vem* (Lisbon, 1993).

—— *Ideia da Prosa* (Lisbon, 1999).

—— *L'Ouvert. De l'homme et de l'animal* (Paris, 2002).

—— *Profanations* (Paris, 2005).

Jan Assmann / Dietrich Harth (Eds.), *Kultur und Konflikt* (Frankfurt / M., 1990).

Alain Badiou, *Abrégé de métapolitique* (Paris, 1998).

Fernando R. de la Flor, 'TT: La puerta de los siglos', in: *W.T.C. – 11-9-01*, organ. Antonio Fernández-Alba & José López Albaladejo. Murcia, 2003 (= Colección de Arquitectura)

O Estado do Mundo (O fulgor da língua). Coimbra Capital da Cultura 2003 [http://www.ofulgordalingua.com/poema.htm]

Manuel Gusmão, *Teatros do Tempo* (Lisbon, 2001).

M. Hardt / A. Negri, *Multidão. Guerra e Democracia na Era do Império* (Oporto, 2005).

Maria Gabriela Llansol, *Onde Vais, Drama-poesia?* (Lisbon, 2000).

—— *Parasceve. Puzzles e ironias* (Lisbon, 2001).

—— *O Senhor de Herbais. Breves ensaios literários sobre a reprodução estética do mundo, e suas tentações* (Lisbon, 2002).

—— *O Jogo da Liberdade da Alma* (Lisbon, 2003).

Sven Lindquist, *Exterminem Todas as Bestas* (Lisbon, 2005).

Montaigne, *Essais*. 3 volumes (Paris, 1969/1979).

Jean-Luc Nancy, *Resistência da Poesia* (Lisbon, 2005).

Edward Said, *Representações do Intelectual. As palestras de Reith de 1993*. Dir. Teresa Seruya (Lisbon, 2000).

Friedrich Schlegel, 'Discurso sobre a mitologia', in: João Barrento (Dir.), *Literatura Alemã. Textos e Contextos*. Vol. I: O século XVIII (Lisbon, 1989).

Carl Schmitt, *Politische Theologie* (Berlin, 1922).

—— *Der Begriff des Politischen* (Berlin, 1932).

Michel Serres, *Ramos* (Lisbon, 2005).

Peter Sloterdijk, *Weltfremdheit* (Frankfurt / M., 1993).

—— *Sphären* (I. Blasen; II. Globen; III. Schäume) (Frankfurt / M., 1998, 1999, 2004).

George Steiner, *A Ideia de Europa* (Lisbon, 2005).

—— *Language and Silence* [1967] (Yale, 1998).

Bernard Stiegler, *La technique et le temps*. 3 volumes (Paris, 1994, 1996, 2001).

—— *De la misère symbolique*. 2 volumes (Paris, 2004).

Ludwig Wittgenstein, *Tratado Lógico-filosófico* (Lisbon, 1987).

The translator would like to thank Professor Kevin Attell, of Johns Hopkins University, for his enormous kindness in allowing access to his forthcoming translation of Giorgio Agamben's article.

Waiting for the Antichrist

JOHN FROW

1

In a recent paper the literary theorist Mary Louise Pratt talks of watching an evangelical preacher performing on television an exegesis of a prophetic passage from the Book of Ezekiel. She is struck by the receptiveness of his 'rapt audience of a couple of thousand', all of whom 'accompanied him, Bibles open in their hands, index fingers following the lines, lips moving as they weighed the powerful words';[1] his work is charged with a sense of vital historical mission, which is enhanced by his charismatic use of the medium.

This is in many ways a peculiarly American story. Although the combination of belief in the literal or coded truth of Scripture with the reach and power of the mass media can be found elsewhere – in the worlds of Islam and of Hinduism, in the mass-produced iconography of Catholicism, and spreading out from the evangelising Protestant churches of the United States to Central and South America and many other parts of the Western world – it works with particular intensity in that country which more than any other is the creature of Enlightenment reason and modernity, and where the tensions between secular and religious versions of the common weal have become pervasive.

During the late 1970s and the 1980s the United States was swept by a cultural revolution at least as formative as that of the 1960s counter-culture, in which millions of Bible believers

> broke old taboos constraining their interactions with outsiders, claimed new cultural territory, and refashioned themselves in church services, Bible studies, books and pamphlets, class-rooms, families, daily life, and the public arena. In the process, they altered what it meant to be a fundamentalist and recon-figured the large fellowship of born-again Christians, the rules of national public discourse, and the meaning of modernity.[2]

The movement was guided and shaped by a small number of fundamentalist preachers, most prominently Jerry Falwell and Pat Robertson, with a command of television that enabled them to reach well beyond their local congregations, seminaries and 'universities' to an audience of millions.

The significance of this movement outwards into public life lay in its challenge to the modern settlement in which religion is allotted a protected place outside politics and the serious business of the state. As Susan Friend Harding puts it, the huge 1980 'Washington for Jesus' rally tore up 'a tacit contract with modern America' which, 'fashioned in the wake of the 1925 Scopes trial, specifically proscribed the "mixing" of ostensibly premodern, that is, Bible-believing, Protestant rhetorics and routine politics. It thus rendered the public arena and the nation as a whole "modern" in the sense of secular.'[3] Now, however, the assumption that a reli-gious premodernity and a secular modernity are neatly separable into a 'before' and an 'after' is barely tenable; as the social land-scape has changed, with religion and politics again forming a globally unstable mixture, we have come to realise that 'moder-nity is unthinkable without the constantly evolving, constantly renegotiated pact between religious and secular knowledge. What appears today as an "undoing of secularisation" is a violent reworking of the pact, whose outcome we cannot foresee'.[4] The central assumptions of enlightened modernity – the primacy of scientific protocols of proof over faith, a non-transcendent understanding of history, value pluralism – are directly challenged by a discourse of Biblical certainty securely anchored in the public sphere. It is not that an achieved modernity has been disrupted by an incursion of 'premodern' elements, but that the separation of religious and political spheres, which has been formative of the modern state since the late eighteenth century, has been replaced by a kind of fusion in which the force of the political is redefined: Jimmy Carter was elected in 1976 as a born-again Christian; the current incumbent of the White House has also undergone rebirth, and has spoken in favour of the teaching of Creation Science in schools. An estimated 70 million Americans call themselves evangelicals, and they gave George W. Bush 40% of his vote. Each one of them wants to bring God into politics. Religion no longer knows, or accepts, its 'place'.

2

'Religion' is a very unitary term, however, for a complex and diffuse phenomenon; let me try to clarify what I mean by it. Our classic understandings are sociological: religion is the translation of a set of social beliefs and practices into an other-worldly dimension where they take on an absolute and authoritative form. Seeking to ground religious belief in a hierarchy of social structures, Bruce Lincoln distinguishes four basic components:

1. A discourse whose concerns transcend the human, temporal, and contingent, and that claims for itself a similarly transcendent status;
2. A set of practices whose goal is to produce a proper world and/or proper human subjects, as defined by a religious discourse to which these practices are connected; these ethical and ritual practices take the form of 'embodied material action', and they are 'the way discourse acts on the world' and on the

practising subjects;

3. A community whose members construct their identity with reference to a religious discourse and its attendant practices;

4. An institution that regulates religious discourse, practices, and community, reproducing them over time and modifying them as necessary, while asserting their eternal validity and transcendent value.[5]

Yet, for all its comprehensiveness, any such schema is reductive to the extent that it subordinates religion to a language which is alien to it. Rosanne C. Euben thus criticises Western scholarly analyses of Islam insofar as 'rationalist discourse explains the appeal of fundamentalist ideas by reference to their function as conduits for processes and tensions in the material and structural realm. In deriving meaning from function, these explanations serve not to make fundamentalist ideas rational – in the literal sense, meaning intelligible – but to divorce explanations of Islamic fundamentalism from the fundamentalists' own understandings of the world'.[6] It is a short step from this to understanding the Islamic fundamentalist 'as the paradigmatic irrational rational actor; that is, the actor apparently rational enough to gravitate toward an ideology that is an effective and therefore appealing vehicle for essentially pathological reactionary sentiment'.[7] Such forms of explanation serve little purpose other than to reinforce the analyst's own framework of values. Don't we need to understand religion first in its own terms, before then taking the next step of translating it into another language?

It is conventional to distinguish between the institutional and doctrinal dimensions of religion and what we might call its *ethos*. Religious affect never floats freely, but the structure to which it is tied need not be that of systematically organised religion. The twentieth-century philosophy of religion, largely accepting this distinction, has sought to apprehend the nature of the experience of the sacred through the concept of the *numinous*. In Rudolf Otto's formulation (1958) there are three aspects to that intense experience of presence that he calls the numinous: first, it is understood as a *mysterium*: it is completely other than ourselves, and cannot be translated into the ordinary categories of human thought; nor can this experience be conveyed to someone who has not undergone it. Second, this *mysterium* is *tremendum*: it inspires awe, even terror at the overwhelming power which is revealed in religious experience, and which threatens to annihilate individual consciousness. Third, it is *fascinans*: it exercises an uncanny attraction, and inspires an emotion which is at once like love and like fear or even revulsion.

Otto's influential analysis operates at the highest level of abstraction to isolate an essence of the religious experience, understood as being the shared foundation of all religions. At a lower level of abstraction, a certain tradition of comparative anthropology seeks to understand the sacred not as an experience in itself but as a taxonomic operation which plays a central role in the formation of a religious cosmos. Finally, there are numerous accounts of socially and culturally specific religious formations, describing an enormous range of variations in the techniques and the cognitive frameworks from which particular experiences of the numinous arise – and indeed, that experience is not necessarily a component of all religions.

For my purposes it is not necessary to descend to this level of concreteness; for now, let me focus on that intermediate level of abstraction at which, in Emile Durkheimian's formulation, the sacred is understood as an empty category defined structurally by nothing but its opposition to the profane.[8] This opposition then comes to govern a series of further structural relations within the cosmos. Against the homogeneous, amorphous, undifferentiated space of the profane world is set the radical heterogeneity of sacred space, which – 'saturated with being'[9] and with significance – interrupts it, breaks its flow, opens out on to absolute otherness. Time is similarly heterogeneous: unlike profane time, sacred time is reversible, because 'every religious festival, any liturgical time, represents the actualisation of a sacred event that took place in a mythical past, "in the beginning"'.[10] But this sheer otherness of the sacred is itself a kind of content; and already in Durkheim it is possible to see the emergence of a positive characterisation of the sacred as it divides internally to produce a distinctive ambivalence, an oscillation between repulsion and fascination, dread and desire, the *tremendum* and the *fascinans*. For Durkheim, this takes the form of a division between the pure and the impure, and between beneficence and malevolence, both of which are the object of interdiction: thus 'the pure and the impure are not two separate classes, but two varieties of the same class, which includes all sacred things'.[11] The sacred, as evidenced in its ambiguous Latin root *sacer*, designates at once the accursed, the outcast, and the holy, a force which is above all dangerous, contagious, and compelling;[12] it is, in Roger Caillois's words, 'what one cannot approach without dying'.[13]

The sacred is thus a force or a presence, whether anthropomorphised or not, which is conceived non-naturalistically as a suspension or rupture of normal time and space by the uncontrollable outbreak of 'spots' of transcendence. Gods are positioned directly in relation to this force, as the force itself or as emanations of it. Within this framework it is 'normal' time which is aberrant, and the time of the sacred that carries the full weight of meaningfulness in a fallen world. Mundane history is subordinate to that other temporality which comprehends but surpasses human time.

3

In listening to the televangelist, Pratt is struck by the similarity of his work to her own as a teacher and an interpreter of texts; the exegesis she hears is 'spellbinding', combining the scholarly elucidation of allusions, etymologies, and historical references with an eloquent and morally informed ability to convey 'the depth and wisdom of the text, the plenitude of its meanings, the higher purposes to which it called them'.[14] Yet what this interpretation is doing is reading the text – Chapter 38 of the Book of Ezekiel – as a prophetic anticipation of an apocalyptic war in the Middle East; the evangelist reads a coded text for an esoteric core of literal truth about the future.

Such an exercise is at the core of fundamentalist modes of understanding the historical world: not as an irreversible and linear unfolding of events without teleology, but as a concordance of sacred time with historical time within a closed order of the universe. Prophecy is what reads the sense of that closed order. The end days foretold in the Bible are always-already inscribed in an order which has the Biblical text as its surface form. Such a placing of the world we live in within sacred time radically undermines non-transcendental forms of reading: 'Current events and the daily news are not neutral, secular phenomena that exist independently and are subjected to religious interpretation by Christians. They are signs of the times. They are inside bible-based history. They are evidence that God and his enemy are coming to final blows over the fate of the Jews and of all mankind'.[15] Everything can be placed in relation to this interpretive schema. The historical time posited by the religious right in the United States draws a fundamental parallel between Israel and America, the two covenanted nations: a Salomonic Golden Age flourishes in the US to the end of the Eisenhower presidency, then declines as the liberal-humanist enemies of religion (for which read in part the counter-culture of the 1960s) force through the 1962 decision banning school prayer and the case that legalises abortion, Roe v. Wade, in 1973. Then follows the presidency of Bill Clinton, the evil Zedekiah who ignores the admonitions of the prophets, and its culmination in the event that parallels the conquest and enslavement of the chosen people by Babylon, the attacks of 11 September 2001.

Biblical prophecy gives tens of millions of Americans a way of construing apparently secular events within a typological perspective; it gives them a line about

the AIDS crisis, the New Age Movement, satanic cults and demonic principalities, about the epidemic of abortion, pornography, homosexuality, divorce, crime, and drugs ... about Israel, about what God has in store for Israel ... about the Persian Gulf war, or the Middle East peace treaty ... [about] what the election and reelection of Bill Clinton meant for America ... about the North American [Free] Trade Agreement, General Agreement on Tariffs and Trade, the European

Economic Community, about borderless travel between
nations, the Internet, transnational business and finance, and
UFOs and alien abductions.[16]

The dominant interpretive framework amongst American fundamentalists – the doctrine of dispensational premillenarianism – sets
out a schema in which history culminates in the 'rapture' of the
saints or chosen ones, who ascend with Christ to Heaven and dwell
there for seven years while those left behind suffer terrible tribu-
lations culminating in Israel in the battle of Armageddon between
the forces of Christ and the Antichrist; the chosen ones then return
with Christ to rule with him on earth during the Kingdom Age of
1000 years. The schema is enunciated in Tim LaHaye and Jerry
Jenkins's best-selling end-time novel (later expanded to a series)
Left Behind, in which the initial moment of rapture is followed by
the story of those church members who were not truly saved, and
to whom the divine order of things is explained in a videotape left
behind for them by their raptured pastor. Dozens of other novels,
and untold numbers of populist doctrinal texts, expound some
version of this pattern.[17]

The reason this matters to those of us beyond these interpretive
communities is that – because of the central role played in it by
Israel and its chosen people – the typological account of the shape
and direction of contemporary history has real effects on US
foreign policy. Cited on the Left Behind website, Mark Hitchcock
says of the recent Hamas victory in the Palestinian elections:

> … These recent events seem to confirm there will be no lasting
> peace in the Middle East until the Antichrist arrives on the world
> scene. According to Daniel 9:27, the seven-year tribulation will
> begin when the final world rulers make some kind of treaty with
> Israel that guarantees her security and access to the temple
> mount in Jerusalem. This peaceful condition for Israel is further
> described in Ezekiel 38:8 and 11… While world leaders should
> continue to do whatever they can to limit violence and blood-
> shed in the Middle East, I don't believe any lasting results will
> be achieved until the Antichrist arrives on the scene.[18]

Questions of justice for the Palestinian people (for example) have no place in this grand scheme; and the political debt owed by the Republicans to the religious right means that, for all its destructive geopolitical consequences, unquestioning US support for the state of Israel cannot be challenged in domestic politics. Similarly, the association of the United Nations with the Antichrist's world government (a recurring theme in the literature) contributes directly to the contempt in which the Bush administration has held it.

4

Pratt's response to the exegetical work done by the televangelist is at once admiring of his ability to bring the text alive and aware that her own work as a teacher of literary texts involves, in part, the need to enter imaginatively into other ways of apprehending the world, including the creation, when reading 'Dante, Bunyan, Sor Juana, Pascal, or Harriet Beecher Stowe' in the classroom, of a 'provisional Christian subjectivity' in herself and her students.[19] This response is part of a larger examination, in the symposium in which she is taking part, of how it might be possible for secular intellectuals to take religion seriously. In a sense, she gives the answer in her understanding of trained literary response as 'provisional': a word that captures all the difference between a reading grounded in the imagination of otherness, and a reading grounded in the certainty of reading for a literal truth.

Yet this is not an answer that can be given *within the terms* of a religious framework, or at least that kind which is convinced of its own revealed truth. How can a secular understanding of the religious experience of the order of the world – the *mysterium tremendum et fascinans* – be possible, when the language in which that experience is couched is so entirely incommensurable with a secular rationality – and when the pact that enforces a differentiation of spheres has broken down? There is no middle ground between Creation Science and the Darwinian theory of evolution, just as there is none between those who hope for a just solution to the misery of the Palestinian people and those who identify them en masse with the forces of the Antichrist. How are we to 'take religion seriously' if we passionately disbelieve its premises?

This is a question that I tried to address some years ago in a paper whose starting point was what I took to be the failure of the discipline of cultural studies – with rare exceptions – to theorise in any adequate way about what is perhaps the most important set of popular cultural systems in the contemporary world: religion in both its organised and its disorganised forms.[20] Religion is an embarrassment to us; it's an embarrassment to me, and above all because we Western intellectuals are so deeply committed to the secularisation thesis that makes of religion an archaic remnant which ought by now to have withered away. This thesis – never more than a polemical one[21] – is plainly wrong. It is wrong as a matter of fact, both because organised religion is flourishing in many parts of the world, and because religious sentiment – the belief in a cosmic order and in the continuing life of the dead – has migrated into many strange and unexpected places, from New Age trinketry through Islamic and Christian and Hindu fundamentalism to manga movies and the cult of the famous dead.[22] Indeed, many of these mutant religious forms have precisely to do with the restoration of that intercessionary realm, the 'vast continuity of being between the seen and the unseen',[23] which, on the Weberian thesis, was eliminated by the Protestant naturalisation and rationalisation of the creation. The secularisation thesis is also wrong, however, as a matter of theory, predicated as it is on a logic of historical progression through necessary historical stages culminating in the achieved rationality of a fully secular and fully Western modernity.[24] We have been told the story of the disenchantment of the world so many times that we have come to believe it despite all evidence to the contrary.

I concluded this earlier paper with three observations about the disciplinary and curricular focus of cultural studies. The first was an argument that among the things we need to know about and to teach our students is the history and sociology of religion. As Casanova puts it, we 'should be less obsessed with the decline of religion and more attuned to the new forms which religion assumes ... in all world religions: to new forms of individual mysti-

cism, "invisible religion" and cults of the individual; to new forms
of congregational religion, from new religious movements to the
global expansion of Pentecostalism and charismatic communities
in all world religions; and to the re-emergence of the world religions as transnational imagined communities, vying with if not
replacing the nation-state for a prominent role on the global
stage'.[25] The second argument, and corollary, was that we need to
take religion seriously in all of its dimensions because of its cultural
centrality in the modern world; and we need to do so without
ourselves participating in those religious myths of origin and presence – the myth, for example, of the great star whose charisma is
the cause rather than the effect of their fame[26] – which are a
constant theoretical temptation in the study of popular culture.
Finally, I made the observation that for many Australian intellectuals these lessons have come from our increased awareness
of Aboriginal spirituality, and our sense both of the need to
respect and honour traditional belief systems, and of the tensions
between a religious cosmology and the Enlightenment ethos
which governs, and rightly governs, our work. That tension is
inescapable, and we cannot pretend not to be subject to it. Its implications are in part political: the legitimacy of Aboriginal claims to
rights in land is based ultimately in their religious ties to country,
and the racist nature of the legislation proposed by the Australian
Government in 1997, to counter the High Court's recognition of
indigenous rights in land held under pastoral lease, lies in part in
its failure of imagination of radical cultural difference. But this is
then also a methodological question: how is it possible for our
knowledge both to ground itself in a hard-won rationality which
must, as a matter of principle, put doubt and sceptical enquiry
before faith, and yet at the same time to enter sympathetically into
forms of understanding which are quite alien to it, and to do so
without condescending to those other knowledges, without
seeking to destroy them, and without seeking to deny the forms
of desire and will to power which are constitutive of enlightened
reason?

5

The imagination of otherness that I take to be central both to literary and to cultural and anthropological studies is far removed from the forms of ethnocentric and in part religious certainty that have reshaped the global political order in the wake of the events of 11 September 2001. That collective event – henceforth 9/11, the hieroglyph condensing 'cultural conjuncture' into 'chronological code'[27] – has come to work as a *casus*, an exemplary case of a larger structure of meaning. It works in the first instance as a historical rupture, an incident without apparent precedent or cause, an anomaly which nevertheless generates new principles, new understandings, new historical generalisations. It carries embedded within it the principles of a change in the course of history, and these principles flow with apparent necessity from the images that constitute the event. Although one possible reading of 9/11 would involve finding in it a confirmation of the wrongs of US foreign policy, particularly in the Middle East, its immediate and contrary narrative message is something like: *evil people are intent on destroying us.* At a higher level of generality, and however bizarre it may seem, it proclaims that world history should be read as the history of a struggle between Islam and Christendom. Story-shaped, the event *exemplifies* this interpretation, with all the consequences that then derive from it.

These messages are, of course, in no way immediate. They were prepared by years of ideological work which created a ready-made explanatory framework, and this is a major part of the point about how the *casus* functions: that apparently random shifts in historical awareness, in the direction and shape of history, are always the result of intense collective effort, or rather of the collision and inter-action of contradictory efforts. We should note in particular the determination and efficiency with which the American right during and beyond the Reagan era – pre-empting the left's Gramscian doctrine of the long march through the institutions – used the resources of well-funded policy institutes and of targeted placements in the bureaucracy, but also of the vast popular movement based in the evangelical churches, to consolidate a massive shift in ideological hegemony which spread well beyond the political establishment to the broad mass of popular culture.[28] In this case, the *casus* of 9/11 crystallises a set of pre-existing cultural tropes about the relation to otherness. Slavoj Zizek thus describes the ways in which the 'terrorist threat' was already libidinally invested in a series of movies from *Escape from New York* to *Independence Day,* in such a way that 'the space for it was already prepared in ideological fantasizing';[29] and to this we should add the evangelical churches' apocalyptic vision of the catastrophes that will announce the end-time, the rapture, and the time of tribulation.

The event of 9/11 worked so powerfully because it was an extraordinary – an exemplary – piece of symbolism. Remember that essay of Baudrillard's in which he asks why there are two towers in the World Trade Center rather than one, and answers in terms of the difference between the singular reality that characterises a mode of production and the specular structure characteristic of a mode of simulation.[30] The towers, in their smooth lack of figuration, their pure and abstract geometricality, are the great architectural icons of non-representation, blankly reflecting nothing other than themselves, stripped of all reference to a world beyond them. The themes of the event of 11 September are the classic ones of Baudrillard's meditations on postmodernity: terrorism as the archetypal liquidation of meaning, the twin towers as the essence, in their specular doubleness, of the realm of simulation, the catastrophic Event as an implosion of meaning; indeed, the implosion of Minoru Yamasaki's towers repeated precisely, but as an effect of random violence, what Charles Jencks calls the defining moment of postmodernity, the controlled implosion in 1972 and 1973 of Minoru Yamasaki's Pruitt-Igoe tower project in St Louis. (Bill Brown argues that the advent of postmodernity must be dated to the latter event, which ushers in a shift from the enlightened belief in the use of design to construct a better world to the Bush administration's 'zealotries and fantasies',[31] corresponding point for point with those of its radical Islamist opponent.) These themes merged in the 11 September script with the Hollywood tropes of the towering inferno and the criminal mastermind striking from his remote stronghold against

the vulnerable heart of Western civilisation. The Bush administration's response, in turn, played to the same script, mobilising
the forces of good against the forces of darkness, leading a 'crusade'
against an enemy defined both as the shadowy master criminal and
an equally shadowy axis of evil; and these themes, this fully familiar
iconography, were accompanied by a secondary iconography: the
heroic firefighter, the sleeper cells embedded deep within the polis.
Beyond all this, the script reinforced the universal sense that
America – the name by which the United States conceals its domination of the Americas – is in some world-historical sense
exemplary, that 'America' is in and of itself a poetic theme, that
the tragic destiny of 'America' carries a significance that Rwanda,
say, or Bosnia, or Bangladesh do not. Yet this thematics of historical destiny too is intertwined with and mirrors its other. The
iconoclasm which was so central a dimension of the destruction of
the World Trade Center towers is already implicit in the towers'
astonishingly specular anti-representationality, and mirrors an
iconoclasm rooted deep in the Puritan and prohibitionist face of
US culture, most recently expressed in its army's complicit tolerance of the desecration of the Baghdad Museum.

The script that underlies the perception of the events of 9 / 11 is
a 'religious' one in the sense that it absolutises political and ethical
judgement. Bruce Lincoln's reading of Bush's speech of 7 October
2001 and bin Laden's reply released the same day uncovers a fully
specular relation between the two: both Bush and bin Laden
'constructed a Manichaean struggle, where Sons of Light confront
Sons of Darkness, and all must enlist on one side or another,
without possibility of neutrality, hesitation, or middle ground'.[32]
The two speeches

> mirrored one another, offering narratives in which the speakers,
> as defenders of righteousness, rallied an aggrieved people to
> strike back at aggressors who had done them terrible wrongs.
> For his part, Bush preferred to define the coming struggle in
> ethico-political terms as a campaign of civilised nations against
> terrorist cells and their rogue-state supporters. Bin Laden, in
> contrast, saw it as a war of infidels versus the faithful. As a corol-

lary, the two also differed in their willingness to couch their views in religious terms…[33]

Bush's language respects the priority of political over religious calculation. Yet Bush's speech, Lincoln argues, is built around 'strategies of double-coding' which allow him to evoke – for the appropriate audience – a quite different dimension. His text contains a religious sub-text, alluding to passages from Revelation, Job, and Isaiah; and 'for those who have ears to hear, these allusions effect a qualitative transformation, giving Bush's message an entirely different status. This conversion of secular political speech into religious discourse invests otherwise merely human events with transcendent significance. By the end, America's adversaries have been redefined as enemies of God, and current events have been constituted as confirmation of Scripture'.[34]

6

It is important to recognise the care with which religion and politics are at once mixed and kept separate in Bush's discourse. The interests of the religious right can be symbolically acknowledged and can constrain political action, but must nevertheless be subordinated to a this-worldly political rationality. This is a familiar pattern in those Western democracies where religious groups – the Catholic Church, in particular – have an input into political representation. Christian Democratic parties in many European states, Solidarity in Poland, the DLP in post-war Australia have all espoused a set of ethical values, centred on the family and reproductive practices, which have nevertheless been relatively peripheral to the real practice of politics for which in some sense they stand in. Conflict over 'values', the 'culture wars', 'history wars' and 'science wars' have at once displaced conflict over socioeconomic relations and encoded it into this space of displacement.

What seems to change after 9/11 is the apparent permanence of the organisation of the modern state around secular Enlightenment principles. It is threatened on the part of Islamic fundamentalists by virtue of their commitment to a theocratic state governed by religious principles; and on the part of the Bush administration by virtue of its contempt for rational scrutiny of policy issues (its deliberate refusal of informed scientific opinion on climate change, for example) together with its casting of the 'War on Terror' in terms reminiscent of the Religious Wars of the sixteenth and seventeenth centuries from which the European Enlightenment emerged. This is not, let me repeat, to suggest that this administration is engaged in anything other than a material calculation of geopolitical interest: on the contrary, its political practice is the usual business of representation of a narrow constituency of monied contributors and key voters, together with a determined global assertion of military and economic supremacy. This is a worldly, not a religious cause. Yet on the 'cultural' level – the level of conflict over ethical and aesthetic values and of the assertion of religious and ethnic identity – American politics is suffused with deeply non-rational positions in which the administration itself is complicit.

Zizek claims, indeed, that religious and ethnic conflict is the transmogrified form in which alone 'politics proper' can now happen.[35] But, as Brown points out, this is to regard religion as a mere means to a more 'real' (socio-economic) end, and to rely on a pre-given distinction between religion and 'politics proper'.[36] That distinction, however, is part of a specifically Enlightenment separation of spheres whereby politics is aligned with social class and economy, and culture constitutes a 'private' realm without effect on the former; it is, in a real sense, a distinction between 'rational' and 'non-rational' spheres of being ('non-rational' meaning the realm of emotions, values, and judgements of taste), and it is grounded in one of the central social processes of modernity: the differentiation of the domains of governance, economy, science, ethics, aesthetics, and so on from religion as the state comes to rely on a specialised political apparatus and relatively autonomous cultural institutions. The differentiation was, however, never complete and never completely accepted by the religiously committed. Thus, as Lincoln puts it, 'the view of religion as delimited, and therefore definable, is ... itself culturally bound, historically recent, and discursively loaded'.[37] To assume distinct spheres of responsibility and truth for religion and politics is to situate ourselves in the enlightened critique of supernaturalism and the perspective of mundane history – precisely one of the sets of values that are at stake in the world after 9/11.

The prospect half-glimpsed before us is of the fusion (or 'de-differentiation') again of those relatively distinct spheres and the end of a secular order based on principles – however inadequately they may operate in practice – of consensual rationality. Although I have tried to emphasise that the role of religion in US politics is restricted to the relatively peripheral areas of the control of fertility and a single field of foreign policy, the specular resemblance between the Bush administration's War on Terror and the war of Islamic fundamentalists against the corruption of the secular West is nevertheless ominous. Islamist and Hindutva ideals of theocratic governance are shared – *mutatis mutandis* – by the American religious right, whose goal is a fully Christian state promoting Christian ethical and cultural norms, and whose 'wilfully mad rhetoric … is a political act, a constant dissent, disruption, and critique of modern thought, specifically of the modern theories of history that shape prevailing knowledge about world events, past and present, in America'.[38]

Yet simply to assert the rationality of the political process against this anti-modernist rhetoric would be not only to assume a transcendental point (the moment of detached reason) from which to speak, but also to ignore the fantasmatic coordinates that structure the realm of the political. Here what matters at least as much as the force of religion is the structural effects of a market society which has transformed the citizen into consumer. The public sphere, spectacularised and rebuilt around a rhetoric of embodiment rather than the classical 'rhetoric of abstract disembodiment',[39] is a field of iconicity and desire in which marketing principles drive the discourse of rational debate. Yet to invoke a 'subject of citizenship' or a public sphere built on conversation about principles as a condition from which we have fallen is still to mistake a normative structure for a reality. Politics is the mesh of desires and fantasies that organise perceptions of real interests.

The slow shift in political forms that we are seeing in the wake of 11 September is not one from the rational to the irrational, but rather a move from one set of fantasmatic coordinates grounded in consumption, the liberal rhetoric of enlightened reason, and the mass media to another grounded in consumption, the transcendental rhetoric of religion, and the mass media.

None of this – finally – gives us a licence either to give up on rational debate and the critical analysis of social interests, or to reduce political action to the mere working out of fantasmatic identifications. But the point from which we speak our analysis has no universally valid authority. It is a part of the game that it describes.

Notes

1 Mary Louise Pratt, 'Subjects and Predicators', *PMLA* 120:3 (2005), p. 881.
2 Susan Friend Harding, *The Book of Jerry Falwell: Fundamentalist Language and Politics* (Princeton, 2000), p. ix..
3 *ibid.*, p.21.
4 Pratt, p. 882.
5 Bruce Lincoln, *Holy Terrors: Thinking about Religion after September 11* (Chicago, 2003), pp. 5–7.
6 Rosanne C. Euben, *Enemy in the Mirror: Islamic Fundamentalism and the Limits of Modern Rationalism* (Princeton, 1999), p. 154.
7 *ibid.*, p. 24.
8 Emile Durkheim, *The Elementary Forms of the Religious Life*, translated by Joseph Ward Swain (London, 1915), p.38.
9 Mircea Eliade, *The Sacred and the Profane*, translated by Willard R. Trask (New York, 1961), p.12.
10 *ibid.*, pp. 68–9.
11 Durkheim, p. 411.
12 For a critique of the notion of the ambivalence of the sacred which nevertheless seems to me not to dislodge it, cf. Giorgio Agamben, *Homo Sacer: Sovereign Power and Bare Life*, translated by Daniel Heller-Roazen (Stanford, 1998), pp. 75–80.
13 Roger Caillois, *Man and the Sacred*, translated by Meyer Barash (Glencoe, Illinois, 1959), p. 21.
14 Pratt, p. 881.
15 Harding, p. 233.
16 *ibid.*, p. 233.
17 James Beauseigneur, *The Christ Clone Trilogy* (New York, 2003–4); Britt Gillette, *Conquest of Paradise: An End-times Nano Thriller* (Lincoln, Nebraska,

2003); Bill Myers, *Fire of Heaven* (Grand Rapids, Michigan, 1999); Pat Robertson, *The End of the Age* (Nashville, 1996).

18 Hitchcock, quoted in St Johnson 'Reactions to Hamas Victory', <http://www.leftbehind.com/channelendtimes.asp?pageid=1258&channel ID=71>

19 Pratt, p. 882.

20 John Frow, 'Is Elvis a God? Cult, Culture, Questions of Method', *International Journal of Cultural Studies*, 1:2 (1998), pp. 199–212.

21 David Martin, *The Religious and the Secular: Studies in Secularisation* (London, 1969), p. 16.

22 Peter Berger, *The Sacred Canopy, Elements of a Sociological Theory of Religion* (New York, 1967), p. 109, while supporting the notion of a process of secularisation, nevertheless allows for the possibility that there may be 'a continuation of more or less traditional motifs of religious consciousness outside their previous institutional contexts'.

23 Berger, p. 112.

24 Gordon Graham, 'Religion, Secularisation and Modernity', *Philosophy*, 67 (1992), pp. 183–97.

25 José Casanova, 'Beyond European and American Exceptionalisms: Towards a Global Perspective', in *Predicting Religion: Christian, Secular and Alternative Futures*, edited by Grace Davie (Aldershot, 2003), p.27.

26 David Marshall, *Celebrity and Power: Fame in Contemporary Culture* (Minneapolis, 1997), pp. 55–6.

27 James Chandler, *England in 1819: The Politics of Literary Culture and the Case of Romantic Historicism* (Chicago, 1998), p. 228.

28 Sidney Blumenthal, *The Rise of the Counter-Establishment: From Conservative Ideology to Political Power* (New York, 1986).

29 Slavoj Zizek, *Welcome to the Desert of the Real* (London, 2002), p. 15.

30 Jean Baudrillard, 'The Order of Simulacra', in *Symbolic Exchange and Death*, translated by Iain Hamilton Grant (London, 1993), p.69.

31 Bill Brown, 'The Dark Wood of Postmodernity (Space, Faith, Allegory)', *PMLA* 120:3 (2005), p. 734.

32 Lincoln, p. 20.

33 *ibid.*, p. 27.

34 *ibid.*, pp.32–2.

35 Zizek, p. 132.

36 Brown, pp. 746–7.

37 Lincoln, p. 2.

38 Harding, p. 238.

39 Michael Warner, 'The Mass Public and the Mass Subject', in *Publics and Counterpublics* (New York, 2002), p. 169.

A World of Museums:
New Concepts, New Models

MOIRA SIMPSON

We have probably all visited museums full of stuffed animals, bones of ancient reptiles, artefacts from archaeological sites, clothing, tools and weaponry from around the world, and art works by the Old Masters. Museums range from national collections, encyclopaedic in scope, to the narrowly specialised, such as the Bata Shoe Museum in Toronto, Canada; the Tattoo Museum in Amsterdam in the Netherlands; the Museum of Cheese in New York, USA; and the Museum of Tap Water in Beijing, China.

In essence, according to the International Council of Museums (ICOM), museums 'preserve, interpret and promote the natural and cultural inheritance of humanity'.[1] Their definition of a museum is 'a non-profit making permanent institution' that is open to the public 'in the service of society and of its development' which 'acquires, conserves, researches, communicates and exhibits, for purposes of study, education and enjoyment, the tangible and intangible evidence of people and their environment'.[2]

As an institution of research and education, the modern museum is embedded within a Western philosophical framework which gives precedence to freedom of knowledge and enquiry and which is dedicated to research and the dissemination of knowledge. This has made it difficult for some to accept restrictions on objects and knowledge which are required in various communities as part of their methods of managing, protecting and transmitting knowledge, particularly in the sphere of ceremonial life. Curatorial responsibilities have also been challenged by Indigenous demands for the repatriation of human remains and material culture from museum collections, which some see as a threat to the integrity of collections and the future of museums. However, these changes have brought new meanings to collections, created opportunities for insightful engagement between curatorial staff and the traditional keepers of culture, and changed the dynamics between the sacred and the secular in the context of the museum. They have also resulted in new models of museums offering local strategies which sometimes challenge conventional approaches to preserving heritage in the museum contact, demanding a reconceptualisation of Western understandings of heritage, preservation and the idea of the museum.

I: Museums, Indigenous Peoples and Colonialism

Since the International Council of Museums was established in 1946, the Statutes have been revised several times and now include facilities whose status as a museum might be less obvious than the examples cited above: for example, natural, archaeological and ethnographic monuments and sites; historical monuments; and institutions displaying collections of live plants and animals, such as botanical and zoological gardens, aquaria and vivaria. In 2001, the list was expanded to include 'non-profit art exhibition galleries' and 'cultural centres and other entities that facilitate the preservation, continuation and management of tangible or intangible heritage resources (living heritage and digital creative activity)'. These additions are significant because the ICOM Statutes now include the development of virtual museums and digital collections, the growth of community museums in various forms, and the inclusion of intangible as well as tangible forms of heritage.

This includes cultural expressions such as languages, oral traditions, artistic skills, religious beliefs, rituals, songs, music, dances, traditional medicine, and sports and games, as well as physical expressions of culture such as objects and buildings. A much wider range of museum activities is recognised than in earlier versions of the Code of Ethics, which emphasised collecting, research and conservation as central activities of the traditional Euro-American or Western museum model. The Statutes now incorporate alternative concepts such as keeping places with restricted access and cultural centres that serve a range of functions, facilities that may be more appropriate than the collection-based, publicly accessible Western model in other parts of the world.

Etymology of Museums
The origins of the museum is a story with several strands and it is not possible here to provide a detailed account but rather to demonstrate the etymological source of the word 'museum' and the provide a very brief outline of the development of the European museum as a collecting institution and its relationship to colonialism.

The precursors of the European museum with its emphasis on objects were the collections of relics, ritual objects and treasures which were stored in medieval temples and churches; but the classical etymology of the museum is derived from ancient Greece. The Muses or *Mousai* were the nine daughters of Zeus and Mnemosyne, Greek goddesses who presided over the arts and sciences and who inspired artists, poets, philosophers, and musicians. The *mouseion* or musaeum was 'a place of contemplation, a philosophical institution or a temple of the Muses'.[3] The Great Library of Alexandria was the earliest known musaeum, primarily a centre for scholarly study and the holding of a large collection of scrolls.

During the Renaissance, interest grew in collecting natural and artificial curiosities: objects, artefacts, art works, curiosities and oddities from around the globe that provided evidence of the wonders of nature, the creatures that inhabit it, and the lifeways and cultural artefacts of the world's diverse cultures. Often thought of as eclectic and disorderly collections, they were referred to as 'cabinets of curiosities' although they varied greatly in size and scale ranging from small cupboards, to rooms and even palaces. In 'Museums and the Shaping of Knowledge', Eilean Hooper-Greenhill demonstrates that these were in fact orderly 'cabinets of the world' which reflected Renaissance epistemology through which the collectors – scholars, scientists, merchants and princes – attempted to give meaning and order to the universe and to position themselves within it and are 'direct ancestors' of the modern museum.[4] In their various forms, 'cabinets of the world' reflected the power, position and worldview of the individual collector: 'the prince at the centre of a political arena, the scholar at the centre of intellectual links, the merchant at the centre of a trading network'. Later, the term 'musaeum' or 'museum' came to be used to refer to collections of objects acquired as curiosities and for academic enquiry such as the collection of John Tradescant who, in 1656 published a catalogue entitled 'Musaeum Tradescantianum: or, a Collection of Rarities Preserved at South-Lambeth near London'. In time, the term 'museum' was applied to the buildings in which the collections were stored and exhibited.

Early private collections that were made available for occasional public viewing attracted both the learned and the curious. Increasingly valued for their potential to inform and educate, governments, learned societies and educational institutions acquired collections and established public museums with an emphasis on 'informing and educating the common man'. The idea of the museum developed as a scientifically-based collecting and research institution primarily concerned with materiality, academic freedom and the open dissemination of information.

Museums proliferated during the latter half of the nineteenth and throughout the twentieth century. They provided a venue in which European powers could recount official histories and achievements and display materials derived from colonial activities, so presenting evidence to the public of the success of government policies for overseas expansion. Closely linked with the ideology of nation-building, museums were also established in European colonies as a means of displaying the growing cultural wealth of the colonies and creating a sense of unity amongst the settler population. The museum concept has continued to grow, and museums are now to be found in virtually every country of the world demonstrating the significance that is given to preserving and interpreting culture and providing education services based upon museum collections. According to *The Dictionary of Museums and Living Displays*, there were 34,987 museums around the world in the mid-1980s, with an estimated expansion rate of 10% every five years; however, accurate assessment of museum numbers world-wide today can be difficult, in part due to the diversity of cultural facilities which may be defined as a museum.

Indigenous Rejection of the Museum

> It shall not be called a museum, for we are not a dead people; let it be called the Skeena Treasure House.
>
> Albert Douse, High Chief of the Kitwancool band,
> naming the Skeena Treasure House in Northern British Columbia[5]

Indigenous peoples in settler societies such as the USA, Canada, and Australia, and newly independent nations of former European colonies have been adopting the museum concept to preserve heritage, interpret their histories and cultures, and to help reinforce cultural identity or forge a new sense of national identity. Simultaneously they may reject certain aspects of museology considered to be inappropriate or undesirable. This may begin at the most fundamental level with the rejection of the nomenclature of 'museum' and the use of alternative descriptors which incorporate cultural symbols or reflect the values and functions associated with the specific cultural facility. Often the terms used emphasise cultural continuity and vitality in contrast to the negativity that many Indigenous peoples associate with the idea of the 'museum'.

The new museum and cultural centre on Thursday Island in the Torres Strait Islands of Australia is named *Ngan Jila*, or 'House of Riches'. *Kluu Laanas*, the name of a museum and cultural centre planned for the community of Old Massett in Haida Gwaii, British Columbia, means 'canoe village' and reflects the importance of canoes in Haida culture. When the Kwakwaka'wakw (Kwakiut'l) people of Alert Bay, British Columbia, established a museum and cultural centre to house ceremonial masks and regalia repatriated from museums in Canada and the USA, they named the centre '*U'mista*' meaning 'something of great value that has come back', a term used in earlier times to refer to the return of community members who had been captured as slaves by other coastal peoples. The *Tr'ondëk Hwëch'in* First Nation of the Yukon in Canada call their cultural centre '*Dänojà Zho*' meaning 'long time ago house'. The Aboriginal centre in Melbourne Museum in Victoria, Australia, is named *Bunjilaka* meaning 'the land of *Bunjil*, the creator', referring to a major creator figure known to the Koori (Indigenous) people of S.E. Australia.[6]

The naming of a museum or cultural centre after a cultural concept, ancestral figure, or architectural form specific to a particular community signifies its cultural meaning to the peoples of that community, and also indicates a sense of community ownership. In some cases, it may also be a deliberate rejection of the term 'museum' because of its associations with death. For some peoples this may be the metaphorical 'death' of objects removed from their culture of origin and placed in a museum showcase or storage facility where they are deprived of the active social life with gives them meaning.

The idea of death may also be inferred from static museum exhibitions of mainly colonial-era material which can give the impression that the peoples and cultures depicted have died out. When the Museum of the Plains Indians was established in Browning, Montana, USA, the Blackfeet named it *Ahkeeneemon*, the traditional name for a memorial lodge to a dead chief or famous warrior. As reported by John C. Ewers in 1943:

> In preparing [the memorial lodge] as the last resting place for a dead hero of the tribe, the tipi was supplied with the finest household furnishings obtainable and the prized personal belongings of the deceased were displayed in the lodge. He was dressed in his finest costume and placed upon his couch in the lodge. Then the lodge was closed and left as a memorial to a recognized leader.

The old Indians say the museum is like that. Here finest specimens of old Indian manufacture are arranged just as they were in the old days when Indians used these objects in their daily lives and sacred ceremonies. The difference is that the old *'ahkeeneemon'* served as a memorial to a single outstanding individual, but its new namesake stands as a memorial for all the tribes of the north Western plains.[7]

A further, direct association with death arises from museum holdings of human remains: the skulls, bones and tissue samples of ancestors whose bodily remains were collected and studied. To this day, museum holdings in Europe, North America and elsewhere contain the remains of hundreds of thousands of individuals collected for purposes of scientific research. As a consequence, Indigenous perspectives of museums often see them as more akin to mausoleums.

There is, then, a certain irony about the appropriation of the museum concept by peoples for whom these institutions hold such strong negative associations. This is even more starkly evident when we consider the relationship between the colonisation and disempowerment of Indigenous peoples, and the ideologies, processes, and politics that underlie the origins and development of museums and the ethnographic collections that they hold.

Collecting the World

For many Indigenous peoples colonialism led to the eradication or near-destruction of the cultural and religious values and social structures which gave meaning to their lives and order to the communities. Colonialism disempowered and dispossessed them, dislocating them from traditional lands and culture *and* stripping them of much of their material heritage. As voyages of discovery, international trade and, later, tourism, took European sailors, explorers, traders, missionaries, colonial administrators and tourists to the shores of far off lands, the circumstances were created for the amassing of vast collections in Western museums.

There were no laws to prohibit the removal of cultural property by armies and occupying forces and it was a practice which had a long history. Victorious Roman armies triumphantly displayed the religious artefacts, statuary and other objects which they had procured from the peoples they had conquered, regarding it as *res nullius* or ownerless.[8]

Not all supported such activities. The Greek historian, Polybius, wrote in the second century BC:

> One may perhaps have some reason for amassing gold and silver. In fact, it would be impossible to attain universal dominion without appropriating these resources from other peoples in order to weaken them. In the case of every other form of wealth, however, it is more glorious to leave it where it was, together with the envy which it inspired, and to base our country's glory not on the abundance and beauty of its paintings and statues but on its sober customs and noble sentiments. Moreover, I hope that future conquerors will learn from these thoughts not to plunder the cities subjugated by them, and not to make the misfortune of other peoples the adornment of their own glory.[9]

However, during the centuries of European colonial expansion, the natural and cultural wealths of the world were seen by Europeans to be rich resources to be exploited commercially, and for scientific, aesthetic and political purposes. This was further driven in the fifteenth and sixteenth centuries by papal bulls issued by the Catholic popes authorising Christian nations to seek dominion over non-Christian peoples and their lands and possessions. The *Dum Diversas* and the *Romanus Pontifex* issued by Pope Nicholas V in 1452 and 1455 instructed the Spanish and Portuguese monarchs 'to invade, search out, capture, vanquish, and subdue all Saracens and pagans... reduce their persons to perpetual slavery, and to apply and appropriate to himself and his successors the kingdoms, dukedoms, counties, principalities, dominions, possessions, and goods, and to convert them to his and their use and profit'.

Following Columbus's journey to the 'New World' in 1492, Pope Alexander VI issued the Papal Bull *Inter Caetera* to put a halt to Portugal and Spain fighting over these and other lands that Europeans had yet to locate. The *Inter Caetera* of 1493, the Treaty of Tordesillas of 1494, and the Treaty of Saragossa of 1529 granted to the 'Catholic kings and princes … lands discovered and yet to be discovered'. Under these treaties, the world was divided into two almost equal halves, assigning Spain authority of most of the Pacific Ocean and the Americas, with the exception of Brazil, while Portugal was granted rights to all of Asia.

The practice of armies acquiring loot and plunder continued and museums became the preferred venues for displaying such trophy collections. During the Napoleonic wars, Napoleon Bonaparte established a systematic programme of collecting art works confiscated from his enemies, which were then taken to Paris and placed in the Palais du Louvre which Napoleon renamed in 1803 as the Musée Napoléon (later to become the Musée du Louvre). After Napoleon's defeat, many art works and treasures were returned to the countries from which they were removed, the first occurrence of a large-scale restitution of property plundered during warfare. It became generally accepted that it was improper for armies and states to acquire the possessions of the private homes, places of worship and public institutions of the conquered peoples and this principle was incorporated into future developments of international law as it related to the protection of cultural property.

Yet there was no protection for Indigenous cultural property rights during the colonial era. In the view of European powers, colonisation was a process not of invasion or war, but of settlement and pacification in the fulfilment of Christian duty. The occupation of new colonies facilitated the amassing of huge collections of ethnographic material by anthropologists. Collecting became more systematic and cultural artefacts became commodities of colonialism, not just through the trading and selling of art and artefacts produced for external consumption, but also the commodification of cultural materials that were intrinsic to the social and religious lives of Indigenous peoples.

The eighteenth and nineteenth centuries marked the height of European expansion – a period during which colonised peoples suffered subjugation and abuse resulting in massive population decline through death in land wars, frontier violence, slavery and the introduction of diseases to which they had little resistance. By the end of the nineteenth century, it seemed that many traditional ways of life and even peoples were doomed to extinction. In a lecture at the Field Museum in Chicago in November 1897, George Amon Dorsey, an assistant curator of anthropology at the Field Museum and one of the main collectors of artefacts on the Northwest coast of North America, described the Haida of northern British Columbia as 'a doomed race. Wars, smallpox, gross immorality, a change from old ways to new ways – their fate is the common fate of the American, whether he sails the sea in the North, gallops over the plain in the West, or sleeps in his hammock in the forests of Brazil'.[10]

Baldwin Spencer and Frank Gillen, who conducted ethno-graphic fieldwork and collecting amongst the Aboriginal communities of Central Australia noted in 1899 that 'No sooner do the natives come into contact with white men, than phthisis and other diseases soon make their appearance, and, after a comparatively short time, all that can be done is to gather the few remnants of the tribe into some mission station where the path to final extinction may be made as pleasant as possible'.[11] In New Zealand and Australia, this idea was commonly referred to as 'smoothing the pillow of a dying race' and was reflected in the paternalistic activities of governments and churches.

For anthropologists, mass collecting was thought to be a neces-sary and urgent process in order to document and maintain a visual record of those cultures believed to be on the verge of extinction. Spencer and Gillen predicted in 1899 that:

The time in which it will be possible to investigate the Australian native tribes is rapidly drawing to a close, and though we know more of them than we do the lost Tasmanians, yet our knowledge is very incomplete, and unless some special effort be made, many tribes will practically die out without our gaining any knowledge of the details of their organisation, or of their sacred customs and beliefs.[12]

Anthropologists and archaeologists undertook urgent rescue archaeology and salvage collecting to record what they could of the 'dying' peoples and their cultures. There was also strong competition between museums in the nineteenth century to acquire the most significant collections of cultural material and, at times, academic rivalry between individual collectors.

Collections and exhibitions in museums and International expositions brought the world to European and American cities, enabling curious visitors to see exotic creatures and plants from other parts of the world and to glimpse evidence of the lifeways and artefacts of peoples from other lands. They even included 'living displays' in which peoples from different parts of the world lived and acted out their lives, becoming a mere spectacle before the curious gaze of thousands of visitors.

Universal Museums: Museums 'of the World for the World'

> It's loot, but it's our loot.
> Lord Gowrie, Former Minister for the Arts in the United Kingdom

The extensive world-wide collecting practices of the colonial era cannot be matched in scope and scale by the collecting activities of contemporary museums which are limited by modern ethical, political and financial constraints. Collecting during the colonial era was a one-way market with cultural objects and knowledge flowing from the colonies into European and American institutions. This included items of religious and ceremonial value, funerary objects and grave goods, architectural fragments, statuary and monuments. Thus the world's major museums hold extensive collections that are universal in scope and represent some of the finest examples of human cultural, artistic and scientific endeavour. As a consequence, much of the rich material cultural heritage of the world lies within the walls of museums and art galleries and in private collections, mainly in Europe and North America.

The UK's 1,823 museums hold around 200 million objects.[13] The British Museum, the world's first national museum founded in 1753, now holds six-and-a-half million objects of art and antiquities, which it describes as 'one of the finest in existence, spanning two million years of human history'. The Museum's website invites people to 'Travel the World: Visit the British Museum'. New York's Metropolitan Museum of Art contains more than two million works of art 'from all points of the compass, covering ancient through modern times', while the National Museum of the American Indian in Washington D.C. has over 800,000 Native American artefacts. The State Hermitage Museum, in St Petersburg, holds over three million works of art which 'present the development of the world culture and art from the Stone Age to the 20th century'. The Australian Museum in Sydney holds important research collections of natural and human history totaling over 14.5 million specimens: more than 1,000,000 are archaeological objects and 111,000 are anthropological objects.

With collections that are encyclopaedic in both size and scope, universal museums are purported to reflect the world and to benefit the world's population in terms of their purpose. This confers on them particular importance as institutions which display the greatest works of art and facilitate comparative research into technological, stylistic and aesthetic expressions across temporal and cultural boundaries. Neil MacGregor, Director of the British Museum, emphasised the importance of the global nature of the collections and the universal status of the museum's collections when he stated:

> At the British Museum we have reaffirmed our founding principles of the museum as a museum of the world for the world; a collection held for the benefit of all the world, present and future... At the universal museum, people can consider their place in the world and see different parts of that world as indissolubly linked, they can find a different way to comprehend the world and see the world as pattern, as process, as system, and where a multitude of truths can be fostered to ensure that the full complexity of issues can be understood, rather than attempting to provide simple and essentially reductive notions of identity.[14]

Universal museums hold so many objects of such artistic and cultural significance that they are regarded as being of world heritage value. Consequently, efforts by source communities to have significant items of their cultural heritage repatriated from museums are seen by some museum professionals to threaten the integrity of the collections. In December 2002, directors of eighteen major museums in Europe and North America signed a 'Declaration on The Importance and Value of Universal Museums', which emphasised the importance of the museums in interpreting objects and providing access to visitors from around the world. The signatories of the Declaration argue against the repatriation of cultural objects acquired by museums in the past stating that 'museums serve not just the citizens of one nation but the people of every nation. Each object contributes to that process.'

Neil MacGregor asserts that universal museums have 'a world-wide civic purpose'. He asks rhetorically: 'Where else other than in these museums can the world see so clearly that it is one?'[15] However, Mark O'Neill, Head of Glasgow Museums, questions whether these really are universal museums or merely museums that hold global collections which are purported to be universal in value merely as a defence against repatriation claims. He suggests that an alternative view of a truly universal museum would be one which 'is open about the conflicted histories of some objects, which acknowledges historical context as well aesthetics, explores violent as well as peaceful cultural encounters, and reveals the Imperial as well as the Enlightenment history of collections'.[16]

Problematics of Western museology
There are a number of important ways in which museums have been problematic for Indigenous peoples. Museums have failed to acknowledge adequately the histories of collections and the ways in which their acquisition was integrally linked with the violent, repressive and destructive histories of colonial contact. Under colonial régimes, colonised peoples were subjected to the imposition of Western government and military authority, and there were deliberate efforts to eradicate traditional religious practices

through the enforcement of the teaching of Christian religion and Western educational, industrial and employment practices. Over time, these policies and practices alienated many Indigenous peoples from the traditional religious, social and cultural systems which had underpinned and structured their individual and community lives.

As Michael Dodson, the Aboriginal and Torres Strait Islander Social Justice Commissioner, said in 1994:

> A people's culture includes all the spiritual and material values which structure its way of life, and the way of life itself. Culture encompasses the whole complex of the identities and products of a people, all that it inherits and transmits, its knowledge, its language, its laws and ethics, its religion and ceremony, its social organisation and kinship structures, its customs, its philosophy and art and song and stories. As Indigenous peoples, we are acutely aware that our survival as peoples depends on the vitality of our cultures. The deepest wound that colonisation has inflicted has come from a process of stripping us of our distinct identities and cultures.[17]

The systematic collecting of artefacts during this period undoubtedly saved many from commercial sale, destruction or neglect as cultural practices changed in the face of Christianisation and other cultural and economic influences. Ethnographic collections in museums now provide valuable, fascinating and informative cultural resources from many periods and places with the potential to enrich our understanding of the world's cultures and the rich artistry of human creativity. However, the acquisition of material culture from colonised peoples was not merely an act of cultural preservation; it can also be seen as a contributory factor in the loss of associated knowledge and the near-destruction of Indigenous cultures. The removal of important cultural objects from communities has left many without the necessary materials to maintain ceremonies, to pass on cultural knowledge and skills, and to preserve the visible evidence of their cultural identity. Ethnographic collectors and museums were therefore complicit in the process of acculturation, along with schools, churches, and government agencies. As Francis B. Musonda, Director of the Lusaka Museum in Zambia, laments: 'decades of colonial rule have left yawning gaps in Africa's cultural heritage'.[18]

Even after colonial rule has ended, the treasures of nations continue to be endangered by the activities of looters and thieves driven by the commercial rewards to be gained by the illicit trade in antiquities and art works on the international art market, the result of 'the power relations that allow rape of the African past'.[19] The international community has attempted to prevent the looting of archaeological sites and to halt illicit trafficking of antiquities and other items of important cultural heritage through the 1970 UNESCO Convention on the Means of Prohibiting and Preventing the Illicit Import, Export and Transfer of Ownership of Cultural Property, 'the first global legal instrument for the protection of cultural heritage from theft and pillaging' and the 1993 UNIDROIT Convention on Stolen of Illegally Exported Cultural Objects. However, these have had limited effect, and looting and trading in illicitly obtained artefacts continues on a massive scale.

While the ICOM Code of Professional Ethics directs that museums should not acquire any objects that may have been illegally excavated or exported from their country of origin, the demand for antiquities and ethnographic materials from both museums and private collectors continues to escalate prices. This drives a huge international trade in stolen and illicitly exported arts and antiquities, fuelling the activities of looters and endangering the heritage of nations. So, asserts author Karl Meyer in *The Plundered Past,* museums are 'indirectly subsidising the devastation of antiquity'.[20]

Ordering the World

> Like Gulliver returning from his travels, the scholar and visitor to the British Museum would see that there are many good ways of organising the world. The original collection contained books, rocks, plants, animals, and scientific instruments – all the world, physical, natural and human, under one roof.[21]

Much ethnographic material was collected during the eighteenth, nineteenth and early twentieth centuries, by various means and by individuals who may or may not have recorded or even known an object's function and meaning. The management of collections in museums involves the ordering of objects and related documentation within taxonomic and classificatory systems based upon function, material, construction method, place collected, culture of origin, etc. Various systems have been devised at different times, each reflecting contemporary scientific and philosophical ideas of how the world can be ordered. These systems give primacy to the objects and their functions as defined within Western epistemologies, whereas in some other cultures classification may be based upon the power with which an object is imbued or the social systems and relationships which are signified by an object. These might include, for example, objects that signify clan or society membership, objects that impart rights and privileges, or objects that embody spirit beings.

Although modern Western epistemology recognises the influence of organic structures, social relationships, and the dynamic nature of 'objective' knowledge, museums still apply classification systems which attribute objects with meanings according to Western scientific and aesthetic measures. The Western museum perspective therefore restricts the accuracy and depth of interpretation of museum ethnographic collections, and the complexities and changed (and changing) meanings that they hold for different peoples in different contexts and at different times.

Consequently, the detail and accuracy of associated museum documentation may lack consistency and reliability. Francis Musonda, an African archaeologist and Director of the Lusaka Museum in Zambia, believes that Western curators who have not been exposed to Africa traditions 'may be unable to appreciate or comprehend' the functional or religious character of certain African objects, and so have been unable to provide a 'meaningful interpretation of objects and their value'. Musonda asserts that, as a result, 'ethnographic collections at the Museum of Mankind, the Victoria and Albert Museum, and other museums in Britain that are quite considerable in extent and important in content, have tended to be badly under-curated'. He emphasises the importance of documenting 'the role of an object in the context of its African society instead of emphasizing only its aesthetics'. More accurate knowledge of the context of African objects will, he believes, provide museum visitors with better information of 'the uses, manufacture, and significance of such objects [and so] will make it possible for the country of origin to be proud of the dissemination of its cultural heritage outside its borders'.[22]

II: Museums and Indigenous Peoples in the Twenty-First Century – Two-Way Cultural Markets

Given this history we might ask why Indigenous people would even consider establishing a museum. Can the colonial foundations and ideological legacy of the museum be overcome? Is the museum an appropriate institution for Indigenous heritage management? And, how can Indigenous concepts of heritage, custodianship, and preservation be accommodated in an institution so grounded in European colonial history and Western epistemology?

Seeking to re-establish control over cultural heritage and the interpretive process, some Indigenous peoples are requesting the return of objects removed during the colonial era. Such moves are regarded by some as a threat to the future of museums and their collections, but have also brought museums and communities into closer engagement with benefits for Indigenous peoples, museums, researchers and visitors.

The ideologies underlying museum development and the methods employed in collecting, classifying and interpreting history, culture and the natural world emanate from, and continue to give primacy to, Western epistemology over those of Indigenous peoples. Museums, while associated with colonialism, are nevertheless effective facilities for protecting and preserving material culture and sites where cross-cultural communication may be facilitated. Many Indigenous peoples are appropriating the basic concept of the museum as a secure storage facility for conserving important cultural objects and archives, an educational centre for the maintenance of cultural knowledge and skills, a meeting place for community activities, and an interpretive centre for interpreting their cultures and histories to visitors. The museum can be adapted to meet local needs and circumstances and inter-cultural dialogue can then be conducted within a framework reflecting Indigenous values, protocols and agendas. This is leading to the development of new museum models and effecting change in mainstream museums: it is no longer a one-way cultural market; rather we are witnessing a two-way flow of cultural objects and cultural knowledge.

Artistic Revival
Until relatively recently, ethnographic collecting and anthropological research generally involved the exploitation of Indigenous peoples as information resources and the appropriation of Indigenous collections and knowledge, with little return to communities. Nowadays, Indigenous peoples are increasingly demanding that researchers undertake community consultation, seek the informed consent of participants, and supply reports and research findings to communities. Many countries have introduced laws which attempt to stop illicit excavations, looting or exportation of important heritage objects. Nevertheless, there are many peoples around the world whose rich artistic and cultural heritage lies in the collections of museums, while little remains within the community.

While repatriation is a growing issue for the museum sector with many peoples seeking the return of important items of cultural heritage, museum collections and ethnographic studies may also provide opportunities for contemporary Indigenous artists to examine and learn about design and construction techniques which may no longer be in common usage or may not be known today. In these circumstances, museum collections can provide resources for Indigenous artists to revitalise traditional arts practices or to rediscover lost styles and techniques.

When the fragile remains of a prehistoric Maori *kawe* or back pack were found in a rocky outcrop on a hillside in inland Canterbury in New Zealand in 1983, staff of Canterbury Museum analysed its materials and method of construction. It was made from woven and plaited strips of the leaves from the New Zealand flax that had been attached to a wooden hoop and closed with a draw-string, a style of back pack which had not previously been seen. By studying the details of its construction, Maori weaver Te Aue Davis was able to replicate the weaving technique, while kaumatua (male elders) John Stirling and Wirimu Solomon assisted her by making the circular framework and providing the spiritual support and gender balance that Maori protocol deems necessary for a project of this importance. Now both the replica and the remains of the original back pack are displayed in the museum and Te Aue Davis is able to use and teach others the re-discovered technique of its woven construction.

Bill Reid, one of the most prominent Canadian artists of the twentieth century, explored his Haida heritage by studying Haida art collections in museums. He honed his carving skills working on a totem pole restoration programme at the University of British Columbia's Museum of Anthropology, carving copies of Haida houses and poles from ancient Haida village sites. He went on to become a master of jewellery and sculpture using both wood and metals, and created many works depicting the ancestral figures of Haida legend. He taught a number of younger artists including Robert Davidson, another prominent Haida artist, who now carves and produces prints of contemporary designs innovative and minimalist in form, but derived from traditional design conventions of Northwest Coast art. Davidson also used collections of Haida material in museums to study the carving techniques and the complex and highly stylised forms of Northwest Coast art, becoming proficient in traditional forms before developing his own innovative and distinctive style.

Each of these artists used museum collections to rediscover cultural knowledge concerning techniques and design conventions, and to revive it through their own work and their teachings. As artists operating in the modern, commercial art world, they are then also able to communicate to audiences worldwide, engendering appreciation of Indigenous art forms, demonstrating innovations in techniques and imagery, and conveying messages of cultural survival and creative dynamism. Museum outreach programmes can also become part of the mechanism for reviving skills and knowledge in Indigenous communities. Alutiiq Museum in Alaska creates travelling exhibitions which are taken to villages by artists who teach skills such as grass weaving, woodcarving, and mask-making and so contribute to the revitalisation of traditional skills. So, the information flow has been partly reversed, from museum to community, enabling Indigenous artists to become proficient in techniques and styles of artistry that may have been almost lost.

Repatriation of cultural property

Many Indigenous peoples remain dispossessed of lands and cultural heritage. The difficulties faced by those who seek to regain control of cultural property in museum collections illustrate their continuing disempowerment and the ongoing inequalities that they experience as a result of the primacy given to the legal and administrative systems of dominant nation-states over Indigenous systems of governance and customary laws. They also highlight the complexities associated with concepts such as 'property', 'ownership' and 'custodianship' which have distinct meanings and legal standings in different cultures.

Take, for example, sacred and ceremonial objects that are regarded in some communities as communally owned. They may be used and cared for by a ceremonialist or custodian, who holds no individual property rights as embodied in Western law but earns or inherits the rights to use the objects through years of learning and ceremonial transfer. That individual holds fiduciary responsibilities to care for and protect the objects for the benefit of their community or clan group and does not have the right to sell or trade the object as if it were a personal possession. According to customary law, such items are inalienable possessions belonging to the whole community.

In recent years significant, although limited, changes in the repatriation policies of some Western museums and associated professional organisations have enabled Indigenous communities to reclaim ancestral remains and some culturally-sensitive objects, such as funerary, sacred and ceremonial objects. Still relatively few in number, cases of repatriation nevertheless represent a change of direction in the cultural flow of heritage items and antiquities, and a weakening of the strictures with which colonialism bound and gagged Indigenous peoples through their dislocation from land and cultural heritage.

Repatriation is, however, more than simply the repossession of property – it arises from efforts by Indigenous peoples to have their human rights recognised, including the right to practise their cultures, religions and languages. This has been the basis for the repatriation of ceremonial objects to a number of First Nations and Native American communities in Canada and the USA. So, rather then merely preserving ceremonial objects in a museum while the associated cultural traditions die out, repatriating these items for use in the performance of ceremonies may contribute to the maintenance and revitalisation of the associated cultural practices and social structures. Actions that lead to cultural revitalisation may, therefore, be perceived as part of the heritage preservation process. In such cases, preservation is an active process rather than a passive one.

However, while some communities actively seek the repatriation of culturally significant items, for others the cultural changes such as conversion to Christianity may have resulted in irreversible alienation from sacred and ceremonial objects, discontinuation of associated rituals, and a preference for the objects to be retained in museum collections. Furthermore, while repatriation has the potential to contribute to the wellbeing of communities, it can also place heavy economic, emotional and logistical burdens on people who lack the financial resources and infrastructure to transport and rebury human remains or to provide secure storage for important cultural materials. A further impediment to the repatriation and ceremonial use of objects such as masks and clothing is the presence of hazardous residues of preservatives and pesticides such as arsenic and mercury used by museum conservators in the past. This contamination poses a potential health risk to Indigenous peoples wishing to handle or wear the objects and requires expensive and time-consuming testing and cleaning, a further and bitter legacy of the colonial experience.

Indigenous Interpretation and Cross-Cultural Communication
Edward Said asked: 'Who writes? For whom is the writing being
done? In what circumstances? These it seems to me are the questions whose answers provide us with the ingredients making a
politics of interpretation'.[23]

In the past, the Western male voice dominated in museum
interpretation, as it did in historical writing, before post-
modernism stimulated greater inclusiveness and enabled
marginalised peoples to become more involved in museum interpretation and collection management. Linda Tuhiwai Smith
contends that 'Indigenous peoples have struggled against a
Western view of history and, yet been complicit with that view.
We have often allowed our "histories" to be told and have then
become outsiders as we heard them being retold.'[24] After decades
of exclusion from history writing and museum interpretation,
many Indigenous communities around the world are now building
their own museums, compiling archives of cultural materials,
conducting oral histories with elders to record and preserve their
knowledge, and establishing language nests to revive traditional
languages and preserve cultural knowledge and stories.

Community museums can facilitate the telling of Indigenous
perspectives of history, cultural practices, and ways of knowing,
and enable marginalised peoples to contradict the dominant
history, present counter-narratives and tell hidden stories.
Indigenous interpretation may tell a story of invasion rather then
settlement, of resistance rather than submission, of continuity
rather than cultural extinction. In contrast to the impression of
unchanging or extinct cultures that were often conveyed in the
past by museum exhibitions dominated by eighteenth- and nineteenth-century cultural materials, many exhibitions in which
Indigenous peoples have had active involvement present a recurring theme of survival and continuity. These exhibitions showcase
contemporary Indigenous peoples and their arts and lifestyles, as
well as Indigenous historical perspectives. The exhibitionary
process enables Indigenous peoples to proclaim: 'We are here –
we are alive', sending a dual message that Indigenous peoples have
survived and are active participants in the modern world, often

balancing Indigenous and non-Indigenous lifestyles.

Another approach to this is seen in some community museums associated with 'reconciliation tourism' through projects designed to bring Indigenous and non-Indigenous peoples together to share experiences and knowledge. These provide opportunities for non-Indigenous peoples to learn about Indigenous cultures and world views, their links with land, and the importance of traditional rights for Indigenous cultural survival. However, they also require careful management to balance economic opportunities with the potential threats that tourism can bring through cultural and environmental impacts, and the danger of exposing restricted cultural practices or sites to what J. Urry calls 'the tourist gaze'.

III: New Museum Models

What is a museum? Museums are no longer built in the image of that nationalistic temple of culture, the British Museum. Today, almost anything may turn out to be a museum, and museums can be found in farms, boats, coal mines, warehouses, prisons, castles, or cottages.

E. Hooper-Greenhill[25]

The new museum is different from the traditional museum in the emphasis it places on territory (environment or site) rather than on the building, on heritage rather than on the collection, on the community rather than on visitors... There cannot be a model for the new museum (or ecomuseum). It is a state of mind and an approach triggering a constructive process rooted in territory...

Hugues de Varine, co-founder of the ecomuseum concept, 1993

As well as the repatriation of cultural objects and the potential for revitalisation of cultural practices, inter-cultural dialogue in the museum sector is leading to a two-way process of cultural influence. Globalisation is taking the concept of the museum to all parts of the world, a process which has had varying degrees of success. At worst, the establishment of a museum may be little more than the imposition of an alien Western cultural model with little relevance to local community circumstances, values, and concepts of preservation. Or it may be adopted and used to preserve cultural materials and ways of life through the recreation of villages that have more to do with artifice and spectacle than historical or contemporary reality. Alternatively, the idea of the museum may be embraced and adapted by a community to suit local needs and values. This is resulting in the indigenisation of the Western museum model through the adoption of indigenous methods of curation and conservation of ethnographic collections in mainstream museums and the development of local, culturally-specific, community museum models within diverse cultural contexts world-wide.

Some Indigenous museums and cultural centres are modelled upon the Western museum using collections of objects for research and conservation, and for presentation in displays within a historical narrative. Others operate within a framework of traditional Indigenous epistemology and their activities and roles may be shaped by various cultural factors such as religious beliefs, customary laws, alternative perspectives regarding the concepts of heritage and preservation, and differing approaches to how objects and knowledge are stored, managed, used and disseminated.

The modern Western academic ideology of freedom of information, scientific investigation, inquiry-based research, and the free dissemination of information which has led to the exploitation of many Indigenous peoples and their cultures, may conflict with Indigenous systems of knowledge management and dissemination. The latter may, for example, involve restrictions on access according to gender, age or status; inherited rights to knowledge and skills; an understanding of the world based upon collective memory, spiritual journeys, ecological knowledge, and 'natural laws of interdependence' (G. Cajete). Indigenous peoples traditionally acquired knowledge and skills through observation and practice, oral recitations, ceremonial initiation, or inheritance. Elders and ceremonialists were custodians of oral histories, skills, culturally-important objects, sacred sites, and the performance of rituals. They were responsible for caring for objects and lands, and passing on the associated knowledge and practices. Indigenous cultural teachings were learned directly from the elders by listening, watching, and participating in the performance of ceremonies, dances and everyday activities.

In these contexts, the knowledge of the elders as custodians of culture, represents the curatorial knowledge of the community, and community museums may continue to draw upon these methods in their approaches to documentation and education. Western epistemology has institutionalised cultural material in museum collections and professionalised the activities of custodians of culture as curators and conservators, but Indigenous museums may continue to involve elders and ceremonialists as key participants in the work of preserving and communicating culture, working alongside professional museum staff. In the Alutiiq Museum and Archaeological Repository in the Aleutian Islands of Alaska, elders and children are regular participants in museum activities. In the age-old tradition, elders pass on traditional knowledge, cultural history and languages using stories, songs and games, but also record them on film and paper to provide archival records.

Realising that the passing of elders meant the loss of traditional knowledge, the Peigan, one of the Blackfoot First Nations of southern Alberta in Canada, have embarked upon a programme of ceremonial and spiritual development using traditional methods and the teachings of elders and ceremonialists, which they hope will stimulate cultural and economic renewal within the community. A museum and ceremonial centre will play a key role in this process as well as providing a venue for non-native people to learn about Blackfoot culture, beliefs and values. Plans for the Centre include a keeping place for material culture including repatriated items, a traditional camp circle of 100 and more lodges (tipis), a centre for ceremonials, and an elders' centre.[26] The Peigan Nation proposals for the Medicine Lodge museum place a clear emphasis upon living culture and upon the adoption of the museum concept, but on Blackfoot terms: 'It will be a "museum" in the traditional *native* sense, but it will also use methods used by non-native museums. This will be a place of living culture and heritage'.

Customary protocols may determine the form of a community museum in ways that directly challenge the conventional role of a museum as a facility in which objects and information are displayed and interpreted. A community museum may include displays that convey the spiritual nature of culture but protect the sacred and restricted dimensions from inappropriate public scrutiny by omitting certain objects or information from displays. Archival databases of Indigenous artefacts and records are being constructed with multiple layers of access, allowing sensitive and restricted images and information to be protected. In Indigenous Australia, traditional custodians were responsible for maintaining cultural knowledge, practices and sacred sites and for protecting restricted ceremonies and sacred objects from inappropriate or unlawful access or use. In some communities this has seen the establishment of 'keeping places' where important sacred and ceremonial objects are stored, accessible only to those holding the appropriate rights accorded by age, gender, or status.

As museology is a discipline which has been largely based upon academic freedom and materiality, these epistemological differences pose challenges for the various professionals involved in the collection, management, conservation and interpretation of heritage, but these developments can also enhance the roles of museums and their social and cultural relevance.

Contemporary Ethnomuseology
In both mainstream and Indigenous museums, there are developments in contemporary ethnomuseology that involve the adoption of parallel approaches to cultural preservation using culturally different and diverse, but complementary, methods. Museum curation and conservation have, until recently, been concerned with preserving the material structure of objects rather than their integrity, meaning and spirituality, but in various societies, attitudes towards preservation may be quite different from those of Western museum curators and conservationists. In some cultures, preserving the materiality of the objects is less important than preserving intangible and living heritages – the knowledge, skills, stories, beliefs, rituals and other practices associated with objects which give them meaning and purpose, and the relationships that they represent. Reflecting this, ICOM definitions of cultural and natural heritage now include spiritual manifestations

of a natural thing, phenomenon or concept, as well as those of scientific significance.

The Maori academic Linda Tuhhiwai Smith explains: 'For communities that value oral ways of knowing ... contested stories and multiple discourses ... are stored within genealogies, within the landscape, within weavings and carvings, even within the personal names that people carried.'[27] The Art historian Dele Jegede notes: 'In Nigeria social, religious, educational, economic, and political factors, separately and in combination, influence the perception of cultural property and the attitude towards its preservation.'[28] 'For a people who place so much importance on oral history, cultural property becomes a living vessel through which history is actualized'.

Indigenous approaches to cultural preservation tend to stress the importance of intangible aspects of heritage, and the need to ensure that culturally significant objects continue to have importance as part of peoples' lives rather than merely being preserved digitally or merely as simulations. In museum showcases, visitors see objects displayed out of the cultural context for which they were made. While curators may try to show them in context, the objects have become something else: a specimen, an art object, a cultural relic, a trophy, a reflection of the viewer's preconceptions, perhaps, and certainly a reflection of the curatorial schema. An artefact in a showcase is no more of a reality than a video tape of a ceremony is the performance of a ceremony: both are artifice, reflections, simulacra.

As Indigenous knowledge systems and religious beliefs and ceremonies play an increasingly important role in contemporary museology, sacred and ceremonial objects, perceived within museums as artefacts of ethnographic or art-historical interest, are once again renewing their role as objects of ceremony and devotion. This may involve the application of intangible aspects of heritage in order to preserve the integrity of the tangible: the performance of rituals, songs, dances, recitations, and prayers, as part of the care of objects, or the use of the objects in such performances in order to re-animate them. The National Museum of the American Indian (NMAI) in Washington D.C. has a large number of Indigenous people on its staff and works closely with Indigenous peoples from throughout the Americas. Native American elders and ceremonialists regularly visit the museum stores and galleries to bless objects and perform cleansing and feeding rituals necessary for the cultural care of the objects. Similar developments are occurring in a number of mainstream and Indigenous museums across North America.

Preservation, then, is an active and changing process; culture is not immutable but is a dynamic concept that adapts to changing circumstances. So the objects and the associated cultural practices are preserved, not with their original meanings but in changed or revitalised forms reflecting the contemporary social, cultural and political contexts.

Preservation through Revelation

Despite the restrictions surrounding certain objects, images and knowledge, some Indigenous artists and cultural custodians are revealing previously restricted images and information in art works, in efforts to protect and preserve their cultures. They hope that by communicating this information to people in Australia and elsewhere, they can engender greater understanding of their circumstances, viewpoints and property rights. In the 1960s, artists of the Yolngu community of Arnhem Land in northern Australia used traditional bark painting techniques and clan designs to present petitions to the Australian Government, asking for their relationship to the land and sea to be understood and their ownership rights observed. Similar objectives have been sought recently by the production of *Saltwater: Yirrkala Bark Paintings of Sea Country,* a touring exhibition of bark paintings that reveal sacred designs that are normally restricted. In the past few years, Aboriginal artists in several remote communities in central Australian have used acrylic paintings to record images depicting their traditional clan estates and presented these as evidence in land claims.

Indigenous community-based art centres provide the resources for art production and an outlet for the distribution and sale of commercial art works, one of the few means by which residents of remote area communities can earn money. The international demand for Aboriginal art also provides Indigenous artists with opportunities to communicate with national and international audiences and some are using the display and sale of art as part of their efforts to achieve political goals. By painting images that depict clan estates and ancestral beings they hope to convey to viewers the important and ancient links between Indigenous communities and traditional lands, and so raise awareness of Indigenous concerns for the protection of the environment and culturally important sites and reinforce their claims to traditional areas of land and sea. These art works, and the culturally sensitive knowledge that they contain, are not being appropriated by outside agencies; they are being deliberately dispatched, their contents revealed to achieve specific political goals. The art centre, as a vehicle in this process, becomes a 'sending place' from which the artists are attempting to communicate with the rest of the world.

Few tourists visit remote communities where many of the artists live, and most visitors to the community art centres are curators from public galleries or commercial art dealers buying works for collections or sale. Commercial and public art galleries in distant cities then also become part of the mechanism for artists to send their art and knowledge to the world, although it is questionable whether many viewers and buyers are 'hearing' or understanding the messages that the artists intend. As the Yolngu artist Galurrwuy Yunupingu explains: 'When we paint – whether it is on our bodies for ceremony or on bark or canvas for the market – we are not just painting for fun or profit. We are painting as we have always done to demonstrate our continuing link with our country and the rights and responsibilities we have to it. Furthermore, we paint to show the rest of the world that we own this country, and that the land owns us. Our painting is a political act. Unfortunately, non-Aboriginal people often remain ignorant of this fact, or deliberately choose to ignore that element in our work.'[29]

Conclusion

> The thematic frameworks defining the [museum] are brittle and their
> spatio-temporal referents are dissolving in a world that affirms the global
> while denying the universal. Any typology is good only as long as its utility
> endures, and utility is measured by approximation to perceived ends.
>
>   H.S. Hein[30]

As discussed earlier, notions such as heritage and preservation are
universal concerns, but they vary greatly in conceptualisation and
realisation. To meet the demands of diverse cultural needs,
museums need to be recognised as multi-faceted, diverse in form,
and with the potential to undertake heritage preservation by
accommodating different ways of understanding what that means
and how it is done. Many Indigenous peoples still carry the burdens
of social, educational, economic, and political disadvantages, and
the sustainability of many community-based cultural facilities may
be dependent upon outside agencies and accreditation
programmes that give access to funding and professional support.
Philosophical rethinking is required to ensure that Indigenous
museums and related cultural facilities are not further disadvantaged by the imposition of bureaucratic limitations derived from
definitions or conceptualisations of museums and their functions
framed within an outdated Western paradigm.

Contemporary ethnomuseology is increasingly becoming a
process of international exchange in which objects, information
and ideas are flowing in many directions, generating cultural interactions from which Indigenous peoples, museums and visitors
have much to gain. An essential element of future museums will
be engagement with living cultures resulting in the active participation of people in museums and of museums in cultural life. In
contrast to their previous focus upon the preservation of objects
and archives, museums must now find ways of preserving the
intangible as well as the tangible heritage. It will be necessary to
continue to develop new approaches to museology that are able
to accommodate alternative concepts of heritage, knowledge
management and preservation with sensitivity and insight.

New museum models can bring fresh understanding of the

multiple meanings of objects, their traditional and transitional significance for traditional owners, and their role in signifying socio-cultural identity, status and rights. They can be sites of inter-cultural engagement, where resources and activities are utilised to reinforce cultural identity and support cultural activities. They can provide insights into other ways of knowing the world and provide a true reflection of the diversity of forms and meanings of human cultural expressions. They offer opportunities for questioning the past and for understanding the present circumstances facing the Indigenous peoples of the world. The challenge will be to ensure that museums are able to actively contribute to the processes of cultural preservation through cultural revitalisation and the re-establishment of Indigenous peoples' cultural, religious and political rights.

Acknowledgements

I would like to thank Steve Charles, Jim Killick, Margie Killick, and Professor Gus Worby for their comments on earlier drafts of this essay.

Notes

1 *ICOM Code of Ethics for Museums* (2004): <http://icom.museum/ethics.html>
2 *ICOM Statutes* (article 2, paragraph 1): <http://icom.museum/statutes.html#2>
3 G. Lewis, 'Collections, Collectors and Museums: A Brief World Survey', in *Manual of Curateship: A Guide to Museum Practice* (London, 1984), p. 7.
4 E. Hooper-Greenhill, *Museums and the Shaping of Knowledge* (London and New York, 1992), pp. 101–32.
5 cited in *Ksan, Hazelton, British Columbia* (Hazelton, n.d.), p. 12.
6. *Bunjilaka: The Aboriginal Centre at Melbourne Museum* (Melbourne, 2000), p. 8.
7 John C. Ewers, 'Museum – The Blackfeet Indians Now Have a Word for It', *Museum News*, 15 March 1943, p. 12.
8 W. Kowalski, 'Introduction to the International Law on the Restitution of Works of Art Looted during Armed Conflicts, Part 1', *Spoils of War International Newsletter*, 2 (1996), p. 6.
9 *ibid.*, p. 6.
10 G.A. Dorsey, in a Field Museum lecture about the Haida Indian nation, cited in R. Loerzel, 'Alchemy of Bones: George Amos Dorsey': <http://www,alchemyofbones.com/who/closeups/dorsey.htm>
11 B. Spencer and J.G. Gillen, *The Native Tribes of Central America* (London, 1938), pp. 17–18.

12 *ibid.*, p. xiii.

13 S. Carter, B. Hurst, R.H. Kerr, E. Taylor and P. Winsor, *Museum Focus: Facts and Figures on Museums in the UK*, issue 2 (1999).

14 Cited in Gareth Binns, 'The Universal Museum', paper presented at the conference *History in British Education* organised by the Institute of Historical Research, 14–15 February 2005: <http://www.history.ac.uk/education/conference/binns.html>

15 Neil MacGregor, 'The British Museum', *ICOM News*, 1 (2004), p. 7.

16 Mark O'Neill, 'Enlightenment Museums: Universal or merely Global?', *Museum and Society*, 2:3 (November 2004), pp. 190–202.

17 Michael Dodson, 'Cultural Rights and Educational Responsibilities', The Frank Archibald Memorial Lecture, 5 September 1994, University of New England.

18 F.B. Musonda, 'How Accurate are Interpretations of African Objects in Western Museums?', in *Plundering Africa's Past*, edited by P.R. Schmidt and R.J. McIntosh (Bloomington and London, 1996), p. 164.

19 Schmidt and McIntosh, p. 3.

20 Karl Meyer, *The Plundered Past: The Traffic in Art Treasures* (1974), p. 46.

21 Neil MacGregor, 'The Whole World in our Hands', *Guardian Review*, 24 July 2004.

22 Musonda, pp. 164–8.

23 Edward Said, 'Opponents, Audiences, Constituencies and Community', in *The Politics of Interpretation*, edited by W.J.T. Mitchell (Chicago, 1983), p. 7.

24 Linda Tuhiwai Smith, *Decolonizing Methodologies: Research and Indigenous Peoples* (London and New York, 2005), p. 33.

25 Hooper-Greenhill, p. 25.

26 *Keep Our Circle Strong: Medicine Lodge Centre Cultural Renewal and Research Program. A Peigan National Proposal.* Second edition (May 1991), p. 13. Prepared by Penumbra Associations for Peigan Nation Chief and Council and the Ad Hoc Committee for Cultural and Ceremonial Renewal.

27 Smith, p. 33.

28 Dele Jegede, 'Nigerian Art as Endangered Species', in Schmidt and McIntosh, p. 133.

29 G. Yunupingu, 'The Black/White Conflict', in *Aratjara: Art of the First Australians*, edited by B. Lüthi (Cologne, 1993), p. 65.

30 H.S. Hein, *The Museum in Transition: A Philosophical Perspective* (Washington, 2000), p. xi.

Culture and Multiculture in the Age of Rendition

PAUL GILROY

To pose analytical questions about the state of our world through considerations of culture and its workings is now a contentious and perilous enterprise. The standard contemporary frameworks for those important enquiries – economics, government, law, war, technology and science – are all routinely approached as if they have no significant cultural dimensions. Immaterial and contingent, in the overdeveloped world at least, culture is now only consumer preference, taste and lifestyle. Globalisation, the master trope of this moment, helps to channel the problematics of culture into a very different discourse centred on the life and conflict of contending civilisations. Each of them is imagined to enjoy a cultural integrity that is essential to its ambitions and its historicity. There, culture remains the ethnic property of national communities and, where religion colours the tale, of their supra-national agglomerations. Sometimes these antagonistic formations are seen to occupy the same present; more usually, they are arranged in a teleological pattern so that command of the future can be allocated unevenly and monopolised by the complacent apostles of necessary and catastrophic development.

To make matters worse, a growing hostility to what is dismissively signalled as the *merely* cultural is evident in the retreat back into academic disciplines made by many of those who were prepared to flirt with the Cultural Studies project in what seemed to be less dangerous times than these. An understanding of political culture is kept alive by the architects of info-war and the engineers of agno-politics – the struggles that grow up from the production and distribution of ignorance.

In some respects, we find ourselves being forcefully returned to an interpretative landscape that would have been familiar during the nineteenth century. Of course, Samuel Huntington and Gobineau disagree about the number of civilisations to be found in the world; but the implicit imperial architecture of race and nation is something that they share. And yet, even to point out this affinity becomes a risky business which invites the accusation of political correctness and the forms of tacit punishment that go along with it.

It is symptomatic that Africa still disappears as completely and efficiently from today's civilisational discourse as it did for Hegel in his famous lectures on the philosophy of history. In his case, there was no need to mention Africa further because the theatre of History was the temperate zone. In our time, Africa must be mentioned obsessively and compulsively: always as a place of chaos, disorder and corruption. These unwholesome results of Europe's colonial withdrawal from the continent are to be borne in mind. The repeated invocation of African corruption and bad governance not only cements the status of civilisationist narratives as popular commonsense and as a default setting for debate, it helps to accomplish two other important tasks. This repetition says, firstly, that remembering Europe's empires need involve nothing to apologise for because they actually made things in that continent better than they would have been; and, secondly, that military forms of humanitarian intervention in its chaos remain a necessary and valuable mechanism for improving the world. Those propositions can only be maintained in the face of a studied refusal to engage the complex histories of Europe's colonial adventures. The politically-saturated memories of empire and its overthrow are rather unevenly distributed. The overdeveloped world has opted to mystify or just forget and ignore these dimensions of its recent past but they remain stubbornly pending elements of everyday life almost everywhere in the formerly colonial countries, particularly in locations where the revival of imperial relations has been proposed as a practical solution to contemporary problems of poverty, development and inadequate government.

Why Racism is Still Important

In this climate, it is unfortunate that scholastic writing has by and large, become disinterested in racial discourse, division and hierarchy. What those formations might reveal about the history of knowing, being and ruling in the modern world has not been thought worth investigating. The history of the race idea gets allocated to esoteric academic specialisms. If the history of *racism* appears at all, it is principally the history of racism's many victims. These lapses represent a missed opportunity especially with regard to struggles over the meaning of human rights: which involves other occasions when questions of race, colony and empire are routinely overlooked.

A few bold thinkers have been interested in analysing the history of racialising bodies, skulls, bones and blood, but they did not often show the same enthusiasm for thinking through the relationships between racism, nationalism and the national state or for exploring the development of legal orders to which the principle of racial hierarchy was intrinsic. In a climate where ignorance of Europe's imperial past and colonial crimes has become a veritable intellectual asset, even those exciting fields can get taken over by timid and drab work. The study of the racialised body is easily reduced to a generic and non-specific enterprise. We can lose the ability to focus on which particular bodies are at stake and the conditions in which they appear as the focus of violent attention. It becomes difficult to address the diverse ways in which the operations of racial discourse makes those bodies meaningful – always in relation to each other. Similarly, racism and nationalism can drift apart and the racialisation of war and law become over-specialised topics relevant only to a few exceptional places where civic and ethnic nationalisms have contaminated each other and produced racialised polities and forms of citizenship that, in turn, institutionalise the forms of exclusionary inclusion which racism facilitates and makes legitimate and desirable.

The reluctance to consider racism as more or less than ideology in general or to see race as anything other than a straightforward effect of nature are extensions of older patterns in which mechanistic assumptions about progress, nationality, and survival were overdetermined by and made congruent with various forms of racial theory.

This is another way of saying that the human sciences have successfully resisted the mid-twentieth-century impulse to be transformed into the sciences of inhumanity. That aspiration has been betrayed by various factors: by a lack of conscience, by conceptions of progress and modernity, cause and effect that are too coarse for the history of colonial violence that culminates in Guantanamo, Yarl's Wood, Campsfield House and Belmarsh[1] to accommodate. The promise of that potential transformation was undone by comparatively shallow approaches to subjectivity and identity that don't seem to be adequate to the fissured and 'diminished' subjects which now narrate themselves and their sufferings in burgeoning post-imperial and neo-colonial archives.

These issues place that archive in relation to its primary objects: the witness, the atrocity, and of course, the camp – a space of exception that has become normative and functional far from its colonial origins. That constellation asks *us* to consider the difference between the archive's role as a historical resource and its contribution to understanding how colonial and post-colonial crimes should be remembered and understood. Are they to be part of the history of our present? And, if so, how are we going to grasp their historicity? Does this contested colonial history have a role to play in the elaboration and defence of the European 'multiculturalism' which has recently been pronounced dead? In other words, how are these histories of suffering to be made useful as guides to action and as interpretative guides to contemporary problems that would otherwise appear perplexing?

Before the bombs of July 2005 formally marked the death of 'multiculturalism' in Britain, we were being told from every quarter that the disruptive presence of immigrants, asylum seekers and refugees had rendered our familiar country unrecogniseable. A discomforting lack of certainty about national culture and identity supplied powerful proof that the alien takeover of the national homeland had already begun to succeed.

The terrifying presence of the 'home grown' terrorist presides over this débâcle. The mid-1960s formula for integrating incomers has been firmly set aside. Governmental pronouncements have returned to older, more authoritarian specifications for how these children and grandchildren of migrants might be assimilated. The workings of culture get reduced to a simple all-or-nothing mechanism just when the bombers' challenging biographies of settlement, accommodation and dwelling demonstrate that a lack of integration could never be counted as the key to their monstrous actions.

Colonial Precedents?

If we are to consider racism as a mechanism capable of linking the colonial past with some unpleasant contemporary practices, it is instructive to return to the work of those exemplary Europeans Primo Levi and Jean Améry as well as various other observers of and commentators on the wartime pathologies of European civilisation. I read their work for its opposition to the corrosive allure of sameness and for its repudiation of proteophobic purity-seeking which gets answered by a historical and moral commitment to the political, ethical and educational potential of human shame and universal vulnerability. That goal can be significant in assessments of the political opportunities opened up by talk of human rights.

Améry was a bold proponent of what he terms 'radical humanism'.[2] He had an intense interest in the politics of a human dignity which could respond to the governmental actions that brought racial hierarchy alive. Perhaps for that very reason he had discovered, through his reading the work of Frantz Fanon, that 'the lived experience of the black man... corresponded in many respects to my own formative and indelible experience as a Jewish inmate of a concentration camp'.[3]

With Améry and Fanon, Levi shares an interest in extracting humanistic and liberatory perspectives from the sufferings he survived in the lager. Analytical insights towards that end flow freely in his writing, especially in *The Drowned and the Saved*, a book that can profitably be approached as an examination of the reductio ad absurdum of key motifs in the history of bureaucratic and military rationalities that help us define the specific attributes of modern governmentality. The figure of the 'Bettnachzieher – bed after-puller' is, in my reading of the text, his cipher for modernity's crowning absurdity. His famous essay on 'useless violence' lies at the centre of an exploration of civilisation's inner tensions and the implication of those de-civilising racial divisions that are not to be dialectically resolved into a reconfigured narrative of progress.

Levi articulates a luminous consideration of the Nazi brutality that, according to standards of rational reflection, appears at first to be without purpose. His argument concludes with the realisation that what he calls 'the outrage motive' intruded into and compromised the more familiar mechanisms of the profit motive which were not altogether absent from the social world of his camp, where slave labour was routine. This distinctive combination of (ir)rationalities is a sign that the power of racism and the order of race-hierarchy are active and potent.

Building on this, one observation that I want to introduce is tied to the proposition that racism has a distinctive and substantive agency and that the colonial archive helps to make its impact recognisable even in the post-colonial present. This observation may, I suppose, be thought contentious, perhaps even vulgar, but I hope it is not trivial. It seems to cut deeply into the problems of how we understand the significance of states of exception and the causality of genocide. It is even linked to how we set about preventing the possibility of genocide's recurrence as well as how we answer the civilisationist commonsense which makes that recurrence more likely and endorses patterns of law and power which regulate those whose lives and bodies count for nothing and who may be disposed of with impunity.

This difficult interpretative agenda set by the survivors of the lager has the additional merit of directing our attention towards two other issues of fundamental import. They can be presented in abbreviated form here as a double concern with the loss and recovery of human dignity. There is firstly the dignity that was stripped away by the bio-political processes which systematically produced racialised infra-humanity. And there is the dignity that might, intermittently at least, be recovered by acts of narration, of oppositional storytelling, even if, as Walter Benjamin puts it, they 'borrow their authority from death'.

Of course, in Levi's exposition of this problem, what appeared at first to be brutality without purpose eventually discloses its secret significance. The value of useless violence can only be seen when we consider the position of its perpetrators who require it in order to complete their tasks with the minimum of emotional and psychological disturbance.

In a memorable conclusion which divorces this particular history from any proscriptive uniqueness and shifts it into an inspiring world-historical mode, Levi raises the possibility that there exists another variety of violence that he hopes will be useful in the longer run. He names this as the self-inflicted suffering involved in inducing himself and others like him, firstly, 'to speak of the fate of the most helpless' in their attempt to reconstruct the alien logic of the murders and torturers and then to move beyond that necessary but insufficient goal into a different stance in which witnessing as psychopathology can unfold into witnessing as ethics.

At that point, talk as trauma would be succeeded by talk as pedagogy and exchange. That conception of utility is something daring and unexpected, upon which a more elaborate conception of what I propose indelicately to call anti-racist pedagogy can, even now, be built.

It should not be necessary to emphasise that the benefits of this proposed ethical exercise can only increase if it is appreciated that it has been summoned, conjured into being in explicit opposition to the racialisation of the world. It is here that hope appears fleetingly to complement a historical analysis of the anxiety, fear and security-talk which bring the prospect of systematic atrocity alive and block the process of working through Europe's disavowed and guilt-inducing memories of vanished colonial preeminence.

Racism and the War on Terror

These problems were not left behind when Europe's empires were overthrown or fascisms faded away. Resurgent notions of racial difference appear to be quietly active within the political calculus that assigns differential value to lives lost according to their locations and supposed racial origins, or considers that some kinds of human bodies are more easily and appropriately tortured, humiliated, imprisoned, shackled, starved and destroyed than others. These obvious distinctions have lately become important in the conduct of 'the war on terror'. In the context of that info-war, they effectively revive a colonial economy in which manifestations of infra-humanity can effectively abolish rights and postpone recognition indefinitely with the unwavering support of the rule of law.

Like the generic, faceless enemies that populate this interminable conflict, the hidden detainees and all the other shadowy third things[4] that race-thinking has lodged somewhere between animal and human, all forms of infra-human waste are best administered under the flexible governance deriving from special emergency rules and exceptional or martial law.

Here we can make use of the incisive reflections offered up by the movements of the enslaved and colonised as part of their past battles for independence, autonomy and national liberation. Their reflections can be used self-consciously to constitute a counter-tradition. They have shown aspects of how racism entered into the process that institutionalised sovereign powers and warranted the belligerent conduct of competitive statecraft, the management of colonies and eventually, the forms of bio-political government that were being developed in the core metropolitan areas where different jungles, savages and degenerate types were being enthusiastically discovered.

The history of how this race-thinking looped back into Europe from the colonial world can still communicate something fundamental and useful about the shifting quality of political life, about the objects of government and the nature of subjection. Something like a historical ontology of races can be used to illuminate all the contradictions – legal, ethical, military – of a civilising mission that had to conceal its own systematic brutality in order to be effective and which has lately been revived as part of how the new imperium will be managed.

Without following Hannah Arendt blindly through the gates of Athens, we can agree with her that race talk and racial solidarity prosper where politics, political institutions, and 'the political' are diminished or compromised. However, there is a sense in which her bold and inspirational linkage of Europe's colonial past with the genocidal ultranationalism of the twentieth century can be misleading.

Though deeply interested in both race and imperialism, Arendt suffers from myopia with regard to racism which remains for her comfortably and tidily ideological rather than metaphysical. It is understandable or it is an error: sometimes both.[5] As is well known, she emphasises that rights come from national states and that the vulnerability of statelessness is compounded by rhetorical appeals to humanity. She moves rapidly on from those insights to elaborate upon another problem which resides in the fact that 'the world found nothing sacred in the abstract nakedness of being human'.[6] Identifying this observation explicitly with the experience of survivors of the Nazi death factories, Arendt – who had not enjoyed the benefits of reading Levi, Améry and the rest – argues that 'the abstract nakedness of being human was their greatest danger'. A repeated preference for the national over the natural dictated that when people appeared outside the protection of their natal political community, their very humanity may even have been an inducement to violence against them: 'it seems that a man who is nothing but a man has lost the very qualities which make it possible for other people to treat him as a fellow man'.[7]

Arendt misrecognises the abstractly naked human as a natural or abstractly essential human. Instead, that vulnerable figure might be described much more accurately as a racialised person: a particular, infra-human creation rather than a specimen of the catastrophically empty humanity that she wishes to repudiate. Her error corresponds to the larger refusal to engage racism as such.[8]

The possibility that abstract nakedness is not so much a cipher of insubstantial humanity but rather a sign of racial hierarchy in operation arises from the work of survivors themselves. Levi who, it bears repetition, sees exercises in brutal racial formation as conducted for the benefit of their immediate beneficiaries, suggests that racism's capacity to reconcile rationality with irrationality is expressed in the dominance of the outrage motive over the profit motive. That combination is enacted, and may even be ritualised, for the psychological benefit of the murderers and torturers who need coercively to make the infrahuman bodies of their victims perform the subordination that race theory requires and anticipates but which those bodies do not spontaneously disclose. The digital camera can now be used to capture this special moment which is not understood properly when reduced to the idea of humiliation.

Human Rights

Many radical voices reserve a special hostility to the project of human rights which gets dismissed both for its misplaced faith in rights and for its naïve projections of universal humanity. The NGO-isation of political struggle is certainly an element in the effective depoliticisation of the contemporary world. And there are certainly tendencies within the field of Human Rights education which should be questioned because of their inability to face the political and strategic processes from which all rights derive and the related refusal to address the analytical shortcomings that arise from the dependence of human rights on an expansion of the rule of law – which, incidentally, was fully compatible with

Europe's colonial crimes.[9] However, histories of colonial power and genealogies of racism help to explain both of these problems and may help to break the impasse into which the analysis of human rights has now fallen. This is why anti-racism remains important. It does not argue naïvely for a world without hierarchy but practically for a world free of that particular hierarchy which has accomplished untold wrongs. It seeks to make the case against racial hierarchy into a matter of politics rather than seeing it as something so deep that it is thought to be pre-political or something so superficial that it can be dismissed as a post-political phenomenon.

Colonial battlefields gave birth to the militarised space of the monocrop plantation which pointed in turn to the legal régimes of protective custody that generated and generalised the camp as an exceptional space. If the life of racism is taken substantively into account, the exceptional spaces that have succeeded the camp, spaces which are now not always adjacent to death factories, become explicable and the racialised government that fuels them becomes an essential and dynamic element in their legitimation.

The political and ethical world of the black Atlantic has generated its own subaltern tradition of comment and opposition to facile rights-talk. That counterculture of modernity still has the power to alter the official genealogy of Human Rights. It anticipates and prefigures the contemporary conundrum of rights and what we can call their tactical deployment. Thinkers like David Walker, Frederick Douglass and Ida B. Wells were alert to what we would now call a deconstructive approach. They tracked the internal problems with rights rhetoric, they grasped the empirical limits of rights-oriented institutional life; but their vivid sense of the power of racism meant that they could not allow themselves the luxury of any casual anti-humanism. They wished to sustain an oppositional figure of the human in discussions of human rights. They did this by keeping the critique of race hierarchy and racism dynamic.

Their critical assessments of the complicity of rights-talk with systematic unfreedom and routine brutality induced them all to try and speak in humanity's name. Their combined efforts help to show how a broad, worldly history of colonial government can be useful in understanding how rights have come to be asserted by torturers and how histories of raciology and colonial rule illuminate the persistent problems in the way that rights are made irrelevant and therefore useless.

Their dissident understanding of the ways in which racism worked to compromise and corrupt politics was supplemented by twentieth-century voices, many drawn from the national liberation movements. This seam of reflection can also, counter-intuitively, show that the entities we know as races derived from the very racial discourse which appeared to be their scientific product.

The special accomplishments of that racial discourse can be explored; its irrational rationalities, elisions and performatives can become historical problems to be understood, rather than simple but enigmatic emanations pulsing out from the decisive world of biology to shape the course of history, the rhythm of culture and the conduct of social life. In particular, we must consider the role of racism and ethnic absolutism in securing the modes of inclusive exclusion that characterise what we might call the age of rendition – a period in which a combination of public and private powers, mercenaries, pirates, contractors and freelance securitocrats harks back to the eighteenth century.

For me, the challenge before us is to maintain and perhaps to refine critical work on these problems in an unstable field that retains heavy investments in the explanatory capacity of race as an abstraction even when the nature of that abstraction has moved away from nineteenth-century bio-logic and towards a different kind of political anatomy re-configured on a molecular scale and oriented to genes. The attachment to race and the refusal of critical humanism conceal and mystify this change. The development of a different political understanding of multi-culture might help to interpret and oppose it.

Multiculture and Multiculturalism

Important and influential strains of political commentary on multi-culturalism have arisen from negotiations with indigenous populations over recognition, reparation and sovereignty. A different though related variety of discussion about plurality – linguistic, religious and cultural – has grown from encounters between 'hosts' and immigrants. The latter may be post-colonial peoples with citizenship claims or they may be refugees, asylum seekers and other guest workers and their locally-born descen-dants whose affiliations are contested on other grounds. The positions occupied by these groups have typically generated a more culturally-oriented commentary on the problems and oppor-tunities represented by assimilation, national identity and belonging. A third variant of multicultural reflection has emerged from a few self-conscious and explicit attempts to undo racial orders. This too crosses several historical cases and has acquired a global reach where, for example, the political legacies of the Third Reich, the overthrow of Jim Crow and the formal destruction of Apartheid were deemed to have more than merely local signifi-cance.

These histories of thought have touched and influenced each other, creating a tacit exchange with the theoretical accomplish-ments of the movements towards decolonisation. Where they interact, multiculturalism specifies a host of discrepant problems. These arise, on the one hand, from a sense that the 1960s paradigm for thinking the fate of immigrants and governing their assimila-tion/intergration has now been exhausted. And on the other, from a sense that Europe is, as far as race, racism and ethnicity are concerned, inevitably tied to a North American future.

As far as the United States' future goes, this connection explains why, behind the figure of the immigrant, lurk images of catas-trophe and conflict derived from north American history. It is the iconic trace of that televised 'race war' rather than the actual wars of decolonisation or the riots and protests inside European coun-tries which communicates to Europe the danger that any unassimilated incomers or denizens now represent.

For many political theorists, especially those based in the United States, the term 'multiculturalism' has been used to identify a 'mosaic plurality'. This is a highly specific conception of diversity in relation to unity. It derives historically from distinctive US conditions of racialised and economic segregation. It promotes a form of analysis in which 'race' and ethnicity are inflated and reified, and in which difference is easily contained within symmetrical social and cultural units that are arranged, in spite of any hierarchy they might compose, so as to form a larger national grouping. That view of ethnic difference and cultural variation should be criticized as a rationalisation of the forms of segregation that are routine in US cities. Ghettoes become enclaves or storehouses of immigrant cultural capital.

Europe's multicultural cities operate under very different rules. A better starting point for our conversations about multiculture can't be defined just through a sense that differences are proliferating, nor by the idea that increased exposure to the otherness of others and the strangeness of strangers should provide the place from which theories of diversity must depart. Those propositions are both shaky. They turn out to be haunted by patterns arising from older conceptions of plurality which were shaped by the brutal imperatives of colonial statecraft and saturated by thinking about race.

Restoring a historical dimension to reflections on multiculture inevitably directs attention towards the fields of colonial history – in particular to the 'small wars' of decolonisation during the twentieth century. The imperial mentalities that fed and justified those wars have been recapitulated in the 'war on terror' which has altered the ways that multicultural society is understood and evaluated as risk and as catastrophe. The failure of multiculturalism is a precondition for the triumph of the securitocracy.

In the United Kingdom, conclusive proof of multiculturalism's demise was first signalled by the appearance of the monstrous shoebomber Richard Reid and the nineteenth hijacker Zacharias Moussaoui.[10] This sequence took in the appearance of British citizens, who were mostly the sons and grandsons of post-1945 immigrants, caged at Guantanamo and then moved through the perplexing biographies of the July 2005 bombers, who seemed to have been fully integrated without being assimilated and who rather inconveniently explained their motivation as the need to strike against the Blair government's neo-imperialist adventures. In Mohammad Sidique Khan's (b.1974) posthumously released videotape, he made it clear that he at least had taken the official rhetoric of war on terror at face value: 'We are at war and I am a soldier... now you too will taste the reality of this situation.'

The return of the first Cuban detainees to England was another event in this grim cavalcade. It was an ambivalent affair that caught the nation frozen between its resurgent anti-war anti-Americanism on the one hand and its hatred of immigrants on the other. With its pseudo-Churchillian jaw set doggedly against the barbaric Muslim world, fearful, anxious views about corrosive immigration and failed assimilation were again being expressed openly. As the panic set in, solidarity and diversity were pitted against each other in a crude zero-sum game. The very idea of convivial co-habitation across cultural, ethnic, religious and racial divisions was thrown into disrepute by the perceived breakdown of assimilation and the crisis of national identity that now frames it.

Terror and racial conflict are explained as the local manifestations of the global clash of civilisations a contentious diagnosis that has been projected ever more widely and authoritatively during the last four years. Islamophobia has increasingly shaped public debate and the figure of the traitor/terrorist has emerged to hold hands with the other well-worn representations of imminent racial chaos and disorder: the violent, feral street criminal, the sneaky benefit scrounger, the duplicitous asylum seeker and the illegal immigrant.

After 1945, Britain found it hard to adjust to the presence of settlers: semi-strangers who, disarmingly, knew its culture intimately as a result of their colonial education. Rather than face up to the reduced geo-political stature embodied in the half-alien presence of these post-colonials, the country developed what can only be called a melancholic attachment to its vanished pre-eminence. The incomers and their increasingly demanding descendants supplied uncomfortable reminders of the history of the empire, which still returns, spectrally, in complex forms that remain as painful and guilt-inducing as they are fascinating.

Memories of lost empire become entangled with the ambivalent prospect of colonisation by another, newer one. Britain cannot be Greece to the USA's Rome. It remains an island outpost, colonised and invaded by America's new Rome. Anglos fret about their overly US-minded children dialing 911 instead of 999 when they want an ambulance, about their appetites for obesity-inducing fast food and the mind-destroying pulses of Hip Hop which represent the best of the USA to many people on this planet.

Of course, employing post-colonial culture-talk – as a means to fix and retain the impossibly-complete national self-understanding which fear of a new colonial predicament demands – will not solve these problems. Culture can never be immobilised in the way that the pursuit of absolute identity demands. To seek to fix culture is a problem because, if we arrest its unruly motion, we ossify it. The US recipe for patriotic solidarity cannot simply be borrowed and imported to glue a fractured polity back together with the aid of flags and prayers.

Post-imperial Britain's problems with identity have been fed by intermittent panics not just over the usual crime, disease and disorder associated with unwanted immigration, but also about falling standards of education which symbolise a generalised 'dumbing down' in media, education and public life. As a result, Britons end up bullying asylum seekers and refugees not so much to force their assimilation but to tell themselves that they're sure the country is still what it is supposed to be.

It seems that, if Britons are to be united and robust in the face of terror, Islam, unwanted immigration and European meddling alike, they must become fundamentally and decisively the same. A new peak of sameness must be attained. In order to reach it we must now become absolutely certain as to who we are, culturally speaking. Nostalgia for war and peculiar fantasies of monoculture secure that comforting outcome.

As in other parts of Europe, the disruptive and unwelcome presence of the country's aliens is almost always explained in racial terms. Conflict is being increasingly described as the inevitable result of illegitimate demands placed upon the white working class who were required to bear the brunt of assimilating dubious incomers into the local way of life. Today, the continuing antipathy towards immigrants, asylum seekers and refugees cannot be concealed. It is now being seen as understandable, even rational on those grounds. The idea that it has anything to do with noxious, violent racism or neo-fascist, ultra-nationalism remains a shocking revelation that induces further discomfort and guilt.

Additional confusion and disorientation arise from a situation in which melancholic and xenophobic Britain can quietly concede that it doesn't much like aliens, blacks, foreigners, Muslims and other interlopers and wants to get rid of them, but then becomes uncomfortable because it doesn't like the things it learns about itself when it gives vent to feelings of hostility.

I think that the xenophobic view of immigrants as an invasive wedge resonated loudly because we all know that Europe was once *out there*, being great in a world it dominated. That basic fact of global history is undeniable. However, grudging recognition of that glorious past now provides a stimulus for intensified hostility. It has been precipitated by the tacit realisation that, even if today's unwanted settlers – for example from Eastern Europe – are not actually post-colonials, they can still carry all the ambivalence of the vanished empire with them. Even if they are 'white', they can be held hostage by the racialised specification that they are immigrants. Poles and Kosovars can reawaken dangerous discomfort in the unhappy consciousness of their fearful and anxious hosts and neighbours. Indeed, the latest incomers may be unwanted and abused precisely because they are the unwitting stimulus for the pain produced by memories of that vanished imperial and colonial past.

For almost four decades, the United States has exemplified the only political and economic future that Britain's punditocracy can imagine for the country. Our politicians have been caught out by their inability to see any future for Europe's racial politics that is not deduced from US history. They have been influenced and encouraged by Samuel Huntington, whose latest work *Who Are We?*[11] presents the flood of overly fertile immigrants from Latin

America as 'the single most immediate and serious challenge to America's traditional identity'.

Europe's recent history tells us that the United States need not be the inevitable destination of our racial politics. Britain has comprehensively outgrown the 1960s model which associated assimilation and immigration in government policy. Two generations beyond that coupling, the anxieties which fuel contemporary concern about the integrity of national culture and identity have different sources. Their origins lie, not in immigration as such for there has been no immigration since the 1970s, but in the broader effects of globalisation, de-industrialisation and de-colonisation; in increased inequality and insecurity, in privatisation and the regressive modernisation that has destroyed the welfare state.

All those forces shaped the chronic turmoil into which immigrants, aliens and more recently asylum-seekers and refugees were thrown and for which they were held responsible even though the large social and economic changes involved were not of their making. The emergence of a better, richer and more satisfying explanation is blocked by the way in which melancholia dictates that immigration can only be experienced as invasive war. From that point of view, successive waves of immigrants to Britain have merely accomplished what the Nazis were never able to do: they wrecked an unsuspecting country from within.

Talk about pensions and the necessity of immigration to answer demographic changes will not address these elemental questions. Culture affords the only effective means to assuage the demands of the post-empire. Widely-read works of revisionist imperial history do more than just airbrush and nuance the rationally-applied barbarity of Britain's colonial phase. Their implicit purpose is now both more sinister and more profound. They seize command of the role of victim which has become such a prestigious item in the moral economy of post-colonial multiculture. Their authors would have us accept that Europeans are the primary victims of their own colonial history. It seems as though that awareness is the best pre-condition for the revival of empire abroad and the rebirth of a homogenous, imperial spirit at home.

Largely undetected by either governments or media, Europe's

immigrants and their descendants can cautiously be revealed to have generated more positive possibilities. Alongside all the usual tales of crime and ethnic conflict there are other varieties of interaction that have developed more organically. They have created, not a mosaic along US lines, in which each self-sustaining and carefully segregated element is located so as to enhance a larger picture, but an unruly, untidy and convivial mode of interaction in which differences have to be actively negotiated in ways that yield civic assets.

At best, civic life has been endowed with a vibrant multiculture that we do not always value, use wisely or celebrate as we should. Note that I say conviviality rather than multiculturalism. By conviviality I mean a social pattern in which culturally different metropolitan groups dwell in close proximity but where their racial, linguistic and religious particularities do not – as the logic of ethnic absolutism suggests they should – add up to discontinuities of experience or insuperable problems of communication. A degree of separation can, in these conditions, be combined with a large measure of overlapping. There are institutional, demographic, generational, educational, legal and political commonalities as well as elective variations that inter-cut the other dimensions of difference and complicate the desire to possess or manage the cultural habits of others as a function of one's own relationship with identity. Conviviality aims to acknowledge this complexity. The term tries, not to banish conflict but to recognise that people are equipped creatively with the everyday means of managing antagonisms in their own interests and in the interests of others with whom they might even heteropathically identify. Conviviality should not suggest the absence of racism but rather that alongside any racism and its unsavoury interpersonal dynamics, resources for its overcoming have also begun to evolve.

In pointing to the political and cultural force of this conviviality as an alternative to Europe's post-colonial melancholia, I am not saying that racial hierarchies and inequalities have been dealt with. Racism is still at work, souring things, distorting economic relations and debasing public life. However, we must also face up to the fact that racism is no longer what it was when the 1960s prophecies of racial war were first offered and invent a political discourse against racial hierarchy that is adequate to the strictures of post-imperial coexistence.

In Britain, this conviviality has promoted everyday virtues that enrich our cities, drive our cultural industries and enhance our struggling democracy so that it resists operating in colour-coded forms. Once it is recognised that exposure to otherness can involve more than jeopardy, conviviality has taken hold. The alternative it represents inspires us to applaud immigrant demands for a more mature polity which, even if it is not free of racism, might be better equipped to deal with racial inequalities as a matter of politics without lapsing into unproductive guilt and narcissistic anguish.

The supposedly unbridgeable gulf between civilisations can be spanned with ease. The same verdict came across strongly in the tales told by homecoming British detainees about their detention at Guantanamo. Though these men were presented in the media as having reverted to alien type, that is as symbols of the failure of multi-cultural society, their return prompted important revelations which have lost nothing with news of the recent hunger strike there.

Jamal al-Harith was one of the most visible returnees. He had been born 37 years earlier in Manchester, as Ronald Fiddler, to a family with Jamaican origins. Bought into captivity in Afganistan, he was held in the Guantanamo Camps for two years before being released and sent back to Britain in March 2004. He is now one of several returnees who are attempting to sue the US government. He recounted his post-colonial life story and in doing so, offered a timely rebuke to all the mechanistic and over-simple conceptions of cultural difference that are currently in circulation.

It would seem that, if we want to find a way out of the impasse of multiculturalism, the fissures, folds and leaks within civilisations deserve more attention than the much-vaunted clashes between them.

It is tempting, in trying to make sense of the predicament of these returned detainees and the arguments about multicultur-alism that are implicit within it, to reach for the old concept of 'double consciousness'. This important idea made a contribution to the now banal notion that people can hold and reconcile multiple identifications. This idea was elaborated by W.E.B. DuBois at the start of the twentieth century. He drew the original idea from Hegel and refined it during his life-changing time as a student in Germany. It was shaped by his sociological reading of the problem of assimilation as it arose there during the nineteenth century.

In DuBois's hands, the concept was tailored both to specific US conditions and to a deeply Hegelian view which presented black American consciousness of freedom as a world-historic force: a precious gift to the planet from the descendants of modern slaves. Much of what DuBois foresaw has proved to be accurate. Black Americans did indeed give a receptive world some new conceptions of freedom derived from their battle against servitude and for citizenship. These fruits of suffering were widely exported and have altered the moral and cultural environments of our planet.

I am happy to draw attention to this process and in some circumstances even to celebrate it. However, I have begun to appreciate lately that it is time to leave the theory of double consciousness where DuBois found it – in the nineteenth century – and specifically to exclude it and its offshoots from the ways that we approach issues of multiculturalism today.

For various reasons, it doesn't seem helpful to try and transplant or reinvigorate the idea so that being a black European or Muslim is thought to be analogous to what being an American and a Negro: 'two warring selves in one dark body' meant when DuBois was writing *The Souls Of Black Folk*.

Another way of posing this problem might be to ask what DuBois's legacy says to the figures of Condoleezza Rice and Colin Powell? That pair doesn't seem either to be gifted with second-sight or disabled by any inner doubleness. Condoleezza Rice in particular is often presented as the terminal point of that DuBoisian double consciousness which is resolved into her embodiment of the successful civil rights movement.

Right now, the flood waters in New Orleans have subsided. Like the poor black denizens of that city who face exclusion from its bright theme-park future, African Americans more broadly have face a different kind of historic choice about where they want to belong, who they intend to be and what to do with the remnants of their broken citizenship.

Some of them must regard the 'war on terror' just as DuBois viewed the outbreak of the First World War: as a welcome means finally to acquire or operationalise long-delayed membership of the national community and to experience the full benefits of formal citizenship which had long been compromised by the effects of racial hierarchy.

Their historic decisions will have important effects far beyond their own shores. However, seeing racial politics in this way risks reducing the contemporary debate over multi-culturalism to an American family quarrel and family romance.[12] It is by no means clear on what terms that romance can continue.

Would-be black Europeans face some parallel and equally historic choices. We need to think about whether, as DuBois implied, that precious gift of African American freedom struggles is something we still wish to adapt or inhabit. To put this question more carefully, we should perhaps ask whether we are, in the name of progress, to embrace the export of US racial systems either as political technologies for solving race problems governmentally or as organisational techniques for generating social and cultural movements that could defeat the racism that still delimits our options.

To try and re-heat the old African American recipes has costs that we should reckon with. I think it has become important to argue explicitly that United States history in the field of racial politics must not represent the future of Europe's minorities.

Many black Europeans, like Europeans more generally, have a deep and symptomatic ambivalence about the US and its abiding racial order. They may dislike its current political leadership, but there is also often something fascinating and exciting about what appears to be its hyper-modern style, its brisk experiential tempo and the exhilarating cultural habits which get fastened on to as indices of freedom, especially in the phantasmagoria of consumer culture that veils imperial adventures in Mesopotamia and elsewhere.

As far as our political hopes are concerned, the era in which the US could plausibly be presented as the future is over. We now need to understand what is involved in removing America from the place that Hegel put it in long ago.[13] That peculiar racial future, those modes of assimilation, with their undiminished segregation and their intermittent liberation need not be ours. We must now be more imaginative and more cosmopolitan than that. So the national story of African American movement out of slavery must be separated from the tales black Europeans need to tell. There are precious narratives of liberation to be gleaned from elsewhere along with vibrant stories of Pan-thinking, conviviality and trans-culture. There are accounts of the movements against slavery and colonialism and for equality that were not centred in the US racial nomos. How might the histories of South Africa, India or Brasil contribute to this de-provincialising reassessment and reconstruction? How can an anti-racist political imagination build communicative networks that facilitate a different variety of worldly conversation on these matters?

Of course, people in the United States are far more likely than Europeans to have accepted 'race' as part of the functioning of their political culture. I can agree that Europeans have something to learn from that acceptance of 'race', providing, of course, that it involves an acknowledgement of the damage done by racism and does not become a blank resignation to the effects of racial hierarchy. But my essential point remains: accepting the salience of the social and political processes that the US knows and sees as a natural phenomenon called 'race' does absolutely nothing to address the multiple mystifications wrought by racism either in US political culture or elsewhere.

DuBois lived a long and complex life. He changed his ideological commitments and political tactics repeatedly. At the end of his days, his commitments to peace and internationalism led him into extensive conflict with the US government over the Korean War, the Marshall Plan, NATO and a number of other domestic issues. Perhaps we can now read *those* parts of his life as a final comment upon or even repudiation of the double consciousness idea he had articulated half a century earlier. We should recall that he spent much of his final decade without a passport, that he eventually joined the Communist Party at the age of 93, that he renounced his US citizenship and embarked on a life in exile as a citizen of newly-independent Ghana which celebrates its fiftieth birthday in 2007. He had found in those treacherous choices a means to activate his long-held and rather Germanic attachments to world citizenship and to world history. What, we are now obliged to ask, are the contemporary analogues of those uncomfortable gestures? How does an emphatically decentred account of the development of diaspora multiculture help us to fulfil *that* discomforting agenda which has remained pending in black politics since the Cold War?

Notes

1   These are the names of some of Britain's detention centres for asylum seekers and prisons for special detainees.
2   Jean Améry, *Radical Humanism*, edited and translated by S. Rosenfeld and S. Rosenfeld (Bloomington, 1984).
3   Jean Améry, 'The Birth of Man from the Spirit of Violence: Frantz Fanon The Revolutionary', translated by Adrian Daub, *Wasafiri*, 44, Spring 2005, pp.13–18.
4   The phrase 'tertium quid' comes from W.E.B. DuBois's much reprinted book *The Souls of Black Folk* (first published in 1903).
5   See Margaret Canovan's discussion of this problem: *Hannah Arendt: A re-interpretation of her Political Thought* (Cambridge, 1992), p.37.
6   Hannah Arendt, *The Origins of Totalitarianism*, p.299.
7   *ibid.*, p.300.
8   The reasons for this can be gone into more deeply.
9   Nasser Hussain, *The Jurisprudence of Emergency* (Ann Arbor, 2003).
10   Paul Gilroy, *After Empire: Multiculture of Melancholia?* (London, 2004).
11   Samuel Huntington, *Who Are We? The Challenges To America's National Identity* (New York, 2004); see also his 'The Hispanic Challenge', *Foreign Policy*, March/April 2004.
12   Destiny's Child, 'Soldier', Sony Urban Music/Columbia, 2005.
13   'America is therefore the land of the future, where, in the ages that lie before us, the burden of the World's History shall reveal itself...' G.W.F. Hegel, *Philosophy of History*, translated by J. Sibree (New York, 1956), p.86.

The New Grapes of Wrath: Post-Communism – Neo-Liberalism – Islamism

PETER SLOTERDIJK

I propose here to take a panoramic overview in the world history style and briefly consider the fate of political dissidence over the last two hundred years in order to place this period of time against the backdrop of a monotheistic millennium. In this process, it will become unequivocally clear that the wrathful God of Catholic teachings and the Communist construct of the anti-bourgeois and anti-capitalist wrathful masses, the two most powerful depositories for metaphysical and political anger in Occidental civilisation, have neither stood the test of time nor the challenge of a change in mentality.

Catholicism only survived the emergence of modernity at the price of a grudging adaptation that continued for more than two full centuries. For a long time, it displayed attitudes that bear a remarkable resemblance to the Islamic-style theocentric anti-modernism we know from present-day sources. During Catholicism's defiant phase, it raged against modernity's alleged presumption in wanting to turn religion into a private affair and battled, as if it were some zealotic God-Alone movement, against tendencies to establish a secularly laic or religiously neutral state culture. The alteration in Catholicism's basic perception of the world, only completed in the second half of the twentieth century, was accompanied by a fundamental theological restructuring; before Catholicism could finally call a truce with modernity, its anti-humanistic and anti-liberal traditions, rooted in an absolutist divine right, had to be hived off. This transformation reached a point at which theology itself could be re-defined as an Organon, a system capable of providing a more trenchant justification of human rights. Naturally, this led to the abandonment of apoca-lyptic threats and eerie *Dies Irae* noises off as degrading intimidations of the faithful. Consequently, the venerable Wrath-of-God teachings and images of vengeful Judgement Days at the end of the world had to be withdrawn from circulation in the Church – and have, in the meantime, become downgraded to curiosities in the history of ideas.

As far as Communism's attempt goes to create a world deposi-tory for adolescent thymotic energies with globally convincing human returns, the disappointments and bitterness in the older eyewitnesses are still too immediate for this case to need re-opening. By contrast, the generations born into a post-Communist world already view the Communist adventure as hardly less of a gothic curiosity than the lost Catholic eschatology of years gone by.

In the earlier parts of my investigation, I considered the motives, procedures and promises of these two major sources of anger. I also discussed the consequences of their dissolution, with a rough outline pointing out how revenge went into a free float in the initial post-Christian situation, and the present essay focuses primarily on anger's political homelessness in the post-Communist world. To avoid any misunderstandings, it should be noted that this essay has no ambitions to investigate potential and real links between Catholicism and Communism – although admittedly, it might have seemed obvious to present Communism as the sacral embod-iment of the Christian wrath theology, and possibly as the materialist transformation of the idea of the Kingdom of God as well. By contrast, given Catholicism's immediate announcement of itself as Communism's moral executor after the latter's demise, it would not be inadmissible to see this as one of Providence's tricks, dragging specific unresolved moments of truth in Communist concerns straight back into the lap of the Holy Roman Church.

Let it suffice to observe that in many respects Communism did indeed take on the characteristics of a second Catholicism, a remark I do not intend to develop further here. The announcement in 1848 in rather self-satisfied tones that a spectre was haunting Europe, a spirit striking fear and trembling into the hearts of governments everywhere between Paris and Moscow, indicated a turn of events ushering in a post-'death-of-God' state where the function of the Last Judgement – in addition to God's numerous other offices – would inevitably be transferred, for better or worse, to earthly institutions. As things turned out, early Communism in particular was well positioned to take on this legacy. However, the movement's 'spectral' character, of which Jacques Derrida makes so much in his book *Sprectres de Marx*, owed less to the fact that Communism presented a rational Utopia (and hence a mental concept which, in any case, could only appear in the spectral mode and never as a figure of flesh and blood) than to the identifiable threat it posed, from the start, to existing relations. When Communism lost this character of menace, its career as a spectre was at an end. At that point, the job of revenging spirit of world history or, put more moderately, universally balancing out suffering, once more slipped out of the hands of human institutions – and hence Catholicism, which had never thought God was dead in any case, had good reasons to strut the stage after its rival's demise, posing as the genuine form of post-Communism, or even indeed as nothing less than the soul of authentic Communism – and it was Karol Woytyla's theatrical mission to grasp the opportunity this presented. Admittedly, the Catholic message incorporates a return to a conservative attitude that claims people today need to free themselves from feelings of wrath and revolt in order to rediscover those qualities lost to modernity since 1789 – namely, patience and humility. Yet this overlooks the fact that these virtues are vulnerable unless buttressed by the menace of violence which is embedded in a seemingly credible Last Judgement theology.

These points surely suggest that the Hegelian idea of the trick of reason (*List der Venunft*) can still claim a certain usefulness, even though the expectations recently directed to indications of some hidden reason in history have been no more than moderate. If one were to summarise Communism's achievements from our present historical perspective, we would be struck, first and foremost, by its paradoxical external effects, which significantly exceed the impact of its internal effects. It is not my purpose here to recall yet again the Soviet Union's efforts, so frequently honoured, in its struggle against the invading National Socialist army; similarly, I do not intend to discuss further its role in the era when two Blocs confronted each other. In truth, its most important effect abroad only became gradually apparent after 1945 when, against the background of a sabre-rattling Stalinist régime and its outposts in central and western Europe, there was the historically unique chance to establish a European social state. Ironically, the Communist World Bank of Wrath achieved its most significant success in the form of an unintended side effect. Accumulating a vast potential of menace, both politically and ideologically, helped the western Social Democrats, formerly its main opposition target, to attain the zenith of their historical effectiveness; it made it easy for moderate socialist parties in Europe to wring an unparalleled range of concessions on wealth redistribution and an extended social net from liberal and conservative capitalist business leaders. In that situation, it even seemed viable for some countries, particularly France and Great Britain, to place large parts of their national industries under state control.

If sovereignty actually describes the capability of a credible menace, the western European workers' parties and unions achieved their greatest sovereignty effect by being able to incorporate the indirect threat of a class struggle in the generally very civilised disputes over union-agreed rates, without ever having to clench their fists themselves. Just discretely directing the employers' gaze to the realities in the Second World proved a sufficiently clear indicator that social peace here had its price. As far as this constellation is concerned, it can be said without any great exaggeration that the social achievements in post-war Europe, the oft-cited *Rheinisch* model of cooperative capitalism, including its extensive social state and a culture of superabundant therapy, were gifts from Stalinism – the Grapes of Wrath that, admittedly, could only ripen to acquire a certain sweetness after they had been exported into a freer climate.

When the left wing's potential on menace fell victim to an irreversible decline, the equation for social peace in the West had to be totally rewritten – not least because the Soviet Union came to be taken steadily less seriously as a transmitter of menace labelled specifically for the West. By the final phase of the Breshnev era, at the latest, the Soviet Union had totally exhausted its entire stock of Lenin's ideological reserves. Moscow no longer had the basis needed to pursue any kind of successful expansion and mission policy. In any case, it was clear that the East had lost the race between competing economic systems. Moreover, in the ten years of fruitless campaigning against Afghanistan guerrillas (1979–89), the Russian Army proved that it was no longer remotely capable of living up to its former reputation. Under these circumstances, the organised workers' institutions in the West forfeited the privilege of profiting from capital's fear of Communism without making any effort on their own part. In the negotiations over the redistribution of income, the liberal-conservative camp gradually realised they were facing an already weakened, if not totally debilitated, opponent. On the one hand, this decay owed much to its own relative saturation and, on the other, to the tensions caused by a progressive deflation in the energetic idealism found in the left-wing camp.

The consequences following from this insight have determined the West's psycho-political atmosphere from the early 1980s until today – with the climate-impacting attacks on 11 September 2001 now adding to their effect and making it increasingly likely that capitalism, against a post-neo-liberal background, will take a neo-authoritarian turn. From today's perspective, the key date in the late twentieth century is the year 1979 – which ushered in the post-Communist world in three ways: the beginning of the end of the Soviet Union after its army marched into Afghanistan, the start of Margaret Thatcher's first term of office and the consolidation of the Islamic Revolution in Iran under Ayatollah Khomeini.

What one dubbed neo-liberalism was, in essence, nothing else but an updating of the costs of domestic peace in countries with a European style capitalist-social democratic 'mixed economy' or the 'regulated capitalism' in the form produced in the USA.[1] Inevitably, this working over of the accounts came to the conclusion that, under temporary political and ideological pressure from the East, western industry had paid too high a price for social peace – and the time had come for cost-cutting measures, all of them designed to fuel a shift from the primacy of full employment to the precedence of business growth. This corresponded to a change in the *zeitgeist*, increasingly accelerating away from the post-war decades' prevailing comfort ethic, equally indebted to revolt and regimentation, to make space for a neo-entrepreneurial ethic of risk – whereby it was thought one could accept the demoralisation of a discarded and neglected underclass as an external cost factor.

The course of the ensuing twenty-five years of the 'economic revolution' in Great Britain from 1979 on, designed by Keith Joseph and implemented by Margaret Thatcher (which rapidly spread to the European continent and to other parts of the world, notably America under Ronald Reagan, 1981–8, and Bill Clinton, 1993–2001), has shown how correct these diagnoses were and how radical the consequences drawn from them have been. The most striking example can be found in the main characteristic of the post-neo-liberal camp – the social policy leitmotiv over the last twenty years reflecting the long march into mass unemployment. The new relations produced a situation that would hardly have been previously conceivable: unemployment rates ranging from eight to ten per cent or more, accepted by the general populations of Europe's capitalist nations almost without a struggle – and even the increasingly noticeable cutbacks in social state provisions have not, as yet, rekindled the fire of the class struggle. Overnight, as it were, the sovereignty relations have been reversed: not only do the employees' organisations hold very few cards that could prove an effective menace, but the privilege of menacing has shifted almost entirely to the employer side, now seeking to present the rather plausible case that if the employees refuse to grasp, and help shape, the new set of rules, they will simply make the situation even worse.

One has to bear this scenario in mind if one wants to understand the conditions under which Islamic terrorism was able to emerge as a new factor on the stage of the powers capable of menace. It had good reasons to characterise itself primarily as a parasite feeding on post-Communism – and indeed it has actually succeeded, almost from one day to another, in pushing itself into place to become, in the post bipolar era, the ersatz enemy, first and foremost, in the USA. It was ambivalently ascribed this role from the start. For those tragic political scientists convinced of a constant need for some enemy, Islamic wrath appeared on the scene like a gift from heaven. Although not especially dangerous in material terms (as long as its agents have no access to ABC weapons), it keeps the bewildered collective's psycho-political tonicity at the desired level. In contrast, Islamic terror remains an unwelcome guest for advocates of the liberal idyll – resembling, in a certain sense, a crazy graffiti artist defacing the façades of enemy societies with obscene slogans.

Yet, however one cares to judge the new terror's ambivalent reception by its western addressees, it would never have been ranked as more than an annoying marginal phenomenon had it not become included as an extraordinarily interesting position in the balance sheet used to re-calculate the costs of social peace in capitalist societies. While, as we have noted, the Communist menace resulted in a dramatic increase in social peace costs in the West, the menace of Islamic terror has an overall cost-reducing impact. By subjecting the weakened collective to foe stress, it helps generate a feeling across social differences, no matter how vast the social divides may be, of belonging to a genuine mutual benefit association: that is, being part of a unit fighting for its future survival. Moreover, thanks to the new terror's undifferentiated enmity towards a western lifestyle, it generates a climate of diffuse intimidation where political and existential security concerns are clearly ranked higher than social equitability issues – *quod erat operandum.*

After 9/11, with the exaggerated rise of the security imperative as the all-dominating theme in the present media democracy, the *zeitgeist* has switched to a new ecosystem of menace and defence measures – whereby at present, as flippant as may sound, from radicalised capitalism's perspective, Islamic terror's menace tendencies do, taken in their entirety, move in the 'right direction'. This time, feeling under threat from those Middle East sources, now so well-known, means acknowledging reasons why one might possibly be ready to come to terms with the West, slowly drifting into post-democratic relations.

The psycho-political destinies of the United States of America during the first and second Bush administrations provide an unfortunate abundance of examples to illustrate this hypothesis. Within the space of a few years the entire world witnessed how, by conjuring up a deliberate and sustainable fictive 'war against terror' to be fought by the entire nation, a tolerably dissent-friendly democracy experienced the sudden extinction of an entire range of species in the arena of diverse political opinion: overnight, as it were, the country's political landscape was de-differentiated and placed under the influence of homogenising and, to a certain extent, war socialist forces. Just as in real wars, the domestic opposition is also paralysed by the patriotic imperative generated in this *drôle de guerre*. This development is largely the work of those neo-conservative Mullahs in the USA who have no inhibitions about vigorously invoking the frightful spectre of a 'fourth world war'[2] to suffocate, as far as possible, every impetus from mounting social inequalities that might lead to a new inner capitalist opposition.

When considering this notion of a redistributed menace potential across present geo-political maps, the obvious question arises of how then the much-cited danger of Islamic terrorism has to be understood. What media disseminate its effect onto the psycho-political fabric of the West and the Islamic states? Does this really have the potential to 'replace Communism as a world dogma', a claim that has also been openly advanced over the last ten years by radical Islamic circles between Khartoum and Karachi?[3] Can a political Islam – whether in conjunction with a terrorist component or not – develop into a new World Bank of Wrath, a globally attractive depository of anti-systemic or post-capitalist energies

and corresponding projects? Can Islam, in some way, really claim
to be capable of writing a further chapter in the central but
exhausted western narratives of the humiliated and insulted rising
against their masters, both old and new? Is it merely sufficient to
contemplate the Jihad concept for long enough until it becomes
transformed into a pseudonym for the class struggle? Or are the
combat scenarios emerging from the Islamic world not actually
characterised by their own distinctive self-will, and can only be
aligned with the western narrative figures of the continuing revolution, spreading universal emancipation, and the progressive
realisation of human rights at the price of misunderstandings and
distortions?

There are three qualities that make political Islam into a potential successor to Communism, and all three can be found
analogously in historical Communism too. The first derives from
the fact that Islam carries within it the dynamic of a resoundingly
rousing mission, enabling it to take a group largely comprised of
new members and create a rapidly growing collective from it: to
shape a 'movement' in the narrower sense of the word. Not only
does Islam address, quasi universally, 'everyone', without discrimination of nation or social class, but it also possesses a particular
attraction for the poor, weak and indignant (providing they are not
women and even, to a certain extent, for them too). A crucial role
here is played by the undemanding admission conditions. Once a
person has been accepted into the ranks of believers, s/he needs
hardly any further preparation to be capable of serving in the spirit
of the communal struggle – and why not serve immediately as an
untrained martyr? The newcomers quite commonly evince the
feeling of having found, for the first time, a truly spiritual home
and a significant role in the world's drama.

Political Islam's second focus of attraction arises from the fact
that – as actually only Communism managed previously – it is able
to offer its followers an aggressive, clear, grandiose-theatrical
Weltbild, based on a distinct friend-foe differentiation, with the
unequivocal destiny of victory and an intoxicating final vision –
reinstalling an Islamic Empire to provide the Islamic millennium
with a global home stretching from Andalusia to the Far East. It is

not necessary to emphasise how here the enemy of Islam replaces the class enemy and how the Holy War stands for the class struggle – especially since it is obvious that both contain variations on the semi-dualistic model of a war of principles: inevitably, a long, drawn-out conflict, requiring many sacrifices, but where, as usual, the party representing good is destined for victory in the final battle. These features point to the fact that what is termed fundamentalism in political usage represents less a matter of belief than an incitement to act, or more precisely, a provision of action roles equipping potential actors with the material to move from theory to practice – or rather, when examined more closely, to move from confusion to practice. As a matrix for radical mobilisations, which here, as usual, are based on the more vehement thymotic drives, Islam is on a par with historical Communism and indeed possibly even superior to it, since it is not only able to present itself to its own source culture as a movement of radical change but also as a movement of revolutionary restitution.

The third and by far the most significant political reason for an inevitable increase in political Islam's appeal over the coming decades (even if, at present, after a series of setbacks, it appears to have lost much of its attraction) stems from the dynamics driving demographic changes in its recruitment arena. Just like the twentieth-century totalitarian movements that preceded it, political Islam is primarily a youth movement and, in particular, a movement of young men. To a large extent, the élan of a desperate surplus of vitality comes courtesy of a vast group of young males between fifteen and twenty-nine (and older), unemployed, unmarried and with no perspectives on society. This group forms the natural body of adherents for the numerous agitators from older generations, whose material for their sermons comes, as if self-generating, from their clients' readiness for a rebellion fuelled by outrage – whereby the Islamic tradition merely provides the semantic forms to textualise the present tensions of anger and violence, with a prime example provided in February 2006 in the way 'spontaneous protests' were sparked by the 'cartoon conflict' between Denmark and some Middle East countries. From this perspective, it is permissible to say that Islam, in Islamic use, is transformed into a theological ready-made offering itself as a route to mobilisation. Admittedly, its suitability for this purpose also derives from specific internal features of Muslim belief which, from the very start, proclaimed a tenet of war against unbelievers – the modern reader of the Koran cannot escape feelings of amazement at how a holy work can threaten, on almost every page, the enemies of the Prophet with the torment of burning eternally. Such astonishment is hardly overcome by the Koran scholars' explanations that the holy writings' polemical tone is due to the historical context – the Prophet was engaged in a kind of early socialist criticism of the rich, arrogant and ruthless merchants in Mecca, who refused to heed the egalitarian values of the traditional Arab tribal culture which, in its Islamic version, was also committed to caring for the weak and disadvantaged.

Given stable birth rates at their present high levels, by the mid-twenty-first century these new mobilisations – whether legitimised by the theology of the Koran or not – could influence a reservoir of between 200 and 300 million young men in the Arabian hemisphere alone, who would probably see their sole existentially appealing meaning in a shift to self-destruction projects under a political-religious guise. Only a tiny fraction of such projects would manifest themselves in external terrorism while, in contrast, the far larger part might well culminate in civil wars of unprecedented size fought on Arab territory – with the Iran-Iraq massacre of 1980–8 providing a foretaste of such wars to come. Today, the truth is that nobody has the faintest idea of how the threat of that approaching *youth bulge*, the largest ever wave of surplus genocide-impregnated young men in the history of the world, could be contained by peaceful means. [4]

This outline of a radical Islamic movement's future mass basis simultaneously indicates the point where comparability with historical Communism ends. Neither the current not the future bearers of Islamic expansionism can be compared in any way with a class of exploited workers, unifying to resist their suppression by restraining or overcoming state power. Instead, they represent far more a disoriented and desperate sub-proletariat; worse still, a movement comprising those surplus to economic requirements, whose leaders will dare to attempt, sooner or later, to bring the pension economies of the Near East under their control to occupy those commanding heights – even if in future they are largely removed from standard business activities – where they can access and distribute the vast sums of wealth from the oil industry. For this reason, rather than their foe images being capable of socio-logical definition, as was the case, for example, in Marx's 'exploiting class', they are defined morally and politically – and the foe images are directed internally against the contemptuous collaborators working, politically and economically, for the West's sake, and externally against the West itself, providing it is portrayed as the epitome of offensive, corrupt and obscene cultural imports.

The more an Islamic theocracy rests on the formal and material totalitarian aspiration of using Koran law to order every aspect of life in the virtual Islamised world society of tomorrow, the less it will be able to meet the economic, technical and cultural realities of the present age on an equal footing. While Communism embodied a genuine expression of western tendencies to moderni-sation, even in a certain sense comprising its avant-garde (as was, to a lesser extent, also the case with fascism), political Islam makes no secret of its lack of temporality with the modern world, gladly highlighting its basic anti-modernist stance – including its broken relationship with occidental-global scientific culture and a decid-edly parasitic relationship with the West's weapons technologies. Yet even its most sympathetic interpreters have, as yet, only inef-fectual ideas of how Islam might find its way out of its self-imposed backwardness. The route most likely to prove successful may be the one that intensifies the separation, in the Islamic world too, between the sacral and profane spheres.[5] Here, the term 'refor-mation' takes on a new meaning with regard to a religion that has always sought renewal by a return to the original sources and not via the positive learning experience of critical dialogue with the spirit of the modern age.

Looked at in this context, the hijacking of the two planes that were crashed into New York's World Trade Center on the morning of 11 September 2001 was in no sense a demonstration of Islamic strength but a symbol of a malicious impoverishment, only to be publicly offset by the sacrifice of human lives. No Marx of political Islam would ever be able to claim that modern technology might have been developed in the lap of western civilisation but could only achieve the fulfilment of its destiny in the hands of Islamic users. Instead, the lesson taught by 9/11 is rather that the most inexorable enemies of the West can expect great things just from turning Western tools against their inventors.

But political Islam's insuperable weakness lies in its basic orientation towards things past, apparent first and foremost in the fact that it can only formulate a romantic concept of tomorrow's world from the elements at its disposal. No doubt with the help of that concept, Islam will be able in future to bring the swelling ranks of the wrathful to their feet. As a force capable of mobilising a vast mass of thymotic reserves, it is certainly far from exhausting its potential. And no doubt the dream of a grand Islamic empire in a revamped medieval form will still prove an inspiration to innumerable fellow dreamers, even if there is no sign whatsoever of the political foundation this would require. Crucially, Islam in its present state remains totally unable to co-formulate, let alone dictate, the next chapter in the technological, economic, political and scientific evolution shaping the life conditions of people in the twenty-first century; it is not even certain that Islam will succeed in modernising its own religious assets in the foreseeable future.

Under such circumstances, one needs to exercise a certain reserve in formulating expectations on Islam to don the robe of a global opposition movement and take over as the potential successor to Communism. Islam will not be able, in any way, to provide a new universal depository of potential dissidence in globalised capitalist countries. In contrast, it can, without doubt, collect massive thymotic potential as a regional bank of wrath. Yet, for immanent reasons, this never moves beyond the level of a black political romantic concept – for instance, with a principle of mobilisation that, via an allegedly fateful and divinely ordered war, is directed towards self-destruction.

Anyone wanting to cling to the notion that world history must culminate in a Judgement Day scenario will have to look for other judges and avengers. Given the situation as it stands at present, this role can actually only be filled by capitalism itself. Only capitalism can develop itself, in its endgame, into its own opponent capable of bringing sufficient pressure to bear so that it will have to be taken seriously as a life-or-death challenger.

Translated by Andrew Boreham

Notes

1   Cf. Daniel Yergin / Joseph Stanislaw, *The Commanding Heights: The Battle for the World Economy* (*Staat oder Markt. Die Schlüsselfrage unseres Jahrhunderts*, Frankfurt / New York 1999), pp. 22–87.

2   Cf. Thomas Pany, *Die Fürsten des IV. Weltkriegs. US-Think-Tanks und das Netzwerk der Neokonservativen*, Part I, Telepolis, 28. 04. 2003; in the western camp the term of a Fourth World War is commonly used by neo-conservative writers such as Eliot Cohen, Irving Kristol and Norman Podhoretz to underline the need to develop a comprehensive plan of war against political Islam. One should not forget that the 'Fourth World War' was previously used by *Subcomandante* Marcos from Chiapas in Mexico as a way of portraying 'globalisation' as a major campaign launched by capital against the poor of the world.

3   Cf. Avi Primor, *Terror als Vorwand* (Düsseldorf, 2004), p. 29.

4   On the genocidal potentials of the twenty-first century, especially in the Middle East, see Gunnar Heinsohn, 'Finis Germaniae?' In *Kursbuch 162* (Hamburg, 2005), pp. 18–29.

5   Cf. Dan Diner, *Versiegelte Zeit. Über den Stillstand in der islamischen Welt* (Berlin, 2005).

Body of Soul Series
The State of the World (2003–2006)

ROSÂNGELA RENNÓ

Eight colour images, digitalised, produced from printed pictures taken from Brazilian newspapers.

Titles:

São Paulo (picture: Pedro Azevedo, Folha imagem)
Senador Camará (picture: Wania Corredo, Agência O Globo)
São Paulo (picture: Renato Stockler, Folha Imagem)
Rio de Janeiro (picture: Salvador Scofano, Agência O Dia)
Rio de Janeiro (picture: Fernando Quevedo, Agência O Globo)
Assunción (picture: Ruben Alfonso, Agência Reuters)
Brasil (picture: Jefferson Rudy, Folha Imagem)
Los Angeles (picture: Lori Shepler, *Los Angeles Times*)

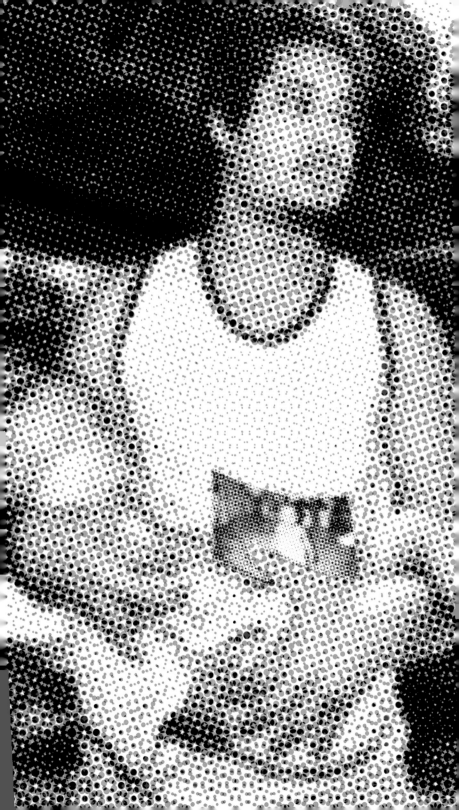

Constructing the Present
The philosophical features of the
concept of trauma

SANTIAGO KOVADLOFF

I

Although it may not seem so, in terms of his creative dimension, man does not come from the past, but from the future. He comes from the future, from his expectation, and moves from there towards the present. In other words, he heads for the present based on the call of his projects.

In my understanding, the future is far from being a concept enveloped in the mists of the distant, the incomprehensible or the abstract. Rather, it is the concrete repertoire of aspirations, needs, concerns, devotions and ideas that encourage us to hope. It is also the demand for a tomorrow, experienced in the present, which enables us to hear (within us) the demand for self-realisation. We try to implement the future by transforming actuality (in itself or as the pure succession of facts) into present (articulating those facts within an interpretative *corpus* that makes them intelligible as a whole and enables us to act upon them).

Actuality is a shapeless flux of everything that happens, every-thing that happens without us ever being able to manage it or place it within a meaning capable of speaking about us as subjects that can make a creative output. Actuality is the real, untrammelled by interpretation. In other words: where actuality rules, in the merciless chaos of its waxing and waning, the subject is dethroned, or rather appears as someone who has still to be established as a reader of events.

In contrast to actuality, the present is construction. The present is a task, a piece of work. This production will only bear fruit if we approach it from the future, from the imperative of a transformative project, from the desire for change that makes itself heard. By configuring the present (and *only* when we configure the present), we move – always with a provisional value – towards interpreting or discerning the underlying trends, the structural lines, the constants and invariables which, at a particular point, define the path that actuality follows in the very core of its convulsion. With its vertiginous power, its mystifying range of signs and its ceaseless wandering, actuality attracts us, distracts us, deprives and absorbs us, confuses and invalidates us, making us the subject of its impact, the material of its traumatic dominance, since its hegemony expands at the expense of our autonomy.

However, it may also be – as indeed happens – that constructing the present is not seen as a task that requires constant renewal. It might be – as indeed also happens – that administering or configuring actuality is done with the feverish goal of once and for all preventing reality's tendency to exceed or expand beyond the field of meanings into which we try to restrict it.

Likewise, it may be – as indeed happens – that man aspires to freeze the flow of time and the dynamic of actuality into some definitive interpretation that is exhaustive and unbending. When this occurs, man no longer comes from the future, but instead from the past. Clearly, this is when the past is understood within the terms I propose here: fixed, written in stone, the complementary and identical opposite of actuality, something that has happened and therefore belongs to the world of the unchangeable. We all know that the other eminent word for the unchangeable is dogma. Dogmatising the present means imbuing it with the vocation of the past, a past that wants to see itself as perpetual, identical to itself and in that sense, beyond temporality. It is precisely because of its unmoveable and atemporal nature that, from a historical and ethical perspective, dogma can be characterised as a social demonstration of the traumatic. Dogmatic reason can be understood as an expression of traumatic logic. Time is crystallised within it, and as such, subjective discourse no longer operates.

Our era yet again encourages the dominance of dogmatic reason in politics. The West is not simply threatened by logic: the West threatens through logic, urged on by the zeal to hang onto, cement and project its global hegemony.

The specific aspect of dogmatic logic is its repugnance for semantic nuances, for interpretative pluralism. Herbert Marcuse's one-dimensional man has now regained his voice. If democratic sensibility now feels threatened, it is precisely because of the level of projection that traumatic logic achieved (in the late twentieth and early twenty-first century) within the context of what are called the monotheist cultures: Islam, Judaism and Christianity. Once again, eternity seeks to overthrow history; once again, certainty seeks to seize control of truth. It is the negation of subjectivity, of the psychical world.

The process of voiding subjectivity that the psychical world has undergone is apparent in the growing volatility of definitions of citizenship in favour of consumerism, particularly in the more developed western nations. It also appears in the anxiety caused by the diversity imposed by the figure of the foreigner, and encouraged by the trend towards uniformity and homogeneity.

If, as Marc Augé states, 'the idea that the multiplication of contacts with the exterior is a threat to identity is stupid', then we must accept that stupidity now abounds. However, the forces that express the feelings of unease and concern caused by this experience of threat are anything but inoffensive, even though we consider them stupid. The idea that one can have one's own identity without incorporating the presence and impact of others is again taking root. In psychoanalytical terms, speaking about 'the others' is a reference not only to the alterity represented by beings external to oneself, but essentially to the alterity of the psychical world, to heteronomy itself.

Marc Augé also stated that 'at the level of large masses, acting correctly means consuming a lot. The consumption index is a country's health index.' On this question, psychoanalyst Germán García said:

> Karl Marx, in his *Outlines of the Critique of Political Economy* (1857), explained that if there is a subject for a product, then there is a product for the subject. [...] The product creates its client and then the client creates the product. Marx is right. Advertising is precisely that: the art of creating subjects for a product. First you create the product, and then the person who will consume it. As Lacan used to say: 'we eat meanings'.

Over fifty years ago, Erich Fromm demonstrated how reducing 'the being' in our societies to 'the having' or 'consuming' would bring profound spiritual alterations in both personal and social terms. A man deprived of subjectivity is a man deprived of discernment; a man who has removed himself from himself, who is excluded from his temporal perception or personal dynamic. In the light of the above characterisation of actuality, when shorn of subjectivity, a man of our times is left at the mercy of an uninterrupted succession of facts, losing his present. When this uninterrupted succession of facts is called 'headlines' or 'news', then the subjectivity-less man who feeds off them becomes a mere passive tele-viewer.

Information flows do not and cannot stop. What happens, happens uninterruptedly, without a single pause, and it overwhelms us. Thus, thinking cannot act on what is happening and cannot restrict it. That is why the flow is crystallised into a perpetual now. As man proves incapable of interpreting this succession, which never elapses as it is identical throughout, he abandons temporality, unable to reveal himself, to present himself.

The psychoanalyst Patricia Leyack is right: wherever trauma dominates, the end result is 'an abolition of the word subjective'. In turn, Oscar González wrote: 'Trauma needs time to be diluted, in that it is always current, like traumatic neuroses [...] The most striking aspect in contemporary neuroses is the absence of psychical time.' In fact, detaching trauma from the present time demands that the victim be reinserted into time, that is, into the future. In order to stop being what it is, the trauma must be affected by time. It has to be made non-present through the action of a path, a flow, a thawing. This essential dynamisation process is naturally psychical time. According to González, it is 'a psychic reality from which trauma benefits'.

Jean-Paul Sartre argued cogently when he established that 'the most important thing is not what history has made of man, but what man has made of what history has made of him'. I believe that he is right because in his diagnosis, the human – in his eminent meaning, the truly human – is the subjective aptitude, the individuality that makes him able to turn what happened into a personal event and the raw material for a personal affirmation. This makes it possible to turn something that is imposed as definitive and terminal into something that can be reconfigured or temporalised. As Oscar González also informs from his Lacanian viewpoint:

> The letter is the read sign. The letter is what remains to bear witness to what the subject read. The sign comes from the Other, while the letter is the subject. The letter is the certificate of birth and of death. One is born as a subject and dies as an object. The space between them, between subject and object, is an adjournment constructed by the action of the signifier.

In the eighteenth century, Goethe declared that the past could only be mastered by whoever transformed it to meet his own needs, needs that will always be of the present, of the subject who is taking action. Should that not be the case, the past – which should be bequeathed or inherited – will devour its heirs. Dissolved or ingested by what was already said or already established, those able to express their own words are transformed into spokespersons for a pronouncement which demands from mere repeaters dual identities (in Otto Rank's terms) of the established, which therefore become a tautology of the dominant discourse. Consequently, actuality will never be a challenge for these people, a call that will stimulate an innovative interpretation. On the contrary, innovative interpretation will never hold anything beyond a definitive profanation of what is written or established. This is the empire of the traumatic wielding its hegemony in culture: preventing culture from being a liberating act, becoming a temporal appropriation of what has happened. Ultimately, it is a mourning that did not take place – but if it had, it would have simultaneously incorporated and overcome the past. I believe that this perspective is closely tied to the following reflection by Isidoro Vegh: 'The problem of trauma is related to a primary identification that does not correspond to any loss of object; it is clear that this is a case in which there is no mourning, there is an identification and there is no loss as there was no relationship with the object. It is clear that this identification is related to the impossibility of not having time.'

II

Among the risks that threaten – both objectively and subjectively – the survival of our species, it is currently possible to conclude that the greatest of all comes from our concept of nature, that alterity that refuses to be subdued and demonstrates its rebellion in so many ways.

If, as Albert Camus stated, the last century was 'the century of fear', it would be excellent – if we still have time – for this century be one of a healthy planetary conscience.

A globalising dynamic now dominates, insistently producing structures that have no nuances (the nuances that give life to individuality) and reducing the multiple to the narrowness of the single, In contrast, a planetary conscience, profoundly orchestral as it inherently is, seeks equitable integration among the parts to cohesively establish genuine diversity.

Evidently, the chances of such a planetary conscience emerging depend on whether or not we take the decision to act according to what we all know: that our forests and rivers are dying; that there are ever more species facing extinction; that the atmosphere is atrophying, debased by contamination, and that climatic change abounds. All the while, visual and sound pollution is becoming more grave in cities that have been transformed into terrifying work camps.

For centuries, man sought to carve out his own space in nature. Now, the balance of power has shifted so far that nature itself needs help if it is not to be razed to the ground by the dynamic of man's culture. Yet for this to be possible, changes must be made to modernity's past and present concept of nature, and concomitantly (as will be shown) its concept of progress.

This modern conception reduces nature exclusively to the status of an object for exploitation and domination. The devastation of nature forces us to confront a pathetic conclusion: highlighting man's treatment of his surrounding environment as a whore simultaneously expresses man's treatment of himself as a whore. Hence, our own current difficult situation largely derives from the aforementioned tendentious understanding of progress.

Anyone paying close attention to the alternatives presented at the recent 'Tenth World Summit on Climate Change' in Buenos Aires will have understood the scale of the difficulties facing this conscience in its call for a radical transformation of what is understood as nature and hence the human condition. We must again ask precisely who man is, and wonder whether he can still be located in the place where he is established by the categories that define him exclusively as a subject of domination and a creator who is unconditioned by the suffering of a creature subject to finitude and to the impossibility of colonising his own unconscious.

What then is the characterising feature of this new vision of nature? It is the characteristic which demands that man must understand that what he calls his surroundings are in fact an integral part of his own identity. We can only develop our aforementioned planetary vision when we realise that our body goes beyond our skin; that in fact, our body includes and is included in everything that transcends it. We have to realise that we are also that which lies beyond us, and that this is as much a part of us as our skeleton. The real is realised within us.

No new reassessment of nature will come about until man proves capable of transforming his self-understanding. Only if this happens will we be able to have an innovative environmental policy. Clearly, this is no simple task. It implies a capacity for ethical and psychical mobilisation that is fundamentally linked to our understanding of time, where time is no longer understood as something that happens, but rather as something that happens to us.

We now know that progress not only fails to impact on us and concerns all human beings in the same way, but also that it is impossible at all levels of human life. The death drive is never defeated; it cannot be overcome 'with time'. In turn, war has not been overtaken as the means to 'resolve' human conflict. We continue to exterminate each other in our determination to suppress alterity, the source of archaic anguish.

As Cicero testified, the root of the word *hostis* (enemy) also meant foreigner. There is no progress if we understand progress as finally overcoming unconscious life, the idealised faculty of transcending it. We learn to develop ever more effective means of mass extermination. Yet we do not learn how to get along without being subject to the anxieties generated by alterity. Our communication is greater in terms of both time and space, yet it is no better, because it is no deeper. The time gained is phenomenic time, a measurable body. But the fact that we are time – the immeasurable in action – torments our spirit with the same intensity now as it did yesterday. We have managed to extend the duration of life. But its meaning still challenges us, and our suffering questions us.

It is known that Freud reflected with tragic lucidity on the effective possibilities of progress. He assessed them from the perspective of the violence of war and the death drive.

He noted that aggression is a bottomless well in the human being. Thus, even though it is transformable, the source is infinite. There is no radical suppression of war. There is no end or definitive sublimation of basic forms of violence. As André Clair so effectively highlighted, they are reborn time and again 'from the ashes where we believed they had been buried by the advance of civilisation'. Freud demonstrated how far the ingenuity of positivism could go, believing that developed nations would gradually but irreversibly move towards controlling their drives. While it is beyond question that 'with great effort, renouncing the satisfaction of many desires, [they] are able to control brutal conflicts by instituting civilisation', this same civilisation is regularly struck by setbacks or regressions which demonstrate that violence cannot be definitively eradicated. As André Clair also said, 'scientific progress and the predominance that man has established over nature and over himself have led us to hope that the end of war will coincide with the continuous and unbroken progress of civilisation'. Clearly, the roots of any such expectation lie in denying what we are, encouraged by the reduction of the most complex to simpler forms, from the real to the ideal:

> The fundamental problem is no longer one of knowing whether civilisation does or does not imply continuous or even inescapable progress. Rather, it is one of knowing whether the inescapable is not the same as aggression itself, that aggression that ceaselessly reappears, creating a barrier that is proof against all reduction or the substitution of violence with rationality.

Freud emphasised that 'the primitive mind is, in the fullest meaning of the word, imperishable'. In that it is not vulnerable to temporality, the primitive mind is part of the traumatic. War is proof of this as, despite its contemporary sophistication, it cannot hide its ancient character. The primary drives to which it responds may be circumstantially submerged, but they are still inextinguishable. 'This also means that death is never defeated and continues to challenge man, or makes man face up to the inescapable: this is the forced return to the inorganic, irreducible violence.'

We again face the traumatic in that – with death and war – we stand before what is immutable, where subjectivity can make no changes because there is no possible semantic feature capable of making war and death subject to time, to a definitive cultural procedure. The immutable and the inexpressible speak to us through the figures of death and war. André Clair adds: 'This origin establishes us as a destination which, like a wheel, returns us to our point of departure.'

It is true that the social contract ceaselessly works to make sure that the original does not recover its prominence. According to Clair, the cohesion achieved by the group (village, kingdom or nation) 'presupposes a renunciation of crime and of declared or manifest violence, where codified laws ban incest and the rule of exogamy. That is the price of the social contract. However, sexual and aggressive drives are not suppressed, they are deflected. As one's own group cannot be the target of such aggression, the focus therefore becomes some foreign group.' Hence, the present returns to actuality and is again updated, 'repetitively substituting the past'. The reason why this happens is that 'if man rediscovers his original situation, this is because it is imprinted onto the subconscious of which he is part'. Clair underlines that 'this remembrance is part of man's archaic heritage' and that, when it reappears, it emerges as a recurrence of the fall into atemporality.

The universe of vital substitutions that we call culture demonstrates its own fragility, even though the desire for humanisation can only find a configuration within this universe. This destiny is clearly the word, the instance in which the primordial failure that determines that man is an incomplete being may be granted a form and therefore a meaning. Lacan stressed that 'dialogue seems in itself to be a renunciation of aggression. Ever since Socrates, philosophy has pinned its hope of seeing rationality triumph on dialogue. However, ever since Thrasymachus's demented performance at the beginning of the great dialogue in *Republic*, the failure of verbal dialectics has all too often been repeated.'

Lacan's observation is also a warning. As Julio Cortazar rightly stated, 'we should live combating ourselves'. If we cannot defeat war once and for all, we can at least constantly reiterate our decision to fight against it, preventing its victory over us from becoming definitive. Ultimately, while recognising the impositions of finitude and the lack that simultaneously deprives us and constitutes us, this means adopting a position which knows how to find a meaning for the word: a word that is capable of establishing a meaning in us, one that is far removed from the anthropocentric omnipotence formalised in the Enlightenment and whose peak appears in *Discourse on the Positive Spirit*.

III

This simultaneously defensive and attacking struggle is proposed for us by a humanism that is not based on man as its exclusive point of reference, the imagined master of himself and of all that surrounds him. Rather, it rests on a dialogical interaction with alterity, an interaction that reveals man as simultaneously creator and creature, as a being who is heard and able to hear this alterity that yearns to be recognised as an irreducible reality, and that appears equally in his surroundings and in his body, as much in nature as in culture and equally in his conscious and unconscious life.

In relation to this new humanism that hopes to project itself as rational criticism of the apostatising sufficiency of lack or finitude and of rationalisation, there are no better words than those spoken almost fifty years ago by Albert Camus when he received the Nobel Prize for Literature: 'Each generation doubtless feels called upon to reform the world. Mine knows that it will not reform it, but its task is perhaps even greater. It consists in preventing the world from destroying itself.'

A hopeful man is not one who believes that things will get better tomorrow. On the contrary, he is the one who sees the nuances and brilliance which prove that reality is not uniform within a present of apparently homogeneous darkness. Consequently, hope does not consist of the expectation that things will move on from their current negative state in the future, but consists instead of the conviction that the present situation does not necessarily have to be constrained by a unilateral definition, since its multiple aspects (while open to integration or incorporation into a global vision) are irreducible to a single criterion or unanimous voice. The hopeful man is always a post-traumatic man.

Just as new perspectives regularly emerge to characterise what we understand by education, new criteria periodically and complementarily also appear to establish what should be understood as ignorance. Like knowledge, ignorance is also renewed and modernised. In fact, I even believe that ignorance is renewed and updated in an intimate and subtle relationship with knowledge. Thus, I believe we must reflect on the new forms that ignorance is now adopting, especially whenever we seek to define the ethical (and not just the epistemological) rules that should guide the configuration of new knowledge.

Two among the most acute forms of ignorance that threaten us merit consideration, due to their interrelationship with the concept of trauma. The first is related to the phenomenon of knowledge; the second, as briefly mentioned above, is the notion of progress.

I will start by examining the issue of knowledge, beginning with the general characteristics of identity that prevailed in the High Middle Ages. I intend to contrast these characteristics with the defining expressions attributable to our times in the field of knowledge.

From its origins until the thirteenth century, the western world's High Middle Ages was a period in which the geopolitical fragmentation that defined a predominantly feudal Europe contrasted with the profound desire for unity from the vision of the cosmos proposed by Christianity. Thus, the fragmentation apparent in the geopolitical order because of the supremacy of feudal concepts and practices was counterbalanced by the Christian vision of the cosmos. The latter wished to create a set of values that could control, on a mutually agreed basis, all the geopolitical fragments that characterised social organisation. In this sense, the intention was to offer the essential unity that these fragments so clearly lacked.

In contrast to this medieval vision, one characteristic feature of our times is that a broad geopolitical unity has been achieved or implemented. Far more so than in terms of any equanimity of social justice, this is primarily ensured by economic interdependence and the development of information and communication technologies. In turn, this unity contradicts the prevalence of the major fragmentation of any vision of the cosmos.

Ours is an age in which growing planetary integration is gradually being achieved on the geopolitical level as a result of the power of communication, consumption and convergent ideological interests. This contrasts with a profound segmentation of knowledge and the lack of any unitary and interdependent vision of the values that underlie the conception and orientation of progress. This orientation of progress is far more targeted at producing consumers than citizens, as so effectively demonstrated by the current crisis of meaning in western democracies.

This contrast between that period from the High Middle Ages and the one we are currently experiencing enables us to start discerning some of the problems on which education should focus. The goal should be to raise professionally ideal citizens, rather than 'experts' or specialists who (as Paul Feyerabend noted) aim to use their segmented categories to gain control over solving problems that impact on the common good and values that transcend their particular specialist fields.

Year after year, every faculty produces teachers, graduates and doctors. Yet they do not produce 'universals'. In its purest form, the word university reflects the idea of universality, of a community whose values are active and discernable in each individual expression of knowledge and in the daily life of its social body.

In contrast to someone who is only qualified to develop as a professional in some specific area, the 'universal' in the word's true sense, while always having proven knowledge that authorises his action in a specific area, is defined by a superior vision of the whole that comfortably exceeds the specific terrain of specialist training. Thanks to this vision, he is able to integrate, from a perspective of strong interdependences, aspects that would otherwise appear as partial, unconnected or falsely autonomous.

With this integrative or transdisciplinary vision, which is perhaps the highest and most profound expression of culture, the true 'universal' develops or achieves his vocation: seeking the essential complementary nature that links fields or features of knowledge which are normally fragmented or unrelated.

The true 'universal' adds an essential openness to epistemological ecumenism to the always vital notion of operative effectiveness. It is this openness to ecumenism that enables him to overcome the temptation of sectarianism, to defeat the irreducible polarisations that are final and permanent expressions of underestimating the Other, scorn for everything that may reduce or compromise the assumed absolute value of knowledge itself and the beliefs traumatically frozen in certainty. In other words, the true 'universal' represents the conviction that the most pernicious blindness now threatening us is idolatry of the fragmentary.

When the 'universal' really responds to an orchestrated vision of knowledge, he immediately understands that the superabundance of specialist pseudo-languages wounds and discredits common speech, and spreads at the expense of the latter's meaning as a collective heritage. This is also weakens the feeling of social integration and spiritual cohesion within a cultural community, demands that are increasingly ignored outside the professional scope where each individual develops. Ultimately, this reflects a growing and consensual atomisation that is surprisingly legitimised by university study centres.

Producing professionals for a job market and empowering individuals to act as educated citizens are completely different, even contradictory, ends. The former currently take precedence over the latter, as demonstrated by the strategies adopted by the still-great western democracies, which form the undisputed centre that radiates the current alienated conception of globalisation. Led and urged on by highly trained technocrats who have no culture, today's dominant globalisation was designed as a process of bringing the planet closer by rejecting individual cultures and any type of specific regional characteristic.

At a time when all manner of intolerances are multiplying in the face of nuances, the essential 'universal' seeks instead to establish a convergent and horizontal concept of the human, one that is culturally pluralist, and that demonstrates solidarity in political and social terms. The anthropologist Marc Augé spoke about this, referring to a need to stimulate the rooting of a 'planetary utopia'. In turn, Edgar Morin insists on the need to encourage the expansion of a 'planetary conscience' that will rise above all the divisions that shipwreck any current notion of identity.

Thus, there is a need for a clearly universal education to regain its leading role, fulfilling a critical function in defence of fertile unity against sterile uniformity. The absence of such an education is now one of the causes of the death throes of democratic sensibilities among those who should be leading the knowledge society.

Without it, the will to achieve equity, complementariness and the sense that all humans are part of a single humanity will be left incomplete.

Modern culture imposes a concept of identity that is linked to developing a possessive attitude, of accumulating the real and manipulating what are called natural resources. This demonstrates how, by defining ourselves fundamentally as owners and consumers, we run the risk of losing our primordial condition as human people, as beings who are open to dialogue with the difference that complements us and that, by so doing, forms us. Sartre was wrong: hell is not other people. Hell is the narcissism that condemns the others.

It is not only nuclear conflagration that threatens the survival of our species and of all species, but also this sordid toil of replacing our dialogical subjectivity with an authoritarianism that pushes us to seek unbridled domination: the exclusive predominance of the desire for power. It is precisely this that threatens the specific features of identity with more than the virtual possibility of extinction.

If we fail to prevent this, we will end up only seeming – and not being – human beings, blind celebrants of the joys of Thanatos rather than of pleasure. The traumatic, understood as that which prevents temporality from circulating and consequently blocks the appearance of the subject, wins whenever the personal enunciation fails. We will survive, but we will not be alive, individually alive, because we will have become indebted to the discourse of some other being whose hegemony demands our extinction as singularised individuals within a vision of the cosmos whose intention is traumatic and therefore paralysing.

Constructing the person is not a task that can be consummated. Only trauma aspires to the definitive. The psychical and moral discovery of our absence, along with its ulterior reversion, is always possible and never terminal. It is achieved by passing through the pain that devastates us and dissolving in the anonymity of the suffering that, while never freeing us from subjection to this alterity that transcends and marks us, operates on the suffering, re-signifies it, and by so doing, enables us to proceed. Each one of us can again proceed as *homo loquens*, subjects that are subjects because they all speak as subjects.

IV

The magnitude of our current ethical absence can be seen in the mirror of our devastated surroundings and of our interiority, impoverished by the denial of finitude.

We also understand that an educational proposal oriented towards creating a citizen capable of reconsidering the meaning and purpose of development and the drama of living in the community demands reflection on the disparities that exist between material progress (which promotes a profound communicative interdependence between the different regions of the planet) and the tragic upswing in intolerance of difference that characterises the style of development of contemporary political and social dilemmas. Information and economic interdependence do not guarantee social integration. We cannot and should not give up on this, but should rather go much further.

Another threat of contamination and oppression that now hangs over man is the result of the destruction of language in the mass media. We have undoubtedly learned to communicate with each other in a broader and faster fashion. However, the expressive quality of our contact is increasingly poor and schematic. Restricting my focus merely to Latin America, the proper use of Castilian and Portuguese is neither of secondary importance nor the preserve of specialists. Instead, it is a question that concerns the quality and consistency of civic identity, and many of the subjective resources that define the potential of interaction. In other words, it is a decisive question for our spiritual health.

In many Latin American countries, the state has started warning us that there will be no real participation in the contemporary world without efficient participation in the knowledge market. Therefore, it should also start showing some concern about the backwardness which leads to the growing linguistic irresponsibility that is perversely paraded in the mass media. The world that we call our own is always correlated to the language that we have at our disposal. Wherever we choose to look nowadays, we see a drastic decline in expressive richness, nuances of interpretation and creative eloquence in the places where they should be most vital. Abandoned and mistreated words do not wither alone: we wither with them. Whosoever neglects them is in effect ignoring himself and his peers. In contrast, whosoever responsibly cares for and nurtures them is revealing both a wish to be heard and an ability to listen.

Without the essential political mechanisms to stem and reverse the draining away of responsibility for elocution that we have endured for so long, it will continue to thrive in the mass media, enjoying the impunity of those who profit from sowing ignorance. Meanwhile, the brothel-like forms of expression and the vociferousness that is an enemy of reflection will be stimulated in the cultural subversion that we suffer. If – on the other hand and as is to be desired – the state does its duty and acts decisively, effective strategies can quickly be drawn up and we can move from rightful protest to essential action. This would be a start to reforming the joyfully linguistic decadence in which our republics wallow.

The purity and plenitude of a language requires the determined application of educational strategies that can help build citizenship. There can be no consolidated civic identity while the powers that prostitute language continue to prosper in the mass media. Obviously, I am not proposing the stimulation of some kind of expressive affectation or academic rhetoric: it is simply a matter of speaking properly, since doing so means thinking properly. My hope is that thinking – that fragile, enigmatic resource for spiritual life – will not be voided and irredeemably wasted by a passive and resigned attitude imposed by habits founded on commonplaces and irresponsible submission to consensus. For the present, educating with proper criteria means proposing a closer relationship between ethics and knowledge, between information and solidarity, between the similar – seen as something whose difference also forms me – and wisdom. The latter is defined as a tool that enables me to have a relationship with the similar without either condemning it or letting it condemn me to intranscendence.

A task of this nature can never be considered to be implemented or complete. Yet it may be constantly undertaken, perhaps because our lives, which react against traumatic occlusion, do not consist of reaching a fixed point but of never abandoning the quest for improvement. It should now be recalled (as already said) why one of our species' most subtle metamorphoses is the one which can place us in a real inexistence, in the sense that was felt, or intuited and proclaimed by Franz Kafka. It concerns our subjective extinction, the fact that we have ultimately become very similar – but only that – to human beings.

The survival of our species neither is nor can be guaranteed. However, without any shadow of a doubt, few threats are greater than the loss of those values which allow us to understand that in order to survive man primarily needs affectively to mean something to someone. In truth, we are the meaningful destiny offered by the eyes of the other. Should the eyes of the other not establish our presence in a shared signification, then we are irremediably absent. Moreover, the loss of personal meaning begins at the point at which we are assessed as an undifferentiated part within a whole. The dissolution of singularity in that whole is the end of the human, because being human means being discerned through our unparalleled singularity. Hence, the combination of ethics with the thirst for knowledge is vital in an educational project where the notion of citizenship must be central, which is to say politically innovative. As Edgar Morin said, one of the greatest challenges facing the present is determining whether we can be 'citizens of the Earth'.

We must educate ourselves in an effort to become such 'citizens of the Earth'. Inhabiting the Earth is not the same as occupying it: above all else, inhabiting the Earth means recognising it and listening to it, approaching it as a presence and not as a mere object.

Intercultural differences should be the guarantee of an authentic, globalising integration. There will be no true planetary integration unless differences are preserved as a resource for communion and convergence, a response for an authentic ideal of living in harmony. One of the fundamental prerequisites for our species' spiritual survival is swept away in places where intercultural differences are abolished in order to achieve integration. We are what we are only in that we are not the same being; we can only be similar in that we are not the same being. If we can in fact recognise each other, it is because we are not all equal. Our family relationship is guaranteed by the irreducibility of one in relation to the other. Our fraternity has nothing to do with tolerance, that gentle demonstration of indifference, but can only spring from reciprocated love of our individual features. In our species, the radical miracle consists – for each and every one of us, and equally for the collective conscience – of having been one for a single time.

Translated by Richard Trewinnard

Is the World Flat?

SURENDRA MUNSHI

Any discussion that concerns itself in some ways with the state of the world must first get one thing clear. Is the world flat? Thomas Friedman (2005) believes that the world is flat: that is the title of his latest book which has already become famous. He opens his book with an entry from the journal of Christopher Columbus. It is generally considered that Columbus put to rest the belief that the earth was flat, a belief that was supposed to have been entertained by the Europeans before him. Columbus tried to go to the 'countries of India' not by the Eastern land route but by the Western route sailing across the 'ocean sea'. He believed that it was possible to reach India by this route in a ship since the earth for him was a sphere; a rather small sphere, going by the provisions of food that he had made. Columbus did not reach India but he showed the way to a place that became known as America later. Friedman, an American, travelled to India more than five hundred years after Columbus's historical voyage. He took the Eastern air route, via Frankfurt. And it is here in India that he discovered that the world is flat. The parallel is significant. 'Columbus reported to his king and queen that the world was round, and he went down in history as the man who first made this discovery. I returned home and shared my discovery only with my wife, and only in a whisper, "Honey," I confided, "I think the world is flat.""[1]

The earth was not generally seen as flat in Europe before Columbus. The Greeks knew the earth was round. Aristotle gave observational evidence in favour of this view. A classical argument pertains to the ships. The bottom of a ship disappears first on the horizon. The ship as a whole does not become smaller and smaller until it becomes invisible as would have been the case if the earth were flat. Even in the middle ages in Europe the belief that the earth was round was not generally given up. Indeed, as Jeffery Burton Russell (1991) has argued, the idea of the 'medieval flat earth' was invented in the nineteenth century. Neither Columbus nor his contemporaries thought that the earth was flat. The concept of the flat earth was invented by extrapolating the views of Lactanitus and Cosmas and then assigning them to the Middle Ages. This was useful for contrasting Columbus with medieval obscurantist ideas. Indeed, the anticlericals of the Enlightenment did not make this mistake. They were well aware that the spherical view of the earth was important for Aristotle's cosmology.

Why then does Friedman claim that the world is flat? Why is it necessary to invent the idea of the flat earth once again? Is our world really round?

*

It all started in Bangalore, India. Friedman came to India in 2004 to find out why the Indians were so successful in work relating to outsourcing in the areas of service and information technology from the United States and other developing countries. Before he came to India, he tells us, he assumed like everyone else that the world was round. But once he was here and had seen for himself what was happening here, his belief in the world being round was profoundly shaken. In the course of his meeting with Nandan Nilekani, CEO of Infosys, 'one of the jewels of the Indian information technology world', he was taken to the global conferencing centre of the company. The conference room is equipped to hold for any project being handled by the company a virtual meeting of all key players from its entire global supply chain at any time. This was made possible by massive investments in broadband connectivity and proliferation of computers and different types of software across the world. This created, as Nilekani explained, a platform for intellectual work that could now be sliced and then put together again for delivery from any part of the world. And what was happening in Bangalore was the culmination and coming together of all those developments. Nilekani said: 'Tom, the playing field is being leveled.' Friedman understood him to mean that a country like India could now compete for knowledge work globally. Friedman kept chewing on this comment. 'What Nandan is saying, I thought,' he tells us, 'is that the playing field is being flattened... Flattened? Flattened? My God, he's telling me the world is flat!'[2]

So this then is meant by the flat world. In Friedman's words: 'The global competitive playing field was being leveled. The world was being flattened'.[3] It means that with the connections that have been established globally more people can now compete and collaborate with people from different parts of the world on more equal terms than ever before in the working of the world. Understandably, the word 'flat' keeps coming up throughout the book. When he sees technology at work at an American command centre in Iraq that makes information available down the line, he concludes that the military hierarchy is being 'flattened', the playing field of the military is being 'leveled'.[4] The fall of the Berlin Wall on 9 November 1989, meant that there was now only one economic system left in the world. It 'flattened' the alternative to capitalism.[5] Around the same time, a critical mass of IBM PCs and the Windows operating system (Windows 3.0 was shipped in May 1990) along with other technological breakthroughs coming together created the possibility of 'the global information revolution'. This made 'the world much flatter than it had ever been'.[6] The Netscape drove 'the flattening process' by making the Internet accessible, going beyond early adopters and geeks.[7] Once Microsoft Word became the global standard, people working in different parts of the world could cooperate more easily, for 'shared standards are huge flatteners'.[8] Friedman uses here the example of PayPal, a money transfer system. It enabled individuals to accept credit card payments. This 'leveled the playing field'.[9]

There are some more instances of the use of the term 'flat' that need to be selectively mentioned here. China is emerging as an important player in the flat world. There are overwhelming advantages in getting into China. 'Either you get flat or you'll be flattened by China.'[10] With China and India moving in the direction of free markets, the world will become 'flatter', benefiting from 'the interconnecting of all the markets and knowledge centers'.[11] These benefits will be greater than those that arose from the efforts made by Western Europe and Japan to become free-market democracies after the Second World War, for the world was not flat then: 'It had a wall in the middle.'[12] Finally, let us go with Friedman to Tokyo. In the winter of 2004, he had tea with Richard C. Koo, the chief economist of the Nomura Research Institute. 'I tested out on Richard', he writes, 'my "coefficient of flatness"': the notion that the flatter one's country is – that is, the fewer natural resources it has – the better off it will be in a flat world. The ideal country in a flat world is the one with *no natural resources,* because countries with no natural resources tend to dig inside themselves.'[13] He goes on to give the example of Taiwan, 'a barren rock in a typhoon-laden sea, with virtually no natural resources', and also Hong Kong, Japan, South Korea, and coastal China which share 'similar flatness'.[14]

Friedman's concept of the flat world will be examined below. For the present, his use of the term 'flat' in selectively presented instances should be helpful in becoming familiar with the range of his thought. Let us look now at his argument.

Friedman believes that the flattening of the world took place while he was sleeping. Actually, it took place when he was travelling to the Arab and Muslim worlds. After 9/11, the olive tree, symbolising forces of identity and nationalism, became important for him. It is therefore important to relate his present book with his earlier book on globalisation, *The Lexus and the Olive Tree.* He has a view of different eras of globalisation. The first era started with the voyage of Columbus and lasted until 1800. The second era lasted roughly from 1800 to 2000. When he was working on *The Lexus and the Olive Tree* in 1998, the Internet and e-commerce were just taking off. They took off around the year 2000, along with other important developments, and then we entered the third era of globalisation. This era is 'shrinking the world from a size small to a size tiny and flattening the playing field at the same time'.[15] What gives this era its unique character, unlike the earlier eras, is that individuals can collaborate and compete globally. This is made possible by the development in software and the creation of a fibre-optic network that connects the world. This era is driven not only by individuals but by a diverse group of individuals. So many more people can now plug and play that one is going 'to see every colour of the human rainbow take part'.[16] He says: you ain't seen nothin' yet. We are entering an era of globalisation that will turn out different from the earlier not only in degree but also in kind. The world has gone flat. 'Everywhere you turn, hierarchies are being challenged from below or transforming themselves from top-down structures into more horizontal and collaborative ones.'[17]

How did it happen? The world has been flattened by the congruence of ten forces. Friedman calls them 'flatteners'. The first is the fall of the Berlin Wall and the coming up of the Windows operating system. While the fall of the Berlin Wall liberated the people of the Soviet Empire and with that the vision of the people elsewhere, Windows opened up the possibility of improving productivity by encouraging a large number of people to use computers. And then Netscape went public on 9 August 1995. This was the second force that flattened the world. It made a call to the world to wake up to the possibility of the Internet. The Internet boom created the need for growing investment in the fibre-optic cable that wired the world. The third force that flattened the world was the coming of workflow software. This made it possible for people not only to communicate but also to collaborate with each other. A completely new set of standards is emerging now to enable workflow. Thanks to the platform that has emerged due to the forces outlined above, new forms of collaboration have been enhanced or made possible.

One such possibility is open sourcing, which is listed as the fourth source. Open sourcing means making available online the source code of a software. There is an open-source movement that involves thousands of people around the world who work together online to create a software and to make improvements in it. The idea is to develop software collaboratively and then to make it available to all those who want it for their own use. While commercial software is protected under copyright and never gives away the source code of a software, open-source software is shared free of cost. This brings us to the fifth force which has flattened the world. It is outsourcing. A major player here is India, which has benefited from its previous investment in higher education and the wiring of the world that has taken place. In the words of Jack Welch, the Chairman of General Electric, who came to India in 1989, 'India is a developing country with a developed intellectual capability.'[18] India further gained from the Y2K crisis that enabled the Indian IT companies to make their presence felt globally. And with the dot-com bust, India benefited further. This brought work to India when the IT budgets of major American companies were cut and there was pressure on every IT manager to get more work done for less money. All this led to the further growth in India of IT companies which started transforming themselves from maintenance to product development, offering a large variety of software services and consulting. The sixth force that has been identified is offshoring. While outsourcing involves taking some specific function from a company, having it done elsewhere, and then integrating the work done with the overall operation of the company, offshoring typically means taking an entire operation elsewhere and having it done there. While India was the destination for outsourcing, China became the favourite destination for offshoring. With China joining the WTO in 2001, more and more companies came to China to set up factories and integrating these factories into their global operations. China has the advantage of what is known as 'the China price'. China, starting from a low base, is not only winning on wages but also improving in productivity and quality.

And that brings us to the seventh force, identified as supply-chaining. Here Wal-Mart fires or rather carries Friedman's imagination. He visits Wal-Mart headquarters in Bentonville, Arkansas. He goes over to the distribution centre and views 'the show' from a viewing perch. It is best to know what he saw in his own words:

> On one side of the building, scores of white Wal-Mart trailer trucks were dropping off boxes of merchandise from thousands of different suppliers. Boxes large and small were fed up a conveyor belt at each loading dock. These little conveyor belts fed into a bigger belt, like streams feeding into a powerful river. Twenty-four hours a day, seven days a week, the suppliers' trucks feed the twelve miles of conveyor streams, and the conveyor streams feed into a large Wal-Mart river of boxed products. But that is just half the show. As the Wal-Mart river flows along, an electric eye reads the bar codes on each box on its way to the other side of the building. There, the river parts again into a hundred streams. Electric arms from each stream reach out and guide the boxes – ordered by particular Wal-Mart stores – off the main river and down its stream, where another conveyor sweeps them into a waiting Wal-Mart truck, which will rush these particular products into the shelves of a particular Wal-Mart store somewhere in the country. There, a consumer will lift one of these products off the shelf, and the cashier will scan it in, and the moment it happens, a signal will be generated. That signal will go out across the Wal-Mart network to the supplier of that product – whether that supplier's factory is in coastal China or coastal Maine. That signal will pop up on the supplier's computer screen and prompt him to make another of that item and ship it via the Wal-Mart supply chain, and the whole cycle will start anew.[19]

Friedman calls this cycle 'the Wal-Mart Symphony'. It has multiple movements, without a finale. It plays repeatedly every day of the year. Wal-Mart has become the biggest retailer in the world because it can handle its supply chain extremely well. It delivers all sorts of goods at lower and still lower prices. Wal-Mart drew $18 billion worth of goods from 5000 Chinese suppliers in 2004.

The last three forces that flattened the world may be discussed now. One of them is identified as insourcing. Friedman mentions United Parcel Service (UPS) here. As Nilekani told him, they are not only delivering packages but also doing logistics. Their slogan is: 'Your World Synchronized'. They are globalising global supply chains with the help of a fleet of 270 aircraft. They ship more than 13.5 million packages a day from one point to another. Not every company can afford to run a supply chain of its own the way Wal-Mart can. This is where UPS comes in. If, for instance, if one ordered Jockey underwear online, UPS employees who manage Jockey products would actually take care of the order, from filling the order to delivery. UPS helps to take the majority of their customers who have small businesses to global markets. Friedman calls the ninth force that flattened the world as 'in-forming'. Here Google has pride of place. Search engines give universal access to information. Google aims to give all knowledge of the world in every language. Google is making about one billion searches per day. This flattens the world, because more and more people are thus able to inform themselves from the convenience of their own homes or offices. There is massive democratisation of access to information taking place here. This affects the consumers as well. Google is not just a search engine but also a profitable business. The advertising is directed by making advertisements relevant to the search topics. And the last force that flattened the world is called 'the steroids'. The steroids are those techniques that enhance all other flatteners. These make it possible, in the words of Carly Fiorina, to do things in a manner that is 'digital, mobile, virtual, and personal'. With the digitalisation of diverse contents and processes, they can be used and transmitted to our computers and supporting systems. Thanks to the wireless technology, this can be done by anyone, from anywhere, using any device that can be taken anywhere. All this happens at such high speed with such ease that one does not have to think about it. And it can be done by a person for himself or herself on a personal device.

All these flatteners started to converge around 2000. This created 'a new, flatter, global playing field'.[20] More and more business and individuals began to adopt such ways of working as to

make the most of what was available. This was the second convergence which flattened the world even more. And then a new group
of people, actually in billions, from China, India, and other places
walked out on the playing field. This was the third convergence.
Thanks to what was being offered in the flat world, these people
could compete directly with others. It is this triple convergence of
'new players, on a new playing field, developing new processes and
habits of horizontal collaboration'[21] that is the most important
development of the century. The entry of new players in such large
numbers alone has serious consequences for the world economy.
Nothing guarantees that Americans or Western Europeans will
permanently lead the way. The world, a global market, is like a
football field. One is a player if one is good or else just a spectator.
The IT revolution that we have seen so far is just the beginning,
the prologue. We are now entering into an era when technology
will transform business, life and society in all aspects.

If this sounds like technological determinism, Friedman is
aware of it. He honestly admits that he is a technical determinist.[22]
Indeed, when Michael J. Sandel of Harvard University heard his
view on the flattening process, he pointed out to Friedman that
Karl Marx and Friedrich Engels in the *Manifesto of the Communist
Party*, published in 1848, first identified the process. While there
has been a different degree of flattening taking place at present, it
constitutes part of the same trend that Marx highlighted in his
analysis of capitalism. Marx was one of the first to see the possibility of the world emerging as a global market under the thrust of
capitalism. That takes Friedman to the *Manifesto*, from which he
reproduces the largest quotation of the book. The passage that he
quotes talks of 'the world market' and how improvements in
instruments of production and means of communication create
universal connections everywhere in place of national seclusion.
All Chinese walls, it notes, are battered down by the heavy artillery
of cheap prices. Some pages later, Friedman talks of the possibility
of new political alignments taking place. He contrasts two possible
configurations: the Wall Party of all those who do not like globalisation and the Web Party of all those who wish to promote global
integration.[23] It is obvious that Friedman belongs to the Web

Party. As an American, he is convinced that the United States as a whole will benefit from free trade. There will be problems for low-skilled workers whose jobs can be moved to China, but they can maintain or improve their living standards by moving vertically. They will have to upgrade their skills. Idea-based workers, on the other hand, will do well, though some of them may have to move horizontally. The growing pie will take care of the problem as a whole. There will be new jobs to do. There is no limit to the creation of such jobs, and America will gain so long as it keeps producing skilled workers who can take such jobs. America can take advantage of the flat world because of some specific features, such as its educational and research institutions, efficient capital markets, flexible labour laws, and so on.

It will not do, though, to be complacent. Friedman sees a quiet crisis here. He finds that the fields of science and engineering are not attracting enough students. He also finds there is an ambition gap, for company executives tell him that outsourcing not only means cheaper work but also better work. The challenge of the flat world is also an opportunity. Friedman presents himself as 'a compassionate flatist'. It is tactful as well as wise to be so. He reminds us that there is always the danger of the backlash, actu-ally a ferocious backlash, if some innovative social security measures are not provided to those who are going to be adversely affected by the process. He suggests measures such as lifelong learning, social activism, and good parenting to help people adapt to a flat world. Leaders have a significant role to play here.

Developing countries get some advice as well. They have to face the challenges posed by the flattening world. They need to carry out broad macroeconomic reforms. Open and competitive markets provide a country with the best way out of poverty. But, going beyond these reforms, there is a need for a deeper process of reform. It is important to consider infrastructure, regulatory institutions, education, and culture. Each country has to ask, in the words of Craig Barrett, the Chairman of Intel, what inherent strength it can offer to the interested parties.[24]

Having brought the readers so far, Friedman throws up an unex-pected surprise. He tells his readers: 'I know that the world is not flat'.[25] He announces that he has engaged in literary licence in naming his book, *The World is Flat*. True, the process of flattening has been going on and it is the most important trend in the world today. But the world is not flat, nor is there any certainty that it will become flat. Not flat? What is the world then? The answer that is given is that half the world is in some way involved in the flattening process. There are on the other hand hundreds of millions of people who have not been touched by the flattening process or who feel overwhelmed by it, and some of them actually use the tools of the flattening process against the process itself. We are told that there is a flat world and there is an unflat world. We are further told that there are people who live in-between these two worlds, in the half-flat world.

Why do some countries succeed and others fail? The difference lies to a significant extent in culture. One major difference that Friedman has noticed during his travels is with respect to the openness of a culture. The more a culture absorbs foreign ideas and practices and blends them with its own traditions, the better possibilities it has in a flat world. The term that is used for it is 'glocalisation'. High on the glocalisation scale are the cultures of India, America, Japan, and more recently China. Muslim countries on the other hand, Friedman notes, do not glocalise well, though there are exceptions. A religious clergy that does not encourage *ijtihad*, the reinterpretation of Islamic principles for the present time, dominates the Muslim world. Tribal culture still dominates in many Arab countries. Tribalism is contrary to globalisation, for the tribalist emphasises exclusion; the globalist asks for collaborative supply chains. It will, though, be a mistake to think of cultures in static terms. As contexts change so do cultures. While Muslim Spain was a tolerant society, Muslim Saudi Arabia is one of the most intolerant societies in the world today. Leaders with vision are needed to take their countries on the path of development. It is important to move forward: that can happen if leaders, in the words of Luis Rubio, the President of the Mexican Centre of Research for Development, think forward and outward rather than inward and backward.[26]

Friedman discusses next those who live between the flat world and the unflat world, in the world that is half-flat. This world belongs to those people in countries like India and China who see, or at times benefit, from the flat world but who are not a part of it. These are typically the people living in rural areas. They need to be brought into the stream, and it is here that a real humanitarian push by 'flat world businesses, philanthropies, and governments' is needed. 'Let's stop here for a moment and imagine how beneficial it would be for the world, and for America, if rural China, India, and Africa were to grow into little Americas or European Unions in economic and opportunity terms.'[27]

One of the sad consequences of the flat world is that it creates unflattening forces. Among the most unflattening forces are al-Qaeda and other Islamic terror organisations of the Muslim world and Muslim communities in Europe. Such forces arise out of frustrations in the Muslim world and in Muslim communities in Europe. The vision of al-Qaeda is to establish an Islamic state, 'a religious paradise'.[28] It seems to offer an ideology to those who are frustrated for different reasons. Osama bin Laden and his colleagues have been able to enlist recruits rather easily. 'I think this has to do, in part,' writes Friedman, 'with the state of half-flatness that many Arab-Muslim young people are living in, particularly those in Europe.'[29] The flattening of the world makes the backwardness of the Arab-Muslim region even more visible.

What is needed then is to tie different countries in supply chains, which promote both prosperity and mutual dependence. This is called the Dell Theory of Conflict Prevention, an upgrade on an earlier theory built around McDonald. Unfortunately, supply chains are used by al-Qaeda as well. It has learnt to use collaboration as well as a company like Infosys. The flat world offers, above all, technical opportunities to both of them. The Dell theory will not apply to al-Qaeda because such terror organisations do not constitute a state with a population to which they are accountable. The world is divided into two forms of imagination, the creative and the destructive. 11 September 2001 was about the destructive imagination, about them, 'the bad guys'. We need to stimulate the creative, positive imagination. The world is being flattened, and we need to manage it. 'On such a flat earth,' concludes Friedman, 'the most important attribute you can have is creative imagination – the ability to be the first on your block to figure out how all these enabling tools can be put together in new and exciting ways to create products, communities, opportunities, and profits. That has always been America's strength, because America was, and for now still is, the world's greatest dream machine.'[30]

★

Friedman has provided an overview of some of the most important trends that are shaping the present world. He writes in a readable and interesting manner for the general reader, and his work is based on a lot of information that he has collected during his travels and conversations with key players. It is clear that he has access to them, and it is widely believed that he has access to their ears as well. He writes with energy and optimism, without being blind to possible pitfalls. Thus, he notes that there is no historical inevitability about the flattening process. Indeed, it cannot be ruled out that those parts of the world that are already flat will not get unflattened by war and other factors. It is for this reason that he brings into play the creative imagination that can take the world forward. It will not do to be complacent.

His strong points, though, have their flip sides. He has packed so much in his overview that there can be questions about the insights he has to offer. His writing at times becomes too familiar and flippant. Thus, for example, he draws a picture where regions of the world are imagined to be neighbourhoods of a city. What would the neighbourhood of Western Europe look like? 'Western Europe would be an assisted-living facility, with an aging population lavishly attended to by Turkish nurses.'[31] He goes on to describe other neighbourhoods. Thus, Latin America is described as the club district where the workday would begin only after ten at night. To take another example: he expects to be taken seriously when he advances a theory, called the McDonald's theory, which suggests that a McDonald's country, a country that has a network of McDonald's, does not go for wars but for queues waiting for burgers. He has travelled much and talked to important persons, but there is not much evidence of his having talked to the people who are on the receiving end. Thus, for instance, when he says regarding his country that low-skilled workers will be faced with problems, there is no single voice from these workers. Instead, we hear Marc Andreessen, the Netscape co-founder, tell us that human wants and needs are infinite. One problem in talking to so may important people is that he tends to define his job as that of putting together what they have said to him. This practice of what may be called here *statement stringing* does not allow for a critical assessment of their positions. If Andreessen says that human wants and needs are infinite, so they are. It is therefore not surprising Friedman's book contains no bibliography: the only book that features with prominence is the author's own earlier book, *The Lexus and the Olive Tree*. True, Friedman does quote from Marx and Engels; it is useful to recall here that he went to that text because Sandel advised him to do so. He is surprised when he finds that Marx and Engels had said in 1848 what he is saying now. This excessive dependence on spoken words may be good for journalism but not perhaps for a deeper analysis. It is to the problems of analysis in Friedman's treatment that we need to turn now.

What is his concept of the flat world? Going by the comment that launched Friedman's ship, Nilekani meant that the global field was being levelled enabling more people to enter the competitive global market on more equal terms than before. A level playing-field, figuratively speaking, is a field on which rivals compete without either side having an unfair advantage. How does a flat world enter into the picture? It enters, as we have seen, through the word 'flattening'. Friedman has a physical vision here. With the dismantling of the Berlin Wall a horizontal surface without structures was created. To the idea of the absence of unfair advantage to any side is added the idea of the flat surface. But then yet another idea is added, as in his advice to get flat under the threat of being flattened by China. This refers presumably to the most basic sense of being flattened, to be knocked down, as one often sees happening in boxing matches. This is not all. Yet one more sense of flattening is involved here. The fall of the Berlin Wall meant not just that the Wall was dismantled but also that any alternative to capitalism was flattened. The idea of the flat surface is moreover conflated to include the flattening of hierarchy. Physical and ideological flattening move together. Thus, we read, 'search engines flatten the world by eliminating all the valleys and peaks, all the walls and rocks...'.[32] These difficult tasks are accomplished without any serious consideration of their implications. It does not take long from Nilekani's making the comment to Friedman's scribbling in his notebook, 'the world is flat'. He is already full of his vision of Columbus.

Friedman pays a price for the conceptual looseness. And so do his readers. What are these flat, unflat, or half-flat worlds? Are they to be identified regionally or by other means? He talks at times quite explicitly as if the flat world and the developed world were identical. Consider: 'children in the developing world – the unflat world – are ten times more likely to die of vaccine-preventable diseases than are children in the developed flat world'.[33] We are told that only half the world is involved in the flattening process. We already have a quotation from Bill Gates to justify this position: 'I am worried that it could just be half the world that is flat and it stays that way.'[34] If poverty and sickness define who is located in the flat world and who is not, as Gates implies, then how do we consider poverty and sickness in the developed world? UN statistics suggest that the incidence of poverty in the United States is the highest among rich industrialised nations; moreover, the incidence of poverty has been on the rise over several past years. If any visual image of this poverty were needed, it was fully provided by the recent devastation in New Orleans. The havoc that was created there was not just the fury of nature; it is said that a contributary factor was the manner in which lucrative building projects were carried out, undermining natural barriers against tidal surges, along with the diversion to the Iraq war of federal funds for engineering work that, if carried out, would have strengthened the defence of the city.

Furthermore, it is unclear how the unflat world is conceptualised. Is it by the consideration of region (developed or underdeveloped; urban or rural), or poverty, or ideology – as in the case of Arab-Muslim young people touched by Islamic terror organisations? Indeed, as Sandel observed, Friedman is basically talking about a smooth global market promoted by capital and technology.[35] To the idea of a frictionless market, it needs to be noted, is then added all this extra baggage. This makes the entire exercise ambiguous.

Thus, contrary to Friedman's expectation of himself, he does not offer a framework, much less 'a nuanced framework',[36] for thinking through and managing the overwhelming changes of our time. His conceptual apparatus turns out to be too weak for that purpose. The world is surely not so flat that it can be analysed with such flat concepts.

Sandel made a suggestion to Friedman to read the *Manifesto of the Communist Party*. It would have been nice if he had asked him also to read Marx's *Preface* to *A Contribution to the Critique of Political Economy* of 1859. In this *Preface* Marx differentiated between, let us say, technological development and property relations within which these developments take place. These relations promote technological development but at a certain stage existing property relations, instead of promoting further development, tend to inhabit it. This conflict is resolved with the change in existing property relations; it becomes explicit in the first place when material conditions necessary for the resolution of the conflict have matured. A familiarity with this thought of Marx's might have provided Friedman with an interesting framework for analysing what is happening in the world of software today. He has covered in some detail the conflict between two principles of software development, open source and commercial. A large number of people formed into communities have shown through different projects that they are willing to develop software and then make it available free to all those who wish to avail themselves of it for their own use. Why do they do it? The reward is often intellectual challenge, reputation, and the satisfaction of contributing to human knowledge. The manner in which IBM showed interest in the software project Apache indicates that there is a recognition of the usefulness of the open-source model of software. The Apache people asked for just one thing – which was that IBM should send people who could meet their standards. As an example of a different kind of project that is being developed collaboratively and made available free, Friedman draws attention to Wikipedia, popularly known as 'the people's encyclopaedia'. The project is not complete yet. Jimmy Wales, who initiated it, wants to expand it to include dictionary, thesaurus, books, manuals, and so on. This goal is simple: to 'give every single person free access to the sum of all human knowledge'.[37] The free software movement relies on collaboration, and it is seen as a better way of creating innovative software. This is also meant to bring users freedom from the grip of global corporations, especially Microsoft. Linux, developed by a student, has posed a challenge for the Microsoft Windows operating system. The argument by Microsoft is that capitalism is needed to drive innovation. Indeed, this is the crux of the problem. To which of the two models of software development does the future belong? In fact, Microsoft admits that certain aspects of the open-source movement are 'intriguing'. *The Economist*, not known for its sympathy for Marx, mused recently: 'some zealots even argue that the open-source approach represents a new, post-capitalist model of production'.[38]

These larger issues do not concern Friedman. He has a single point to make. Whatever is happening that promotes global markets is good and needs to be supported. He observes with fascination what he calls 'the Wal-Mart Symphony'. As he sees thousands of boxes move on conveyor belts forming long conveyor streams, he thinks of the river of boxed products, but there is hardly any thought about what these boxed products are doing to our environment. There is hardly any thought about whether that is our collective future, and whether that future is desirable or sustainable. What kind of symphony is this that goes on round the year with monotonous regularity? This does not bother him, for all that he is concerned with is the consumer; and he has heard from Andreessen that human wants and needs are infinite. Is it our future ideal that more and more Wal-Marts ensure that rivers of boxed products keep flowing to feed infinite human wants and needs? In India, there was a man whom the nation reverentially called Mahatma Gandhi. He differentiated between need and greed, and he said that it is the greed of man that is unending.

This is of no concern to Friedman. To get an idea of the greed that is involved, one has to consider Wal-Mart more closely. While Wal-Mart can boast of making nearly $20,000 profit per minute everyday, it has attracted considerable public attention for labour abuses across the world. Its former Vice-Chairman, Thomas Coughlin, is going to plead guilty, according to the reports available at the time of writing, for charges of fraud. He seems to have been paid in millions, yet he misappropriated $500,000 through improper use of gift cards. Corporate America still remembers Bernard Ebbers whose massive fraud dumped WorldCom into bankruptcy. It has been noted that excessive respect for free markets tends to reduce ethical concerns.

It would have been useful for Friedman to see what Max Weber has to say on what capitalism has become when 'material goods have gained an increasing and finally an inexorable power on the lives of men as at no previous period in history... In the field of its highest development, in the United States, the pursuit of wealth, stripped of its religions and ethical meaning, tends to become associated with purely mundane passions...'[39] In discussing these mundane passions, Weber mentions in a footnote, often overlooked, the life of a leading storeowner dealing in dry goods in an Ohio city. He could not be satisfied with his substantial income. He wanted to expand further his store and worked hard for it. He went to bed early when his wife and daughter read together in the evenings. On Sundays, he looked at the clock every five minutes to see when the day would be over.[40] A futile life?

There is another Marx from whom Friedman could have learnt something useful. Friedman tell us that he discussed the theme of his book with his religious leader, Rabbi Tzvi Marx of Holland. Rabbi Marx's words deserve to be quoted: 'The heresy is not that mankind works together – it is to what ends. It is essential that we use this new ability to communicate and collaborate for the right ends – for constructive right aims and not megalomaniacal ends. Building a tower was megalomaniacal. Bin Laden's insistence that he has the truth and can flatten anyone else's tower who doesn't heed him is megalomaniacal. Collaborating so mankind can achieve its full potential is God's hope.'[41] There are many impor-

tant points to note in this wise statement. We need to be clear
about our ends: the ends have to be right. We need to collaborate
for the purpose of realising our full human potential. The view that
I have the truth and that gives me the right to flatten others is
wrong. It would have been relevant if Friedman had asked himself
as he watched the conveyor belt of Wal-Mart to what end this
gigantic supply chain was built. Was it helping humanity to realise
its full potential? It would have been helpful if he had asked himself
whether he had the truth on his side. Could it be that the process
of globalisation that he was hailing uncritically had to be understood not only in terms of the globalised world and the
unglobalised world but also in terms of inequalities that it had
created within and across nations? Could it be that the forces that
make the playing field less than level arise from the West? As
Joseph Stiglitz says in his review of the book, 'the new "rules of the
game" that were part of the last round of global trade negotiations
– notably intellectual property regulations requiring all countries
to adopt American-style patent and copyright laws – are almost
surely making the playing field less level. They will make it easier
for those who are ahead of the game to maintain their lead.'[42]
Could it be that globalisation was not only creating a flat world but
also flattening people and alternatives? The process of turning
everything into commodities is directed towards leaving nothing
untouched. These questions do not trouble Friedman. And when
he does raise questions they are disarmingly dumped into a chapter
that is appropriately called, 'The Great Sorting Out'. He poses
problems and then admits 'it is going to take a lot of sorting out',
or just 'sort that out', or, even better, 'somebody, please, sort all
this out'.[43] Friedman says that imagination has not been, to use an
ugly word, commoditised. He then goes against his own
contention and unwittingly gives evidence to the contrary. All that
his imagination offers is how to create products and profits.

Even though he is not a supporter of George Bush, Friedman is
unable to go beyond American biases shown by his régime. He
offers the same naïve play of the bad guys and the good guys, the
destructive forces and the creative forces. He does not see that the
Iraq adventure of Bush has contributed to al-Qaeda, making Iraq,

in the words of Fawaz A. Gerges,[44] a new opening to make inroads into the hearts of outraged Muslims. In the ringing words of Harold Pinter, the truth is not that Saddam Hussein possessed weapons of mass destruction (WMD) which could be fired within less than an hour. The truth has to do with the manner in which the United States sees its role in the world and enacts it. Friedman does not recognise that fundamentalism comes in different forms, including market fundamentalism. In the words of Jeff Faux, Friedman behaves like 'the pied piper of global free market fundamentalism'.[45]

We do not only need supply chains but also *soul chains* that will bind human beings together for the purpose of achieving the potential of humanity.

This is, then, the right time to attempt answering the question posed at the beginning of this paper. Why does he invent the idea of the flat earth once again? It is possible that Friedman re-invents the idea of the flat earth for the reason it was invented in the nineteenth century. It is to highlight his achievement in the manner in which the achievement of Columbus was emphasised earlier. Moreover, literary hype does not hurt in this flat world of instant success. But this story is not so simple. Friedman tells us that his advice to his daughters is to do their homework because people in China and India are hungry for their jobs. It is now Columbus himself who is under threat. If the map that has surfaced in Beijing is to be believed, according to a report in *The Independent,* 15 January 2006, it was not Columbus who 'discovered' America but a Chinese admiral, Admiral He, who was a eunuch and a Muslim. It seems his fleet sailed the oceans between 1405 and 1435, much earlier than the fleet of Columbus. Even if the map turns out to be a forgery, we need to examine more closely the claim made by Gavin Menzies.[46] What next?

★

The general belief of our age is that the earth has a spherical shape, though not exactly so. Planet earth, it is believed, has an oblate shape, a little flattened at the poles and slightly bulging at the equator. Direct space explorations of the second half of the last century have made it possible to look at the earth from outside. The flattening and the bulging are only slight. It is with the help of technical observations recorded through these space explorations that it is possible to do precise calculations. In any case, the difference is insignificant. The diameter of the earth is about 40 km longer through the Equator than from North Pole to South Pole.

In the words of Aleksei Leonov, a Russian astronaut, 'the earth was small, light blue, and so touchingly alone, our home that must be defended like a holy relic. The earth was absolutely round. I believe I never knew what the word round meant until I saw earth from space.' Others who have gone into space have come back with similar experience. They have come back with the belief, in the words of Donald Williams, an American astronaut, that what we share in our world is more important than what divides us (*see* Earth from Space). We share, among other things, the threat that our planet faces from our own activities. There is mounting evidence to suggest that our planet has been warming over the past century and temperatures are now rising at a higher rate. Enough weapons of mass destruction of all kinds have been amassed by us to wipe out all humanity. Along with the risk of a nuclear war on a global scale, there is the threat of nuclear or other deadly strikes by irresponsible states or terrorist groups. This is the time when we need to look at the earth from a great height and to think of it as a whole and all the living beings that are supported by it. This is the time when we need to go outside our tribes and tribal mentalities. We also need to look at the earth from a lower height. We need to see lands and oceans, peaks and valleys. In this view, it does not appear very small any longer. This is the world of diversity, some colourful and other colourless. While it shows the rainbow of different human colours, it also shows inequality: opulence and poverty. This view of the world is as real as the earlier view.

If we want to survive, we have no option but to think of our earth as a whole. What we do with diversity of all kinds is something we shall need to put on our agenda for serious consideration. Our world is round, and we shall have to figure out how best to make it go round.

Notes

1 Thomas Friedman, *The World is Flat: A Brief History of the Globalized World in the Twenty-first Century* (London, 2005), p. 5.

2 *ibid.*, p. 7.

3 *ibid.*, p. 8.

4 *ibid.*, p. 39.

5 *ibid.*, p. 51.

6 *ibid.*, pp. 54–5.

7 *ibid.*, p. 56.

8 *ibid.*, p. 77.

9 *ibid.*, p. 78.

10 *ibid.*, p. 125.

11 *ibid.*, p. 127.

12 *ibid.*, p. 127.

13 *ibid.*, p. 262.

14 *ibid.*, p. 263.

15 Thomas Friedman, *The Lexus and the Olive Tree: Understanding Globalization* (New York, 2000), p. 10.

16 *ibid.*, p. 11.

17 *ibid.*, p. 45.

18 *ibid.*, p. 106.

19 *ibid.*, p. 128.

20 Friedman, *The World is Flat*, p. 175.

21 *ibid.*, p. 181.

22 *ibid.*, p. 374.

23 *ibid.*, p. 221.

24 *ibid.*, p. 322.

25 *ibid.*, p. 375.

26 *ibid.*, p. 336.

27 *ibid.*, p. 380.

28 *ibid.*, p. 395.

29 *ibid.*, p. 397.

30 *ibid.*, p. 469.

31 *ibid.*, p. 316.

32 *ibid.*, p. 158.

33 *ibid.*, p. 377.

34 *ibid.*, p. 379.

35 *ibid.*, p. 204

36 *ibid.*, p. 222.

37 *ibid.*, p. 95.

38 *ibid.*, p. 103.

39 Max Weber, *The Protestant Ethic and the Spirit of Capitalism* (London, 2001), pp. 123–4.

40 *ibid.*, p. 260.

41 Friedman, *The World is Flat*, p. 438.

42 Joseph Stiglitz, 'Global Playing Field: More Level, but It Still Has Bumps', *The New York Times*, 30 April 2005.

43 Friedman, *The World is Flat*, pp. 208, 212, 219.

44 Fawaz A. Gerges, *The Far Enemy: Why Jihad Went Global* (New York, 2005).

45 Jeff Faux, 'Flat Note from a Pied Piper of Globalization', *Dissent* (Fall 2005), pp. 83–6.

46 Gavin Menzies, *1421: The Year China Discovered the World* (London, 2003).

Some Questions about the Historical Explanation of Contemporary China

WANG HUI

China's economic reforms since the 1980s have brought about tremendous achievements, but have also led to social re-differentiation. During the same period, Chinese intellectuals have been debating how to interpret these contradictory phenomena. Since the middle of the 1970s, the discourse of developmentalism centred on neo-classical economics has come to dominate in many countries. This discourse challenges state interference and the tradition of the welfare state with such ideas as private property, the free market and formal democracy, replacing the social system in post-war Western Europe with the political power of Reagan-Thatcherism. In the latter half of the 1980s, this trend of thought reverberated powerfully in socialist countries. The ideas of private property, the free market, and formal democracy became the most powerful weapon against the socialist state system, centred on the planned economy, and against socialist ideology. During the historical process in which the Cold War came to an end and the socialist system disintegrated, 'neo-liberalism' came to be interpreted as one of the main forms of momentum propelling reforms in China. After the world-wide events of 1989, almost every historical interpretation of the various social movements and of the progress of reform in China was subordinated to the mainstream discourse of 'neo-liberalism'. This mainstream discourse, however, cannot adequately explain the drastic differentiation between classes, strata and regions taking place in China and worldwide. Nor can it provide any alternative plan to the developmental model, mainly in the form of market expansion, which caused environmental crisis and social disintegration. Therefore, the market economy of 'neo-liberalism' encountered powerful resistance from various different directions.

The mainstream discourse of 'neo-liberalism' is based on the polar oppositions between the free market and state intervention, capitalism and socialism, globalisation and anti-globalisation, private property and state ownership. However, if we consider Chinese intellectuals' debates in terms of these dualities, the discourse will take on different connotations.

First of all, the formation of China's market system embraces two basic directions: internally, through transfering rights and profits from the central government to local governments, nurturing the decision-making power of enterprises, reforming the finance system, and privatisation, the state allowed market mechanism to permeate into all fields of social life; while, internationally, through reforms in international trade and the finance system, the state gradually brought China into the global market relationships that are dominated by the WTO and the IMF.

This process was related to profound transformations in China's social structure, and it also ignited profound social crisis. In the second half of 1988, because of social instability caused by inflation, price reform had to be stopped. 1989 is therefore often regarded as a brief interval in China's urban reform. But this interval happened to overlap with the time when the state adjusted its policy in face of the first cycle of crisis, and so it became a period of preparation for further market expansion. In September 1989, the price reform that had twice been aborted began to be implemented again; at that time, major adjustments focused on prices, the exchange rate and the interest rate. The events of 1989 and the changes that took place subsequently demonstrate the paradoxical relationship between market expansion and the state. On the one hand, nurturing and developing the market is almost unthinkable without the policy adjustment, legal system, and political support of the state. On the other, the market's dependence on the state is simultaneously the premise for dealings between power and the market. From this perspective, we discover the internal historical relationship between the reforms of the 1980s and the post-1989 period, and see a peculiar interaction between the traditional socialist system and market creation – the expansion of the market relied on an 'anti-market' power (namely, state intervention), and the state overcame the crisis of its legitimacy precisely through market expansion. In this sense, the duality of market/state cannot explain the process of market expansion in China. The 'neo-liberalist' idea of the state's retreat cannot explain the great achievements accomplished since the reform because of effective state policies regarding price and industries. Nor can it explain the exchange of power for profit and the social stratification that took place in the large-scale privatisation of state-owned properties.

Secondly, since the end of the 1980s, the social conditions in which the state system has functioned have changed so acutely that the system itself and the social interest relations that it represented have been thoroughly reformed. During China's high-speed economic development, the income gap between various social strata, groups and areas expanded, and the destitute population rapidly increased. The state's old ideology (namely, the socialist ideology based on equality) and practice were rendered contradictory by this historical transformation, and the state was consequently unable to perform its ideological function. It is within this context that 'neo-liberalism' became a new dominant ideology. Therefore, the traditional socialism/capitalism duality basically cannot be used as a framework for historical analysis. It is in the process of the ideological transformation that the following phenomena in the field of thinking may be understood: new social criticism was resisted and denounced as old ideology, while the simple socialist element in the social movements that took place at the end of the 1980s and their internal relationship to appeals for democracy were covered up by the pattern of reform and anti-reform, etc.

Thirdly, the social movement at the end of the 1980s tried to accomplish organic interaction between society and the state through popular participation. But after 1989, the system of inter-action between the market and the state replaced the interaction between society and the state. In the 'neo-liberal' discourse, the concept of society was gradually replaced by the concept of the market, and the basic driving force behind the reform of the state system and the transformation of the legal system was no longer 'society' or 'the people' but the domestic and international market. Therefore the connotation of 'politics' itself changed greatly: the state became the major executive power to maintain the market system, and to reconstruct the legal system according to WTO regulations. In such a historical perspective, the relationship between social movements, the reform crisis and the role of the state need to be reconsidered. The social trend of thinking that was developed in the 1990s under the slogan 'reflecting on radicalism' replaced the view of democracy as based on popular participation with the view of democracy as a step-by-step and formalistic process. As a result, the real momentum of democratic practice is theoretically negated, and social protection movements from different social levels have been excluded from the field of democ-racy since the 1990s.

Fourthly, when privatisation becomes a trend, and private prop-erty becomes a key point in constitutional reform, there is a need to establish a historical differentiation between the two forms of 'privatisation'. The first kind is the private economy developed from local social relations and small markets: for instance, market relations based on regional and family relationships in the Wenzhou area, and market expansion propelled by the production of small goods and low-profit production. This economic form proved to be particularly vital after the financial crisis of 1997. The second kind is the large-scale privatisation that took place under the supervision of the state, in which large numbers of state-owned properties were misplaced or illegally transferred. Corruption, large-scale unemployment, social injustice and the disintegration of social security in contemporary China took place largely through the second kind of 'privatisation'. This is a process of power reform dominated by the state, but in the form of 'state withdrawal'.

According to the above observations, three basic differentiations must be made.

First, we must differentiate between the notion of the market that competes freely or adjusts itself and the historical process in which the modern market economy came into existence and functioned.

Second, we must differentiate between neo-liberalist market ideology (often characterised by the demand for complete state withdrawal) and neo-liberalist market order and economic policies (often characterised by reliance on state policy and enforcement).

Third, we must differentiate between the category of the market and the category of society.

1. According to the first differentiation, the market society and its rules are formed and function in the interrelationship between state intervention, institution innovation, monopolisation, social customs and historical events. Free competition is only part of its conditions. Therefore, criticism of the market society and its crisis in reality does not equal the negation of the market system.

2. According to the second differentiation, neo-liberalist ideology requires the state to adopt a non-interventionist policy, i.e. the state should give up its duty of social welfare and social security, abandon its economic methods to adjust market activities, and furthermore sever the link between politics and the economy. But surrendering these duties is itself the result of arrangements achieved through institutions and policy. The crisis of China's state-owned enterprises and agriculture is the result of active institutional and policy arrangement. Therefore, the slogan of anti-state intervention happened to be based on the premise of state policies, the essence of which is another form of active 'intervention'.

3. According to the third differentiation, market rules and regu-

lations do not equal social rules and regulations, and the social democratic system does not equal the market's operating system. Thus, the orientation of the state toward democracy does not equal the transformation of the state into political organs that will set up a market system. The crisis of 1989 demonstrated that market expansion under the supervision of the state created social crisis, while social crisis became an opportunity for the state to control society (and not only the market) in all aspects, and that the market system was established when society (not the state) completely withdrew from the field of 'politics'.

Given the above analysis, I will outline some orientations here.

First, economic inequality caused by market expansion is always closely related to inequalities in other fields, such as politics, economics, and culture. Hence, struggles for freedom (including labour contract freedom, freedom to exchange, political freedom, etc.) must at the same time be struggles for social equality. The discourse that directly opposes appeals for equality to appeals for freedom must be rejected.

Secondly, resistance to monopolisation and domineering market tyranny cannot be simply equated to the struggle 'against' the market, because such social resistance itself includes the efforts that strive for fair competition in the market and for economic democracy.

Thirdly, the resistance to economic hegemony and multinational monopoly does not mean closing the country off, and a certain degree of trade protection does not equal being 'anti-market'. Social movements regarding the WTO and the conflict between rich and poor countries in WTO negotiations demonstrate a new form of struggle that does not oppose international organisations and international adjustments as a whole, but promotes the democratisation of international institutions (including the WTO) and of international regulations through participatory social movements. Furthermore, it aims to equate domestic economic justice with international economic justice.

Fourthly, economic movements are always embedded in politics, culture and other social conditions, so striving to achieve fair market competition does not equal getting rid of the state political system, social customs or any regulating mechanism. On the contrary, perfecting market conditions aims to reform, limit and expand these systems so as to create social conditions for fair interaction. In this sense, the struggle for social justice and fair market competition cannot be equated with opposition to state intervention. Rather, it requires social democracy, namely to prevent the state from becoming the protector of the domestic monopoly and multinational monopoly through society's democratic control of the state. In this case, participatory and popular democracy is still the real momentum for contemporary democracy. The method that opposes popular democracy with formal democracy must be rejected. On any scale – no matter whether it is on the scale of a nation state or of the world market – the struggle for freedom will manifest itself as the struggle for democracy and freedom.

I have summarised these orientations as a way of thinking about the democratic system of the market, a way of approaching the development of society and not just the development of the economy. Only within this framework can the struggle for economic justice be connected with the struggle for social justice and political democracy and with the discussion of different models of development.

Acknowledgements

General Curator
António Pinto Ribeiro

Cover Design
R2Design

Translation
Carlos Pacheco: Richard Trewinnard
Ghassan Zaqtan: May Jayuusi and Alan Brownjohn for East-West
    Nexus / PROTA
João Barrento: Richard Trewinnard
Peter Sloterdijk: Andrew Boreham
Santiago Kovadloff: Richard Trewinnard

Linguistic Revision
Wang Hui: Richard Trewinnard

With additional thanks to
Alexandra Pinho, Felicity Luard, Mahmoud Abu Hashhash